Women and
Culture Series

*The Women and Culture Series is dedicated to books that illuminate the lives,
roles, achievements, and status of women, past or present.*

Mary Carr Moore, American Composer

Mary Carr Moore, American Composer

Catherine Parsons Smith and
Cynthia S. Richardson

THE UNIVERSITY OF MICHIGAN PRESS

Ann Arbor

1990   1989   1988   1987   4   3   2   1

Library of Congress Cataloging-in-Publication Data

Smith, Catherine Parsons, 1933–
  Mary Carr Moore, American composer.

  Biblography: p.
  "Catalog of compositions by Mary Carr Moore": p.
  Includes index.
    1. Moore, Mary Carr, 1873–1957. 2. Composers—United
States—Biography. I. Richardson, Cynthia S.,
1947– . II. Title.
ML410.M7755S6   1987   784′.092′4   [B]   86-24953
ISBN 0-472-10082-3

Preface

Music historians have been slower to draw on the new scholarship of women's studies than have historians of other areas of Western culture. Prevailing social and economic patterns have cast women largely as patrons or audiences for art music and as composers and performers mainly within the confines of their domestic roles. Written music history has concentrated until quite recently on the creative output of a handful of "great composers" to the exclusion of more widespread popular and nonprofessional aspects of the art, including the areas in which women most commonly functioned. This narrow approach has been all the easier because of the ephemeral nature of music as an artifact. Until the advent of recording technology, the basic evidence of music history survived primarily in the form of music notation, and secondarily in written or pictorial accounts. At best, music notation is never complete; notes committed to paper cannot represent the composer's finished product. The creative act in music is only completed when the composer's work is performed before disinterested and reasonably informed audiences. The composer's artistic growth depends upon feedback yielded by such performances. Thus music is a highly social art, particularly sensitive to the separate roles assigned to women and men in any society.

Female composers in the nineteenth century were so inhibited by Victorian values from developing their creative potential that few even attempted to compose the ambitious, extended works understood to be characteristic of the Romantic century in music. In the United States it is difficult even to identify by name many woman composers who were active before the final third of the nineteenth century. Of the many who emerged after about 1870, relatively few ventured beyond the accepted limitations of songs and short piano pieces suitable for use in the home. Their work is largely outside the traditions of art music, theater music, or popular music as they have thus far been chronicled. Those who did emerge in this period could not entirely break out of their culturally reinforced isolation, and beginning around 1920, there was a gradual decline of interest in their work.

The authors are therefore pleased to bring forward this biographical study of an American woman composer who tried to accept the limitations of Victorian ideals of womanhood while at the same time creating a substantial body of music. Mary Carr Moore's creative career spanned six decades. Born in Memphis, Tennessee, in 1873, she received most of her training as a musician in San Francisco and passed most of her life on the West Coast. Her talent and drive were such that she wrote not just one opera (as several other woman composers did), but several full-length operas, a feat unmatched by any of her female contemporaries in the United States. Her relatively provincial existence, away from New York City and the great European music centers, guaranteed her present obscurity, but also offered her opportunities that were not available in those great centers. How she dealt with both the limitations and the opportunities in her life and how they affected her as a creative artist form the substance of our study. We have chronicled her life and described her most important music, concentrating on the operas. We have tried to show the close relationship between Moore's musical development and her encounters with the various discriminatory barriers, both internal and external, that she and other American composers of her time faced. The indigenous culture of American art music, which quietly subsisted in the shadow of the dominant European art music culture of the late nineteenth and early twentieth centuries, provided the environment in which Moore functioned and in which her music may properly be understood. We have described this culture in the cities where she worked as much as seems necessary for her story.

We have not attempted to create feminist theory about music history, about American music in our own century, or about music in relation to the other arts. Feminist as well as Americanist themes are present in the materials we explored and have clearly provided the organizational framework for substantial parts of the book. Theorizing beyond this seems premature. Not only are biographical studies of American woman composers still too few in number, but critical evaluation of their music has scarcely begun. Much more music and biographical information must be rescued from oblivion before a viable feminist theory about American music history can be formulated. We view the present study, then, as an important part of the foundation for such a formulation.

We have been fortunate in attempting the project, for the process of research and writing about Mary Carr Moore has stretched into a remarkable six-year voyage of discovery. It was surely a fruitful coincidence that both authors, previously unknown to each other, converged at almost the same moment on Moore as a potential topic. Smith located Moore's daughter and first visited the garage in southern California where most of Moore's music and other important documents from her life lay in two rusting file cabinets and five water-stained cartons. Moore's daughter, Marian Moore Quinn, graciously welcomed us and patiently answered our questions about her mother, the family tree, and nuances of her family life from the moment of her own birth. A scrapbook that Quinn produced turned out to contain Moore's handwritten catalog of her music and a wealth of biographical information, another example of the extraordinary good fortune we have had at almost every turn. A bundle of datebooks discovered in the Quinn household, covering a quarter-century of Moore's activities in Los Angeles, represented another stroke of luck. Most of this collection soon found its way to the Music Library of the University of California, Los Angeles, forming, with a box of music already there, the Mary Carr Moore Archive.

Marian Quinn also provided the names and addresses of old friends who had once been her mother's students and friends and who were unfailingly eager to talk with us. They brought out their own scrapbooks and address books, sending us to more people who had known or worked with Moore. The circle widened until we had interviewed, either in person or by telephone, more than eighty people. We corresponded with many more. The search gradually spread to special collections of related materials, some in private hands, some in libraries.

Unearthing the facts about Moore, stimulating as it was, formed only the first part of our odyssey. We then had to address the questions that the facts had raised. Why did she make the choices she made at various critical junctures in her career? Which of them were in fact choices and which were dictated by circumstance? How good a composer was she? We quickly found that we could not begin to answer these and similar questions without approaching the aesthetic question that underlies any qualitative judgment about music. We needed to understand what she was trying to achieve as a composer, what means were available to her, what means she chose, and, on these terms, how well she succeeded. Conventional formulations about twentieth-century music history seemed increasingly irrelevant as we became familiar with her music and her world. We joyfully concluded that we really *had* discovered an unknown talent of substantial importance to the history of American music in the first half of this century. We intensified our efforts to understand Moore's aesthetic rationale. Our conclusions about her very likely extend to many other of the women who were active as composers during the same period, though the extent of the documentation in Moore's case is, at least so far, unique. Since the events of Moore's life and her music are so closely bound together, it made sense to integrate them in our narrative rather than separate them as is often done in biographies of composers.

A catalog of compositions is included in this volume, both to document the extent of Moore's achievement and to assist others in seeking out her music. As mentioned above, nearly all of her music that survives may be found in the Mary Carr Moore Archive of the Music Library at UCLA. A few works are more readily available for those who wish to see, hear, or perform Moore's music themselves. A modern reprint of the opera *David Rizzio* (New York: Da Capo Press, 1981) is readily available. A new collection, *Twenty-Eight Songs* (New York: Da Capo Press, 1987) includes most of the songs and one aria mentioned in the text. Cambria Records (P.O. Box 374, Lomita, California 90717) has issued an album of Moore's songs and arias (C-1022) and will release some of Moore's chamber music on a future recording (C-1025). A sixty-minute tape, drawn from a lecture-recital on Moore's music and funded by the Nevada Humanities Committee, was prepared for broadcast on National Public Radio in 1984. The cassette is also available through Cambria Records. The authors hope that these represent only the beginning of renewed interest in Mary Carr Moore's music.

Acknowledgments

This book could not have been written without the help of many individuals. First among them is Marian Moore Quinn, who has given generously of her time, delving into her family's history, answering our endless questions, and offering corrections on factual matters. In cooperation with Moore's four grandsons and musical heirs, Clyde B. Hudson, Robert Wray Hudson, Richard Carr Moore, and John David Moore, she arranged the donation of Moore's music and many of her papers to UCLA, where they have been designated the Mary Carr Moore Archive. Those materials that Quinn retained she has generously allowed us to microfilm for the archive. Stephen Fry of the UCLA Music Library not only welcomed the Moore materials but made them easily accessible to us and helped us repeatedly in many ways.

Other librarians and archivists have also been enormously cooperative. Robert Riley, formerly at the Los Angeles Public Library; Joan Meggett and Helen Azhderian, formerly at the University of Southern California; Wayne Shirley and Rodney H. Mill in the Music Division of the Library of Congress; John Emerson at the Music Library, University of California, Berkeley; and very many others went out of their way to help us. Interlibrary loan departments at the University of Nevada Reno and Western Washington University tracked elusive out-of-print volumes penned by Moore's relatives and many other obscure items with remarkable persistence and success. Private individuals also made their own collections of materials available to us. The Manuscript Club of Los Angeles, Mary Carr Moore, Founder, made its archive available, and we were helped by members of the Dominant Club and Mu Phi Epsilon as well. In addition, we visited or corresponded with the following libraries or associations, all of which house special materials that helped us in our research: American Music Center, New York; American Music Research Center, San Rafael, California; Arnold Schoenberg Institute, University of Southern California; Bancroft Library, University of California, Berkeley; Brand Library, Glendale; California Academy of Science, San Francisco; California Historical Society Library, San Francisco; California State Library, Sacramento; Department of Special Collections and Archives and the Music Resource Center of the Department of Music, California State University, Long Beach; Chapman College Library; Detroit Public Library; Ella Strong Denison Library, Scripps College; Free Library of Philadelphia;

George Arents Library, Syracuse University; Honnold Library, Claremont College; Huntington Library, San Marino, California; Archives and Manuscript Collections, Knox College; Lemoore (California) Public Library; Los Angeles County Museum of History, Science, and Art; Marin County Historical Society; Miami University (Ohio) Music Library; Multnomah County (Oregon) Library (Library Association of Portland); Music Library, Yale University; Napa (California) Public Library; National Archives and Records Service, Reference Services Branch (NNIR); Natural History Museum of Los Angeles County; New York Public Library; Newark (New Jersey) Public Library; Newberry Library; Pasadena Public Library; Penrose Memorial Library, Whitman College; St. Helena (California) Public Library; University Archives, San Diego State University Library; San Francisco Public Library; Seattle Public Library; Sibley Music Library, Eastman School of Music (University of Rochester); Society of California Pioneers Library, San Francisco; Stanford University Music Library; University of Southern California; Research Library, University of California, Los Angeles; and University of Washington.

Individuals whom we interviewed or with whom we have corresponded have gone far out of their way to make unique information and materials, mainly dealing with Moore and Moore's Los Angeles, available to us. We extend our thanks to Catalina Ortiz Acosta, Pauline Alderman, Verna Arvey, Ernst Bacon, Ruth Orcutt Bacon, Florence Bardell, Leon Becker, Lucienne Biggs, Jack Blake, Marie Woods Bohnhorst, Radie Britain, Frank G. Brown, John Browning, George Burchette, Grace Callahan, Nelle Gothold Carlson, Paulena Carter, Vivian Cheverton, Dorothy Compinsky, Sydney Cowell, Frank Cron, Emil Danenberg, Ivor Darreg, Hugo Davise, James Deese, Paul Delp, Matt H. Doran, Dorothy Miller Dunlap, Edward Earle, Mrs. Albert Elkus, Brice Farwell, Celeste Grunn Feliciano, Etheleen Brown Fiske, Florence Billinghurst Flagg, Rose Freedman, Lillian Steeb French, Lorene Dales Frost, Ted Gilbert, France Goldwater, Albert Harris, Elizabeth Usigli Harsh, June R. Howard, Clyde B. Hudson, Julie Hudson, Robert Wray Hudson, Stiles Johnson, Phil Kahgan, Marjorie Lange, Herman Langinger, Cornell Lengyel, Lois Linn, Ray Linn, Mrs. Theodore Koller Lucke, Alfred J. Mapleson, Carol Maves, Olga Webster Michel, Harlow John Mills, Elena Miramova Moore, John David Moore, Richard Carr Moore, John Morganthaler, Leonard Morganthaler, Jerome Moross, Helen Nash, Dika Newlin, Martha Locker Nisberg, Adelaide Pouliot Onassis, James Patrone, Marie Melore Patrone, Mary Green Pauloo, Emily Hardy Peluso, Ralph Pierce, Paul A. Pisk, Winifred Leftwich Pointer, Jane Church Porter, Margot Rebeil, Grace Good Reed, Mae Gilbert Reese, George N. Reeves, Naomi Reynolds, Beth K. Robinson, Kay Robinson, Dane Rudhyar, James Sample, Margaret Ryan Sampson, Dorothy Schulner, Roger Sessions, John A. Sherman, Constance Shirley, Dorothy Spensley, Judith Anne Still, Franklin Stokes, Gerald Strang, William Teaford, John R. Thompson, Elthea S. Turner, James Utter, Virginia Vallines, Clifford Vaughan, Elinor Remick Warren, Dorothy West White, Bert C. Williams, and Eleanor Howett Zimmerman.

The help of those with secondary information, and of those not already mentioned who have given us advice and encouragement at various stages, is likewise gratefully acknowledged. These include Doris Allen, Martin Bernheimer, Karen J. Blair, Adrienne Fried Block, Edith Borroff, Lance Bowling, Phyllis Bruce, Malcolm Cole, Evelyn Davis Culbertson, Evelyn De La Rosa, Susan Finger, William B. George, Marlene Jameson, Jane Johnson, Andrea Lenz, Harry Perison, Vivian Perlis, Jeannie G. Pool, Sister Mary Dominick Ray, Clare Rayner, Betty Roleder, Arnold T. Schwab, Nicholas Slonimsky, and Robert Stevenson. We thank Nancy Taylor of the Text Processing Center at the University of Nevada Reno for her painstaking and tireless cooperation in preparing the manuscript. We thank our friends and families, who have heard a great deal about Mary Carr Moore and her world over the past several years and who have helped us in many ways. We extend our apologies to anyone whose assistance we have inadvertently failed to acknowledge here. We are, of course, responsible for the way in which the information we have gathered has been used in this book.

We acknowledge the following with thanks for permission to quote directly from written materials, published or unpublished, or for the use of photographs: Verna Arvey; Beacon Press; Chapman College; Hugo Davise; James Deese; Celeste Grunn Feliciano; *Halcyon;* Clyde B. Hudson; Robert W. Hudson; The Huntington Library; John David Moore; Richard C. Moore; *Musical America;* Winifred Leftwich Pointer; Marian Moore Quinn; James Sample; Margaret Ryan Sampson; Art and Music Department and Special Collections, San Francisco Public Library; James E. Seaver; Judith Anne Still; Unitarian Universalist Association; Mary Carr Moore Archive, UCLA Music Library; Bessie Bartlett Frankel Papers, Department of Special Collections, UCLA Research Library; The Bancroft Library, University of California, Berkeley; University of Nebraska Press; University of Washington Press; Warner Brothers Music, a division of Warner Brothers, Inc.; Northwest & Whitman College Archives, Penrose Memorial Library, Whitman College; and Charles Ives Collection, Music Library, Yale University. All photographs are courtesy of Marian Moore Quinn unless otherwise noted. We have made every effort to trace the ownership of all written material quoted in this book and to obtain permission for its use.

Smith was fortunate in receiving summer grants and a sabbatical leave from the Graduate School of the University of Nevada Reno, as well as a fellowship from the National Endowment for the Humanities. These allowed her to visit more libraries, conduct more interviews, and do most of the writing after the initial research was completed. Richardson carefully documented the opera *Narcissa,* whose initial production and two revivals mark critical turning points in Moore's career. Her professional skills helped us deal with the challenge of organizing and evaluating the wealth of primary source material and presenting a catalog of Moore's music. Both authors have edited the text repeatedly, so that the book is now a collective product.

Contents

CHAPTER 1

Manifest Destiny

All her life, Mary Carr Moore held an exalted view of her forebears. The Carrs on her father's side and the Pratts on her mother's were literate and capable individuals who honorably filled their roles in nineteenth-century America. The men were models of enterprise and patriotism. The women were paragons of duty to home and family. At different times, grandparents and cousins, uncles and great-aunts were members of her immediate family circle. The composer-to-be formed lasting perceptions about American history and about her own future in terms of their experiences. Railroading, the Civil War, and Republican politics all figured strongly in her family's scheme of things.

Family records have the first Carr ancestor coming to Rhode Island from London in 1635. Around 1800, Rev. Clark Carr, Moore's great-grandfather, moved to New York State, first to the Catskills and later to Buffalo, where he is supposed to have delivered that city's first Protestant sermon. His son Clark M. Carr (another of many Clark Carrs in the family) settled on a farm near Buffalo, producing a family of five sons and a daughter, by two different wives. Moore's father, born in 1832, was the second son of Clark M. Carr. By 1850, when Byron Oscar Carr (always called B. O.) moved with his prosperous parents to Galesburg, Illinois, he had already taught school for a year. In Galesburg he attended Knox Academy and Knox College for two years, then left school to serve as a surveyor's assistant on the new Chicago, Burlington and Quincy line as its rails approached Galesburg. After that railroad was completed, he worked as clerk and then conductor of a passenger train between Chicago and Galesburg. When the Civil War began, B. O. and two of his brothers became officers in the same Illinois regiment. Horace was the chaplain and Eugene the commanding officer. B. O. served in Missouri, Arkansas, and Louisiana, winding up as quartermaster to the Army of the Southwest. With his sociable good humor, and the competence born of a photographic memory and plenty of experience with railroading, he made many friends.

B. O. had married Mary E. Buck in the late 1850s. He was already a widower when he went off to the war, for she had died in 1861 while bearing their second child. After the war, his two sons stayed on with their grandparents in Galesburg while B. O. sought his fortune in the West. For a while he traded in lands and cattle in Butte County, Kansas. Then he became a conductor with the Union Pacific, working out of Omaha. In 1868 the state of Illinois issued a certificate authorizing him to practice law. The Union Pacific and Central Pacific railroads had only recently connected their lines in the first transcontinental railroad when B. O. went to work for the Central Pacific in Nevada. There he met and married the much younger Sarah Amelia Pratt.[1]

Of B. O. Carr's four brothers, Horace, a minister, eventually became chaplain general of the Grand Army of the Republic, the Union veterans' organization. George Pitt Carr was a carpetbagger after the war, becoming a judge in Louisiana. George published a volume of poetry that includes a blood-thirsty battle poem, probably known to Moore.[2] Clark E. Carr, the third brother, stood at Lincoln's elbow on the platform at Gettysburg, a privilege earned through his early support of the Emancipation Proclamation as well as through his Illinois political connections. Later he made a career as an attorney, postmaster, and Republican party functionary in Galesburg. Clark Carr became U.S. Minister to Denmark for four years around 1890, then retired to write several volumes of biography, fiction, and history.[3]

The career of B. O.'s older brother, Gen. Eugene A. Carr, is itself a chronicle of the settlement of the American West. After West Point, he served in Texas in 1854 and Kansas in 1857. During the Civil War, he served west of the Mississippi, winning the Medal of Honor at Pea Ridge in Arkansas.[4] In the following decades, he led or fought in a series of Indian campaigns in Kansas, Nebraska, and Colorado. It was in his service that Buffalo Bill Cody achieved fame as a scout. After the Battle of Cibicu Creek, Arizona, in 1881, General Carr was mistakenly reported in the national press to have been massacred. Not expecting a battle, he had taken along his fifteen-year-old son, who wound up shooting at Indians alongside the cavalrymen.[5] Moore, who was then eight years old, remembered the incident well enough to give a brief account of it in her autobiography.[6]

Moore also records at least one childhood visit to Uncle Eugene, probably in the late 1880s. The visit created a lasting impression:

One Christmas it was down to Phoenix, Arizona, for our entire family on Grandfather's special car; then we went on to New Mexico, to Fort Wingate, where we were the guests of Father's oldest brother, General Eugene A. Carr, then in command.

There I saw a sham battle, heard the blood-curdling Apache war-whoops, (which I have tried to re-create in the last act of *Narcissa*), and had a brief and thrilling glimpse of Army life. My aunt (Uncle Eugene's wife) was said to be the most beautiful woman in the regular army at that time. (Moore, p. 33)

Uncle Eugene believed that the Civil War had yielded some worthwhile benefits, besides preserving the Union.

But if you look at the results of the late war, and most other wars, you find, notwithstanding its admitted evils, an increase in material prosperity, in intelligence, energy, and manliness, in the breed of children, and even morality! which compensates for all. . . .

What can equal the pleasure, *for a man*, of risking life, and hoping for fame, in upholding a cause he deems just?[7]

The Spanish-American War came along after his retirement, but the general whom she had learned to admire supported it wholeheartedly: "We are grown up, and cannot only take care of ourselves, but of other people. . . . England has been doing this for ages, and it is our turn now."[8] "Only the most enterprising foreigners emigrate, hence the American is superior to the European in enterprise. For the same reason the West is ahead of the East in energy. It takes an energetic man to pull up and move west."[9]

While the Carrs were fighting the Civil War and subduing the western Indians, the other side of Moore's family, the Pratts, were settling California and helping connect it to the rest of the Union by building the transcontinental railroad. The first American Pratt had arrived at Weymouth, Massachusetts, in 1623. Moore's great-grandfather, Simeon Pratt, was born in Maine in 1797. In addition to being at various times a storekeeper, bookkeeper, fisherman, and school

Carr Family Tree

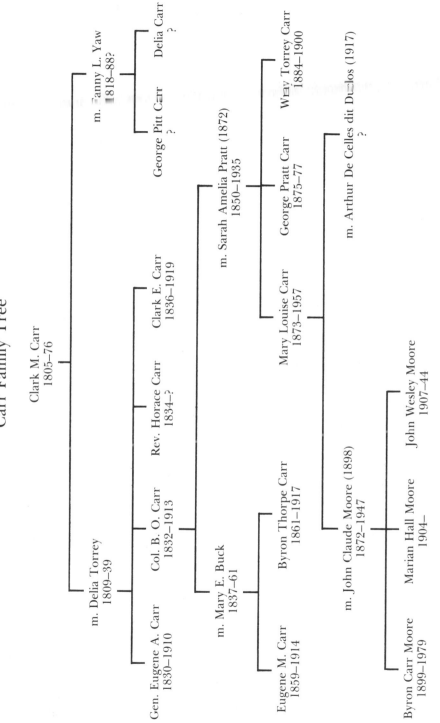

Clark M. Carr
1805–76

m. Delia Torrey
1809–39

m. Fanny L. Yaw
1818–88?

George Pitt Carr
?

Delia Carr
?

Gen. Eugene A. Carr
1830–1910

Col. B. O. Carr
1832–1913

Rev. Horace Carr
1834–?

Clark E. Carr
1836–1919

m. Sarah Amelia Pratt (1872)
1850–1935

m. Mary E. Buck
1837–61

Eugene M. Carr
1859–1914

Byron Thorpe Carr
1861–1917

Mary Louise Carr
1873–1957

George Pratt Carr
1875–77

Wm. Torrey Carr
1884–1900

m. Arthur De Celles dit Duclos (1917)
?

m. John Claude Moore (1898)
1872–1947

Byron Carr Moore
1899–1979

Marian Hall Moore
1904–

John Wesley Moore
1907–44

Pratt Family Tree

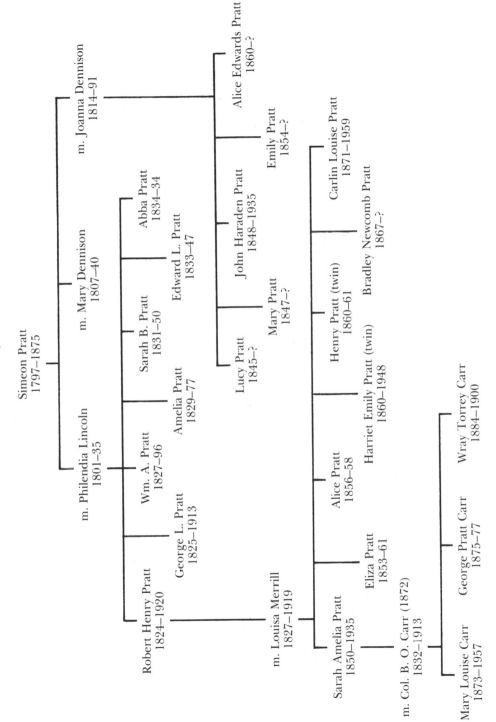

teacher, he was town selectman, town clerk, justice of the peace, and a colonel in the state militia. Colonel Pratt was also one source of his great-granddaughter's musical talent.

For many years he [Simeon Pratt] was the teacher of singing-schools for the whole country-side . . . One of Colonel Simeon's former pupils, an elderly lady, . . . describes her teacher as "at least six feet tall, handsome, cultivated, a fine singer, and withal a great ladies' man." It is said that his voice was the best tenor of that neighborhood—a voice which developed to the age of forty-five, held its own for ten years, and never wholly left him. His children still remember the evenings when their father "sat by the hearthstone and poured out a stream of song, as he loved to do when all was quiet and the day was done."[10]

Colonel Pratt planned to live out his last years in California with his children, but drowned accidentally as he went aboard the ship in Boston Harbor when Moore was a year old.

Simeon married three times and fathered twelve children between 1824 and 1860. The eldest, Robert Henry Pratt, Moore's beloved grandfather, was only eight years older than her father, B. O. Carr. The youngest, Alice Edwards Pratt, was only thirteen years older than Moore. Older than Aunt Alice were Aunt Emily, who played the organ at the Baptist Church in St. Helena; Uncle John, who became Moore's composition teacher; and Aunt Lucy Pratt Lillis. As a girl Moore visited the Lillis family on their enormous Spanish land grant ranch in the central valley of California.

Robert Henry Pratt and Louisa Merrill Pratt, Moore's grand-parents, were among the early settlers of California. Robert Henry had already been to sea as a navigator when he married Louisa Merrill in Freeport, Maine, in 1849. Following the discovery of gold at Sutter's Fort, he left by ship for California in a party with his brothers George and William and about a hundred other New England men. A mutiny by his fellow goldseekers early in the voyage left Robert Henry as the *Crescent's* first officer. Under his leadership, the trip around Cape Horn was rapid and uneventful. In six months, the *Crescent* arrived at the Golden Gate and sailed up the delta to Sacramento. It still lies buried in the levee at the foot of M Street, alongside many other ships of that era.

In a year of mining along the Trinity River of northern California, the Pratt brothers did well enough to buy a ranch on the Sacramento

River. There they built a hotel, operated a ferry, and helped organize Colusa County, Robert Henry becoming the first county auditor. Louisa and baby Sarah Amelia could now afford the safest and easiest route available from New England to California. They shipped to Panama, crossed the Isthmus on muleback, and sailed north, arriving in 1851.

Louisa, a former schoolteacher, became a pioneer wife, living ten miles from the nearest white woman and forty miles from a doctor. The Pratts dipped their own candles and paid exorbitant prices for occasional fresh fruit. Once an epidemic destroyed livestock worth $100,000 in a few weeks. Another time, Robert Henry needed to deliver $20,000 in gold to Sacramento. To avoid bandits, he put the gold in a gunny sack, dressed in shabby clothes, and took passage on the lower deck of a river boat.

After a few years, Robert Henry sold out to his brothers and moved to the Santa Rosa area, where he farmed for a time. According to one source, he went to Europe, perhaps after the death of two of his children in 1861.[11] In 1863 or 1864 he became involved in the trans-Sierran railroad project, when there was still some doubt about its feasibility. As "the Big Four's man," he rebuilt and ran the Dutch Flat and Donner Lake Wagon Road, the profitable but rugged route used for traffic from Sacramento to Virginia City, Nevada, before the Central Pacific (soon the Southern Pacific) Railroad was completed. The wagon road also supported the railroad construction as it crept up the ridges toward the crest of the Sierra Nevada. Pratt kept his family with him during the years when he worked on the railroad's construction. Sometimes they lived in a boxcar, parked on newly laid rails. Afterward, he was based in Sacramento and then San Francisco. In later years it was his job to lead the crews to the rescue of trains that were blocked by massive winter snowfalls in the Sierra. He retired from his final position as assistant general superintendent in 1896, at age seventy-two. After the great San Francisco fire of 1906 had destroyed the company's records, Pratt's detailed recollections were accurate enough to be accepted as evidence by both sides in an antitrust case against the Southern Pacific.[12]

R. H. Pratt and Louisa had seven children. Moore's mother, Sarah, was the eldest, born in Maine and raised on the frontier. Louisa, a former schoolteacher who wrote poetry and painted watercolors in her spare time, took great pains with young Sarah's education.[13] At four, Sarah recited a short poem of her own in Sunday School.[14] As Sarah grew up, the headquarters for the railroad moved farther up the mountains, from Newcastle to Dutch Flat to Colfax. But her parents saw to it that she graduated from Sacramento High School. Louisa records that Sarah read an essay of her own at a benefit for the Sacramento Library Association in 1868.[15] If there had been any opportunity for further formal education, Sarah would have jumped at it. As it was, she found herself teaching school in Colfax. She later wrote wistfully on a biographical form, "further study desultory, and alone."[16] Two of Sarah's siblings, Harriet and Carlin, were especially important in Moore's life. Much younger than Sarah (Carlin was only twenty months older than Moore), they were more like cousins than aunts.

Moore gives an account of how her mother met the widower B. O. Carr.

After the War, Father went into the West, and there into railroading— becoming, of course, well acquainted with Mother's father, who was then Superintendent of Construction of the old Central Pacific, and was working day and night to meet the schedule. Grandmother, who had been a New England school-mistress, and a beauty, always made Father welcome at the little home on wheels, which moved forward every day to the end of the track. Mother was a buxom, rosy-cheeked girl, very assured; and as Grandmother had a new baby (her seventh), Mother was in charge of the household. . . .

Naturally, Mother was spoiled, being one of about four "single" girls among that vast army of builders. Father was very courtly, awfully good-looking (in his Eastern way), and accustomed to leadership. So, after inviting Mother to several dances and "socials" and getting nowhere, he finally asked her to a dance to which, unbelievably, she hadn't been bidden! It transpired that *after* getting her promise, he arranged with their "set" to give the dance. Of course, Mother's "regulars" found her already engaged. . . . They were married in the little box-car house; the Overland Limited backed up to their "front door," took them on, and sailed through the station. (Moore, pp. 2–3)

CHAPTER 2

The Sixth District

Sarah Amelia Pratt and Col. B. O. Carr were married in the remote railroad community of Carlin, Nevada, on February 15, 1872. The nearest preacher was the agent at the Pyramid Lake Indian Reservation, two hundred miles west. The new couple traveled briefly to San Francisco and then took up residence in Wadsworth, Nevada, another tiny sagebrush-surrounded railroad town. But before long B. O. abandoned his job as a conductor on the primitive new railroad across the wilds of Utah and Nevada, for he had landed a federal appointment from President U. S. Grant. His old military connections, his knowledge of the transportation industry, and his ability to get along with everyone all probably helped him become supervising inspector of steam vessels for the Sixth District, covering the heart of the Mississippi–Ohio River system, approximately from Louisville, Kentucky, south to Memphis, Tennessee. The safety of the steam-operated riverboats and the certification of their officers was in his charge.

B. O.'s new headquarters was Memphis, where Gen. Carr's family made their home. B. O.'s sister-in-law now welcomed the new family. B. O. and Sarah, who was by then pregnant, were joined by B. O.'s two sons by his first wife, fifteen-year-old Eugene and thirteen-year-old Thorpe. Sarah quickly made friends of her stepsons, but she was not comfortable in her new role of running a household in a southern city. Moore later reported: "It was a summer climate where vegetables and fruit bought in the morning were crawling away by night! House-keeping??? Mother learned, later on, the knack of handling her colored help. Poor little thing—far away from everyone she knew, homesick, ill, but ever valiant!" (Moore, p. 4). Presently, on August 6, 1873, Sarah had an attack of "cholera" that turned out to be labor. It was the new mother's idea to give the name of B. O.'s first wife, Mary,

9

to their first child. Decades later, Moore marveled at her mother's extraordinary generosity. "Could I have done as much?" she wondered about this first, continuing example of devotion to duty and family. " 'Fraid not" (Moore, p. 7). The middle name, Louise, came from Sarah's own mother, Louisa Merrill Pratt.

Within six weeks of Moore's birth, the Carrs left Memphis. A yellow fever epidemic supplied the excuse. B. O. moved his headquarters as far north as he could, to Louisville. Sarah's opinion of southern city life may be inferred from the fact that B. O. installed his family across the Ohio River from Louisville, first in Jeffersonville, Indiana, and then, when Georgie was born two years later, in New Albany.

Like other women of her generation, Sarah probably drew many of her ideas about her responsibilities to her new family and her household from *The American Woman's Home: or, Principles of Domestic Science, Being a Guide to the Formation and Maintenance of Economical Healthful, Beautiful, and Christian Homes,* which appeared in 1869. Catharine Beecher and her better-known sister, Harriet Beecher Stowe, were coauthors of this very popular and lengthy tract. The volume, which went into details about household design, proper ventilation, child-rearing, cooking, and other essentials of domestic life, is now viewed as a cornerstone of the domestic feminism movement of the late nineteenth century in the United States.

> The authors of this volume, while they sympathize with every honest effort to relieve the disabilities and sufferings of their sex, are confident that the chief cause of these evils is the fact that the honor and duties of the family state are not duly appreciated, that women are not trained for these duties as men are trained for their trades and professions, and that, as the consequence, family labor is poorly done, poorly paid, and regarded as menial and disgraceful. . . .
>
> Woman's profession embraces the care and nursing of the body in the critical periods of infancy and sickness, the training of the human mind in the most impressible period of childhood, the instruction and control of servants, and most of the government and economics of the family state. These duties of women are as sacred and important as any ordained to man; and yet no such advantages for preparation have been accorded to her, nor is there any qualified body to certify the public that a woman is duly prepared to give proper instruction in her profession. . . .
>
> During the upward progress of the age, and the advance of a more enlightened Christianity, the writers of this volume have gained more elevated views of the true mission of woman—of the dignity and importance of her

distinctive duties, and of the true happiness which will be the reward of a right appreciation of this mission, and a proper performance of these duties. . . .[1]

The necessity for the proper "training" for one's position in life was a concept that Sarah took very seriously in educating her own children and that she often reiterated in her own writings much later.

From the start, Mary Louise, who was always small of stature, was considered a delicate child. Recollections about her infancy appear in the autobiography.

It seems I was rather puny, and Mother wasn't a good provider in some ways; so, when Yellow Fever began to menace the City, my father hustled us all out of there and on the last boat before quarantine. . . . Our boat broke down, and no milk was to be had. . . . The Ship Doctor didn't seem very enthusiastic about me; I'm sure I didn't look worth saving. . . . Anyhow, we got over into Illinois and when Papa's mother saw me, she said, "Poor little thing; she's starved to death"—and gave me a nice juicy piece of steak, which I sucked until it was white. That, I believe was the beginning, although I still remember old ladies clasping their hands over me and saying to Mother: "She looks delicate, my dear. I'm afraid you'll never raise her!" (If they could see me now!!) (Moore, pp. 4–5)

At one point in her early years, it was thought that she suffered from "hip-joint disease."

Then began those dreaded treatments (to which I undoubtedly owe my escape from crutches!) when, during a period of about six months, every few days my left hip was pierced to the bone by a set of fine needles, released by a spring. Dr. Long was very gentle and suffered more than I did, I'm sure, but I still awaken from a dream where the dreaded needles are about to be released! . . . Finally, the danger was averted. I was allowed gentle exercise, and later was sent to a dancing school, which I loved. (Moore, p. 20)

Delicate or not, Moore loved to climb and had no fear of heights. At one point, she was reproached for hanging by her knees from a horizontal bar in front of a crowd of picnickers and felt "thoroughly ashamed of my exhibition. . . . *I should have been good.*"

Which reminds me of other "stunts," when we lived in the Studio Flat. The entire block was one building, and in front of each flat was an iron balcony, connected by a ledge as wide as the length of a brick. Mother used to tell how she would be sitting by the window, sewing or reading, when she would notice some lady on the opposite side of the street, stop and gaze up at our building in horror. She would realize that I was doing the "human fly" act, and would step out on the balcony and gently remind me to step inside at the next balcony. It seemed that it was an almost incurable habit with me, and I really needed, as Papa would say, "a little of the oil of spank." (Moore, p. 22)

Moore was also inclined to sleepwalk. Several times she traveled with her mother by rail to California. On one of the trips, she had opened the door to the platform at the rear of the sleeping car, and was just stepping out as the porter reached her. Thereafter, mother and daughter slept loosely tied together in one berth.

When Mary Louise was two, her brother Georgie was born. These are her recollections about him.

Georgie was one of those glowing, adorable children . . . everyone loved him on sight; and I was his adoring slave. Sunshine and sparkle were in his big blue eyes . . . and even then there wasn't one of the nursery rhymes he couldn't rattle off at top speed, altho I generally had to translate to make them intelligible to the uninitiated. . . .

Georgie and I used each to draw up our little chairs before the grate fire in the library on winter evenings, and he would help me sing the dolls to sleep. Soon it would be our turn, and I in my father's arms and Georgie in Mother's would grow drowsy, listening to "There's a Land that is Fairer than Day," and "Listen to the Patter of the Raindrops on my Cottage Chamber Roof." . . .

One Sunday we all started out for a walk. Georgie wore a sash of vivid blue, like his eyes. My sash was of dark brown. I felt so *terribly* about it but couldn't express my feeling. I thought, "I am so spindly and ugly—a red sash would be something pretty to look at. . . ." We walked on slowly, as Father had been delayed. Then, as he came breezing down the street, shoulders back, his long golden-brown beard blowing to either side as he walked, he came straight toward me! Stooping, he picked up my handkerchief which had fallen, handed it to me with a courtly little bow, and we all four moved on together. Father loved me—even if my sash was brown! "God was in his heaven." . . . (Moore, pp. 6, 8)

At age two, Georgie died of "brain fever." His death was the first and most traumatic of several family deaths that touched her closely as a child. She remembered Georgie in his casket, her parents' tightly clasped hands after the funeral, and her own failure to understand what had happened. Afterward, the family moved across the river to Louisville. Sarah read Schopenhauer and struggled with her despair. From this time, Mary Louise was the only child at home, for her older half-brothers had by now gone away to college or work. Except during Georgie's short life, she was far more often with her parents and the household servants than she was with other children.

Sarah and B. O. feared that Mary Louise, too, might develop the brain fever that had taken Georgie. They adamantly refused to teach her to read and threatened to fire any of the servants if they helped her.[2] The prohibition lasted surprisingly long, but it did not extend to music. Within a year or two of Georgie's death B. O. arranged for her to have a music teacher, although she was allowed only two fifteen-minute practice sessions daily including improvisation time. Emma Dewhurst, an assistant to the well-known New York piano teacher William Mason, came to live with the Carrs as Moore's first governess.[3] To the young Mary Louise, she was a tall, robust, gray-haired lady with nose glasses, "who took me at once into her heart and arms. She taught me my notes. . . . She taught me to love music, spoke a little German with me, read me lovely fairy tales and poems, and sometimes—just sat and held me in her strong arms—a refuge against loneliness for both of us, I suspect" (Moore, p. 14). They called her "Miss Dew" and she took part in family musicales: "Miss Dew played accompaniments for Father, and the evenings were *lovely*. Father's rich baritone in Mozart's 'In this Celestial Dwelling'; 'Oh, Hush Thee, my Baby'; and 'It will be Summertime, Bye and Bye'— Miss Dew singing a capable alto" (Moore, p. 19).

Moore's talent for music was confirmed by a visit from one of her future teachers.

About this time, Mother's uncle (her father's half brother, only a year or so older than Mother) returned for a brief vacation from Leipsic, where he had been for several years studying organ and music theory under such men as Richter, Reinecke, Jadassohn and Rubinstein. Being an amateur phrenologist, he felt of my "bumps" and concluded that I was destined to become a musician, and Mother was to leave no stone unturned. In this opinion he and Miss Dew were in accord, together laying plans for my future.[4]

Moore made her career intentions known early: "When she was five . . . she announced her intention of being a music teacher. . . . 'I'm going to be a music teacher,' she replied in a confident voice; but spying her mother, added in a less confident tone, 'If my mama will let me.'"[5] She had already made a debut of sorts, when she was no more than four. Someone stood her on a table in their Sunday School room to sing before an audience: "I was frightened to death, but having been accustomed to obey, I started in a high, quivering little voice—something about a 'Robin'" (Moore, p. 7). While Miss Dew was with them, they lived in a sizeable house, located on a principal street. The house was on the route taken by black funeral processions in Louisville. "When 'old Hannah,' the devoted cook, would cry, 'Fune'al comin', Mamie!' two pairs of flying feet would run down the walk to the front gate. Hannah would lift the child to one gatepost and she would flank the other, while the flamboyant funeral of some prominent colored citizen would pass, the number of bands deciding the importance of the deceased. Both 'children' were equally delighted."[6] Similar funeral processions in New Orleans became the immediate predecessors of American jazz, but they seemed to have held no musical interest for Moore.

Music, literature, theater, and art were a natural part of family life to both parents. In addition to hiring Miss Dew, they read to Mary Louise, told her stories, sang to her, and took her to plays and concerts. Among other things, her father could recite and/or sing many of Thomas Moore's popular Irish ballads from memory.[7] His business took him to other river cities; Sarah traveled almost yearly to her family in California. Often they took her along with them, so her opportunities for exposure to music and theater were extensive. All kinds of theatrical productions, including the circus, the minstrel, the museum, and the legitimate stage, as well as the musical theater and the opera, were widely popular, with both resident and touring troups, amateur and professional, in towns far smaller than Louisville. Distinctions among the genres were blurred, but all had plenty of music as a matter of course.[8] These early experiences with the theater must be considered an important source for Moore's later approach to opera and her easy movement from operetta to grand opera to vaudeville and back.

Moore was very interested in the social events in her own home. In Louisville, the family moved several times, living sometimes in a flat, sometimes at the Galt House (the city's major hotel), and at least once in a large house with several servants.

This time, on our return, Father had taken a house out on Broadway, which was then quite a fashionable part of town, though not one of the large mansions. Our house was the usual style—four stories, the upper a mansard roof, marble steps, kept shining by constant scrubbing. The household consisted of, besides ourselves, my beloved Hannah, the old style type whose "fambly" was her chief concern. Hannah presided over the kitchen. Then there was Lucy, new style housemaid, with immeasurable scorn for Hannah! . . . Ridley Reed, the boy of general utility, hitched the pony to the phaeton, kept the stoves filled, ran errands, and waited on table in a starched white coat! (Moore, pp. 13–14)

Her parents had a wide acquaintance and entertained often. They kept very late hours, and she quickly picked up their habit. As a child, she slept away the mornings after her late evenings; only later would she learn to do with very little sleep at all.

One night I awakened late, and hearing merriment below, I slipped down the stairway and peeking over the newel-post saw a very gay company just rising to go into the dining room for supper. One gentleman, glancing into the hallway, spied me, and at once claimed me for his supper partner, carrying me out, and placing me on his knee. Mother, of course, thought I should go back to bed, but Father thought I could stay awhile. So I was wrapped in a shawl and spent the evening on the knee of "Colonel" Barnabee, later of "Bostonians" fame. (Moore, p. 18)

Henry Clay Barnabee's presence attests to the Carrs' enthusiasm for the theater as well as their taste, for Barnabee's productions of Gilbert and Sullivan's operettas rivaled those of touring English troups. Perhaps Barnabee's ideas about the value of the theater as an educational tool, as opposed to the competing contemporary view of it as inherently sinful, helped influence Sarah to try her hand at writing plays later on.

Although the Carrs' friends often had some interest in the arts, the "close friends" whom Moore lists as having come to their home in her childhood were more likely to have been politicians, former officers in the Union Army, or entrepreneurs. She mentions President U. S. Grant, Gen. William Tecumseh Sherman, Gen. John A. Logan, President Garfield, Col. Henry Watterson, and Robert Ingersoll.[9] The list certainly reflects B. O.'s interest in Republican politics and, less certainly, the possibility that he may have entertained political ambitions beyond the appointment he then held. They must also sometimes have been joined by B. O.'s brother Clark E. Carr, who was active in Illinois politics. Events would show that Moore was deeply impressed by these early visitors to her parents' home and by her position as a member of a family that was a part of the social and political aristocracy the visitors represented. The Carrs seemed to have had more room for uncertainty and eclecticism in their religious than in their political views, as Robert Ingersoll's presence attests.[10]

B. O. was far from the remote and distant father figure often described in portrayals of Victorian American families. Sarah remembered him and his relationship with his daughter this way: "Colonel Carr was a genial, lovable man with a quiet, gentle wit that bubbled through his conversation spontaneously, in illness and in health, with never a sting in his joke. And the little girl of a dozen quaint or funny pet names, always could understand and meet his jokes with some of her own" (S. P. Carr, p. 2). B. O. was her earliest model as a performer both at home and in public:

> He had a beautiful high barytone voice and a repertoire of songs that ranged from grand opera to gospel hymns; and he sang to her snuggled in his arms, many of the evenings when his affairs permitted him to be at home. . . . But as he was called to assist in many church and other amateur musical entertainments, she became accustomed to hearing him in public. (S. P. Carr, p. 3)

Mary Louise adored him, and he was clearly devoted to the daughter who bore his first wife's name. Of course he was absent from home often, so their relationship was less troubled by the frictions of day-to-day living than was her relationship with her mother.

Sarah managed to instill an exaggerated sense of propriety in her daughter from an early age.

> My first positive memory must have been when I was about two years old! Sitting in the sunny bay window of Mother's bedroom were my "Aunt" Minnie Groseider (I always called her all of that during the years we knew her) and Mother, who looked relaxed and "different," not my usual lively Mother! I stood at Mother's elbow, feeling quite one of the group. As they talked, Mother reached over and WIPED MY NOSE FOR ME! Right before company!! I remember feeling utterly crushed and insulted, and the day was spoiled! Mother later recalled that this must have been about the day before my little brother Georgie was born, although she never suspected until many years later that my dignity had been so upset. (Moore, p. 5)

Sarah herself remarked rather ruefully that Moore "early knew that she could win her father to almost anything she wished to do" (S. P. Carr, p. 3). Or, as Moore put it: "Later discussions revealed that Father was spoiling me outrageously and that for my own good *some-*

body must discipline me, and that would probably have to be Mother" (Moore, p. 17).

When B. O. got tickets to the opening of one of the circus companies that wintered in Louisville, he flatly overturned her mother's system of discipline in order to see that she attended.

> Father arrived . . . in a state of wrath such as I never beheld before or after, and in his turn "pounced" on Mother. It transpired that I had done something or other that Mother had strictly forbidden. Father said, "Why didn't you spank her and send her along?" But Mother answered, "You know, B. O., that I will never spank that child again." "Well, I will," said my splendid Papa, suiting the action to the words and turning me across his knee. A few rather mild spats, and he stood me up and told me to get my hat. I have never forgotten his oration to Mother: "Madam, it is the inalienable right of every American child to attend the circus whenever it is available; and we will understand, here and now, that if punishment is necessary, some other means are to be found." And Father hurriedly drove us back to the circus himself, deciding against a return to the Custom House, and personally supervising the "tour," even to peanuts and elephants, and a visit to the famous Mr. and Mrs. Tom Thumb. (Moore, p. 17)

At various points in her autobiography, she refers to B. O. as "altogether modest and lovable," of his "naturally kingly aspect," of his bravery in the Civil War ("reported by others, not by him"), of his devotion to Sarah in the wake of his first wife's untimely death. Her descriptions of Sarah have much less to say about her mother's personality in the abstract, and more about her everyday activities.

Poor Mammy Hannah used to be dreadfully distressed by Mother's manner of marketing; to Mother it was a business matter, and she went in the phaeton in the simplest of morning costumes. Hannah would protest, "Mis' Cyarr, efn you all go lookin' like that, they'll think yo're nothin' but po' white trash"! But Mother just couldn't see silk and ostrich plumes, with diamonds, in the Market of a morning and stuck to her own ideas. (Moore, p. 14)

Her mother's continuing model of what a lady should be, her unfailing sense of duty, and her later position as aesthetic mentor and artistic collaborator would have a decisive influence on Moore's career.

Although Moore remembers her mother in those years as lively, a good horsewoman who liked to "circus" for the neighborhood children, Sarah's health became a source of concern during the years in Louisville. The many trips to California were intended to relieve the noxious effects of eastern winters and Louisville coal smoke, as well as Sarah's loneliness. Finally: "Mother's lungs got to a point where the doctors could give no hope. Dr. Long felt that if she went to California, she might live six months or a year and be happier at any rate. Mother demanded the truth of the doctors, and finally said, 'If I can ever get to California, I'll outlive all of you'" (Moore, p. 22). Meanwhile, the fickle winds of political controversy showed signs of blowing against B. O. It was no easy task to hold a political appointment from an administration that was becoming famous for its corruption, while maintaining one's personal integrity and performing one's duties in the public interest.[11] Inspectors of steam vessels worked on a fee basis, collecting license fees to support the system of inspection and certification deemed essential for public safety, and administering the system in their various districts. B. O. had to steer a careful path to establish a good safety record in his district and earn the respect of the people involved in the river's commerce, especially given the obvious possibilities for corruption built into the fee system. His relatively close association with presidents Grant, Hayes, and Garfield made him vulnerable, regardless of his own personal record, as the public demand for civil service reform grew stronger.[12]

By 1881, B. O. counted a coal mine in Iowa and some acreage in the Napa Valley of California among his assets. At fifty he could afford to resign his position and spend more time with his beloved wife and daughter. He seemed happy enough to leave the general neighborhood of his own family connections and his political friends and go to California, where he took up his position among Sarah's numerous and similarly prosperous clan.

CHAPTER 3

St. Helena

San Francisco had boomed after the discovery of gold in the nearby Mother Lode country in 1848. It was a cosmopolitan cultural center from its early days, hearing its first opera as early as 1851. The Napa Valley, which drained into San Francisco Bay, was soon cultivated as a convenient source for fresh fruits and vegetables for the new metropolis. Readily accessible by steamship, the favored means of transportation within the region for decades, mild in climate, and surrounded by wooded hills, it quickly attracted the prosperous as a location for elegant homes and vineyards. Grandfather R. H. Pratt and his two brothers had ranched there from the late 1850s; the brothers had remained there and grown comfortably rich while R. H. was drawn to the railroad enterprise. Thus there were already several well-established Pratt family homes and farms in the upper part of the valley around St. Helena when B. O. paid the sum of five thousand dollars for twenty-three acres and started his own vines several years before the Carrs left Louisville.

Eventually the Carrs acquired a total of thirty-five acres on the west side of the valley, a few miles south of St. Helena. The property forms a long rectangle. Today, part has been subdivided but most is still planted in vineyards, as it was when the Carrs owned it. At the rear is a knoll with a grove of eucalyptus trees. A small stream runs across the west side of the property. The large house they built was just below the knoll, still above the vineyard. The house is gone, but the hillside above the property remains wooded and undeveloped, as it was a century ago. To the north and south are other large nineteenth-century homes, also just at the edge of the valley, facing their own vineyards. Perhaps half a mile to the east, the one-room Vineland District School that Mary Louise attended for a time is still to be found, though its use has changed.

A volume of lithographs printed in 1878 shows a number of large Victorian homes in the valley even then. The town of St. Helena itself consisted of a broad dirt main street with a row of wooden one-story businesses on each side. Many of the early homes and businesses in St. Helena have been restored, though parts of the valley adjoining the property the Carrs named Valle Vista have been subdivided, and there is strip development along the highway. The now-decaying barn erected by B. O. a century ago is a reminder of the idyllic beauty and quiet of their Napa Valley.

In contrast to the lively descriptions of life in St. Helena in the mid-1880s, the Carrs' first years there were marked by illness and death. Sarah was thought to have tuberculosis and not expected to live when B. O. brought them out to the property in 1881. The diagnosis was wrong, for she soon recovered enough to design their large house around the small one already on the property.[1] Within the next year or two, Harriet's young husband died of cancer at Valle Vista. Soon after, Thorpe's bride and her infant both died there, she after a lingering infection resulting from the birth. At the same time, B. O.'s older son Eugene, by now a Seattle attorney, disappeared for some months while prospecting for gold in Alaska.

Extracts from the *Napa Register* and its rival the *Reporter* give an idea of the lives led by the elder Carrs, once they were established at Valle Vista. Now a gentleman farmer, B. O. first occupied himself by supervising the construction of the large house Sarah had designed. He became commander of the local post of the Grand Army of the Republic, and in that capacity helped get the veterans' home at nearby Yountville turned over to the federal government. Mary Louise remembered his uniformed, mounted splendor as he led the annual Decoration Day parade and delivered his formal oration at the cemetery.[2] He invested in the Bank of St. Helena and in a community water system. His vineyards prospered, and he was regarded as a good, strong man, closely identified with the community's business leaders. He remained interested in politics, accepting the Republican nomination for state senator for Napa and Yolo counties when it was offered in 1886. The *Register* supported him, but the rival *Reporter* raised some issues that "will not tend to bring to him strength other than that of his own personal popularity."[3] He was said to support a constitutional amendment that would give the railroads "a chance to assess themselves and pay what they are [of] a mind to in the shape of taxes." He was also charged with supporting the use of Chinese labor, a sore point with Caucasian workers in the western states.[4] Her father's politics were already too conservative for the voters. B. O. lost the election in spite of his personal charm.

For her part, Sarah put her illness far behind and became every bit as active in local affairs as her husband. Soon she was state president of the Woman's Relief Committee, the ladies' auxiliary to the Grand Army of the Republic. She worked for a home for "worthy widows, wives and mothers" of Union veterans, and "to support and relieve deserving women who served as Army nurses." After her election, the papers report that over a hundred friends gathered at Valle Vista to greet her as she returned home from the state convention. The "spacious parlors" were "quickly opened up" and an impromptu entertainment, all a "complete surprise," was organized. A farce was presented and there were recitations. B. O. and "Mamie," as little Mary Louise was often called, sang a duet, and there were solos from her and others.

Sarah contributed to women's magazines.[5] Drawing on her experiences of Louisville, she also wrote her first play, "Kentucky Belle." It was staged as a fund-raiser for the Woman's Relief Committee. The *St. Helena Star* reported that she herself was a hit in the role of Aunt Hannah.[6] The *Napa Register* reviewed the production on its front page.

We are scarcely prepared to believe this is the lady's first effort at holding the mirror up to nature, because its construction is so good and the sentiment so well developed. Unfortunately, perhaps, the setting and performance do not do the play any justice . . . and with all the credit and allowance to which amateurs are entitled it must be said that the parts were imperfectly learned. . . . In our humble opinion, "Kentucky Belle," if Mrs. Carr so chooses, will become a popular play. The "limbs and outward flourishes" only need trimming, in order that the author's work may find its most perfect expression.[7]

B. O. took a role in another entertainment organized but not authored by Sarah, *Esther, the Beautiful Queen*.[8] Apparently such amateur productions were quite common in St. Helena in those years, so the young Mary Louise had further exposure to the theater, this time amateur dramatics in the community as well as at home.

Early on at St. Helena, the family's efforts to prevent Moore from reading ended, largely because she had learned in spite of them. She quickly took advantage of her newfound access to the family library. "Mother took charge of my history, and *I* took charge of my reading" (Moore, p. 25). Immediately she absorbed Shakespeare ("in the original," as she proudly told a visiting senator), Thackeray, Dickens, George Eliot, and Jane Austen. Later she admitted that much of it had been over her head. Though her ability to read was formally sanctioned only when she was nine, at ten she published her first story. Without telling her parents, she wrote "Adventures of an Indian Maid" and sent it off to a magazine for which Sarah wrote, the *Woman's Magazine,* where it duly appeared in 1883.

There were also activities more characteristic of children, and some friends her own age. The activities included her large and well-clothed doll collection, begun when she was two with her beloved "Miss Tyree." The dolls reenacted her father's steamship voyages on the Mississippi, as well as scenes from the novels and plays she happened to be reading. She also had a dog named Frank, a loved companion. Once when she decided to run away, she dutifully tied Frank up, carefully packed her bag, and got almost to the far edge of the vineyard before changing her mind. Sarah later used the running away incident as an illustration of Moore's very strong, and possibly sometimes misplaced, sense of duty: "And prescient of her lifelong faithfulness to duties as she saw them, she quickly asked if her bag was safe and if we had untied Frank" (S. P. Carr, p. 5).

Seven years after Georgie's death, Sarah became pregnant for a third time. Mary Louise took a very enthusiastic part in sewing the layette. She would always feel very parental toward her younger brother Wray Torrey. The mixture of strong filial and maternal feelings she must have had toward Georgie, Wray Torrey, and her own parents all doubtless contributed, much later, to the determined enthusiasm with which she welcomed her own children. Perhaps her strongly maternal feelings about Wray Torrey Carr disquieted her parents. Whatever the reason, her need for interests and activities outside the home finally outweighed their fears about her "delicacy."

At age eleven, Mary Louise began to attend the nearby one-room school, located near the far end of the family vineyard. Frank, the dog, was her escort. Her home education, in which Sarah had figured so large, had both strong and weak points in comparison to the school. She could read and spell with the oldest children. Her considerable knowledge of geography, at least in her own country, came from her many rail and boat trips and required some adjustment to reconcile it with textbook information. In arithmetic she started with the youngest children, for despite her father's experience as a surveyor and quartermaster, the Carrs had scarcely introduced her to mathematics. It quickly became evident, however, that she was a lightning calculator; she digested all the arithmetic offered in the school by the end of the single term she spent there.

At some point Uncle John Haraden Pratt returned for good from Leipzig, bringing her some children's songs by Reinecke, which she and B. O. sang together.[9] The next fall she went daily to the Armstrong Academy in St. Helena, two miles away. Once a week she took the train to Napa for voice lessons with Walter B. Bartlett. There were also piano lessons. Her voice was high, very strong and precocious. B. O. made her sing for friends and family from the start. "But I was terribly timid before people, and I remember once singing before some relatives, with the tears running down my cheeks, for Father had threatened to stop my lessons if I declined or had to be unduly coaxed to sing when I was asked" (Moore, p. 26). She soon overcame her shyness and stage fright. She took part in local concerts and sometimes cantatas in church. From this point, "No one doubted that I had an operatic future" (Moore, p. 34). Soon she became a boarder at Miss Darling's Seminary in Napa, some twenty miles away, going home on weekends and suffering from loneliness during the week. Her serious music study, her intensive reading habits, and her long association with adults left her little in common with the other girls.

In the middle of the following year, when she was fourteen, Miss Darling's School was closed by an epidemic. Mary Louise joined her Aunt Carlin as a student at Miss Chase's School in Santa Rosa, another town to the north of San Francisco in neighboring Sonoma County. There she was assigned to room with her great-aunt Alice Edwards Pratt, then a young teacher with a bachelor's degree from the University of California. Aunt Alice had been the first woman in the family to go to college. She taught at the Santa Rosa Seminary for ten years and later earned the Ph.D. in English literature from the University of Chicago.[10] Though Moore said only that the roommate assignment must have been hard on her older great-aunt, Sarah thought that the serious and scholarly Alice had exerted a permanent influence over her teenage daughter. Later Alice taught at Vassar for a year before becoming head of the English department at San Diego State Normal

School, where she remained for some years before retiring.[11] At Santa Rosa, Alice posed the basic issue confronting her young female students.

> To every soul must sometime come the day
> When, standing on youth's threshold, h... i... f...
> To choose from all the myriad lives that be.
> . . . .
> What is the burden of your soul's request?
> Who sits upon your heart's most secret throne?
> Power, or Love, or Wisdom—which is best?[12]

Alice chose to remain single.

Uncle John came weekly from San Francisco to give a theory class, in which Moore was the only student. He worked her hard: "The barrels of tears I shed because, try as I would, the parallel fifths and octaves *would* creep in" (Moore, p. 36). But there were no voice lessons available in Santa Rosa. The only singing was in the church choir on Sundays, involving a rigorous schedule.

Sunday School was at ten, Church at eleven, and then back to the Seminary for a *cold Sunday dinner*. Bible Study was from three to four, young people's meeting from six-thirty to seven-thirty, and Church afterward—getting home late to bed and pretty tired. I sang in every session of course. There were no weekends at home. (Moore, p. 36)

The Carrs had taken an eclectic approach to Moore's religious education. Sarah's struggles with religious belief had probably begun after Georgie's death and continued through the rest of her life. B. O.'s religion was more easygoing. Some years later, he sent his daughter a telegram after she had sung at a series of evangelical meetings: "Congratulations to you and Dr. _____ for bagging so many sinners with song" (Moore, p. 47). In Louisville, Mary Louise had often attended the Episcopal Church with Miss Dew or,

For a change, I sometimes got permission to go to church with Hannah, where it was very exciting, as so many took part. "Yes, Lawd"—"Bress de Lawd," "I'se comin' to Jesus, Lawd, sho' as yo' is bawn." And then, at other times, I went with Lucy to her stylish church, where the service by the old colored pastor was formal, and the utmost decorum was observed. (Moore, p. 15)

She continued to attend a variety of churches in St. Helena, though none was as colorful as Hannah's had been.

At home, in St. Helena, I had gone to church when and where I pleased. One Sunday perhaps I went with Katie to her Catholic Church, where the organist always took me up in the choir loft, and generally I sang an "Ave Maria." Another Sunday I went with Bruder, the hired man, and his wife to the Lutheran Church. Next, I would go to visit Aunt Emily Pratt [really great-aunt] at the Baptist Church and help in the choir; and still another time I would go with my friend Etta to the Presbyterian Church, in the Bible Class. (Moore, pp. 36–37)

Presently, Moody and Sankey staged a week-long revival in Santa Rosa.[13] Sarah searched diligently for religious truth throughout her life, but Mary Louise now embraced the teachings of organized Christianity without question: "I poured my whole soul into that revival, being thoroughly converted (I think, I hope—I have never become 'unconverted' even though that revival cost me a lot)" (Moore, p. 37). Moore gained a lifetime of faith, but lost in that week her remarkable and precocious voice. She sang every night after her classes,

but on Sunday night, when the revival was over, I was "finished" too. Monday, I couldn't speak—Tuesday, I couldn't speak—I wanted to die. I asked to telegraph home, but Miss Chase thought it was only a cold and would soon pass away. Finally, my sensitive mother sent Father over to see me. (He crossed my heart-broken letter on his way: "my voice is gone forever!") Father was one very disgruntled man when he found me voiceless and hysterical. He told Miss Chase that if she would confine her attention to her pupils' health and education, he felt sure their parents could handle their "immortal souls." He took me home with him, and that ended my education in schools. . . . Only one who has sung with freedom and joy—and then cannot—knows what I suffered. (Moore, pp. 37–38)

The compensations for this abuse of her voice, which permanently cost her the top four notes of her range, were that she now turned her attention more fully to the piano, and that she began to compose. Her "little experiments . . . were very crude and annoyed Uncle John, as he felt I was neglecting my Harmony and Counterpoint studies. However, it comforted me to write a few songs with the despair of one who has 'lived and loved and lost'" (Moore, p. 38). Though none of Moore's early attempts at composition survive, the habit of writing songs that reflected her emotional state stayed with her for another three decades.

B. O. and Sarah had planned to take Mary Louise to Europe, probably to Madame Marchesi's school in Paris, to complete her training as a singer.[14] Now, when she was sixteen (or as soon as her voice recovered sufficiently), would have been the suitable time. Instead, B. O. found himself facing financial ruin. Part of his capital was invested in a coal property in Iowa; now the coal seam that had provided a steady income turned off the property, leaving him empty-handed. At the same time, a phylloxera epidemic, which nearly destroyed the wine-making industry in both the United States and France, deprived him of income from the vineyard and greatly reduced the value of the Valle Vista property. The final blow came when B. O. had to cover a note he had cosigned for a friend, who defaulted. At fifty-six he was forced to abandon the congenial life of a gentleman farmer and return to work.[15] The Carrs' beloved Valle Vista was offered for sale, and B. O. became the manager of a bank in San Francisco.[16] Moore later recognized how devastating all this was for her father.

From that time on, Father's gaiety and spirit gradually lessened, although he gallantly tried to hide his anxiety. He felt himself a failure! As if he were in any way responsible for these calamities. He had always thought only of his family. It was chiefly because of my future that he grieved; he had planned to take us all to Europe, to "finish" my musical education. I have always felt, and many times told him, that had he kept his money, I probably wouldn't have been "worth the powder to blow me up." (Moore, p. 40)

Sarah observed more formally, "The most poignant sorrow accompanying loss of fortune for Colonel and Mrs. Carr was their inability to send Mary Louise abroad as they had intended to do" (S. P. Carr, p. 8). Bankruptcy had been avoided, but family loyalty and pride prevented the Carrs from seeking help within the larger family circle for Mary Louise to study abroad. Instead, B. O. returned to work to support his family, and Mary Louise began to work to recover her voice. In 1889 they joined the Pratts in San Francisco, and Moore's music education began in earnest.

CHAPTER 4

San Francisco, 1889–95

For something over two years, B. O. worked as secretary and manager of the People's Home Savings Bank in San Francisco. The Carrs and their two children, Mary Louise and Wray Torrey, shared a large house at 1131 Laguna Street with the Pratts, whose youngest daughter, Carlin, was still at home. Grandfather Pratt, who was only eight years older than B. O., still held his prestigious position with the Southern Pacific Railroad. Aunt Carlin, but twenty months Moore's senior, was "going in for society" and was allowed to stay up much later than her career-bound niece. Her own career as playwright and novelist was still twenty years in the future.[1] Carlin's callers might leave around midnight; then the elder Pratts and Carrs would enjoy their own game of cards before retiring. Moore, who had already become a confirmed night person, did not appreciate her own ten P.M. bedtime.

The curfew was imposed after Moore had spent a month near Seattle in the summer of 1889 with her half-brother Eugene and his new wife, Alice Preston Carr. Part of the visit was passed at the state militia's summer camp, where she was allowed "grown-up" status, meaning that she could receive male callers. Eugene expressed some concern over his sister's enthusiasm for this arrangement, urging her to remain a little girl for a while longer. This visit resulted in her first surviving composition, a lullabye dedicated to a new baby born to some of her friends from that trip a few weeks after her return to San Francisco. "Lullabye" is listed as opus 1, number 1 in her catalog and was later published; Moore sang it often in public.[2]

With the coming of 1891, her living arrangements changed once more. B. O. was offered a better job in Lemoore, a rural community in the San Joaquin Valley, several hundred miles from San Francisco.[3] Sarah welcomed the opportunity for her own reasons. The Carrs permitted their daughter to remain behind with her grandparents, but only reluctantly. The Pratts, who had lived at the Lick House before the Carrs left St. Helena, now moved back into a hotel, this time the Bella Vista, "one of the best family hotels in the city" (Moore, p. 49). Carlin and Mary Louise shared one large room, while the elder Pratts, whom she came to regard as a second set of parents, took over an adjoining suite. Mary Louise remained at the Bella Vista for most of the rest of her training, although she spent summers and holidays with her parents.

San Francisco's musical life in the 1890s was probably second only to that of New York in richness and vigor. Mary Louise's dedication to opera may well have resulted from having been taken there to see and hear Adelina Patti or Lillian Nordica in one of Colonel Mapleson's famous touring companies of the 1880s, even before the move to San Francisco.[4] She may even have seen Emma R. Steiner's *Fleurette,* which was produced in 1889.[5] The Tivoli Opera House offered performances almost nightly from the time it opened its doors in 1879 until it was destroyed in the earthquake and fire of 1906. It occupied three different locations in those years, but it was dark for only forty nights the entire time. Opera was sung in English. *Otello* ran for thirty-four nights, and *Faust* for forty-two. In the 1890s, the Tivoli's five most popular productions were *Il Trovatore, The Mikado, Aida, Faust,* and *H.M.S. Pinafore.*[6] In summer the fare was somewhat lighter. Gertrude Stein, who grew up across the bay in Oakland in the same years, remembered going to Buffalo Bill's Wild West shows at the Tivoli.[7] Mary Louise saw his shows and met Buffalo Bill, who had once been Uncle Eugene's scout.[8]

As in other American cities, opera was the province of the Italians, while orchestral playing was dominated by the Germans, a situation that continued well into the twentieth century. Although there were pit orchestras, symphony concerts were not presented in San Francisco on a consistent, season-after-season basis, as opera was, until several years after the 1906 earthquake.[9] Hence Moore's listening experience focused on theater, opera, and song; she probably heard little orchestral music except from the theater pit, which meant abbreviated string sections and condensed orchestrations. H. B. Pasmore, her teacher, confirmed this by listing the instrumentation of one of the leading San Francisco orchestras: four first violins, two seconds, two cellos, one viola, and one double bass, somewhat smaller than a modern chamber orchestra and top-heavy in balance.[10] Thus she was not introduced to the repertoire of the Classical and Romantic symphonists, nor did she gain a feeling for the subtleties of orchestration.

Moore's earliest music teacher had been Emma Dewhurst, back in Louisville. In St. Helena, she had commuted to Napa for lessons with W. B. Bartlett, probably the person who persuaded both Moore and her parents that Moore should develop her voice. At some point she had some voice lessons in San Francisco with Louisa Marriner-Campbell, a soprano with a high, flexible voice like her own.[11] But her main study over this five-and-a-half-year period was with Henry Bickford Pasmore and John Haraden Pratt.

Mr. Pasmore and Uncle John, as she called them, had in common several years of study in Leipzig, as well as similar interests in composition, singing, and keyboard. Both were very highly regarded as musicians and teachers in San Francisco. Generally, Mr. Pasmore had charge of her voice, while Uncle John, with whom she had already been working, taught her theory, counterpoint, and composition. These two teachers made a serious, coordinated effort to give her training similar to that she would have received in a formal conservatory. Sarah had dreamed of university study for her daughter as a substitute for foreign study, but Mr. Pasmore convinced her that a university was not the place where Moore could develop her talents. He was probably right, although one consequence of this decision was that Moore did not receive any kind of formal diploma for her study.

Pasmore had grown up on a farm in Wisconsin, where his chances for music study were slight. In his late teens, he went to Oakland, California, where he began to study piano and organ and taught to support himself. By 1882 he had saved enough for the compulsory voyage to Leipzig. There, "Jadassohn went so far as to say that young Pasmore had the most talent for composition of any American who had ever attended the conservatory. The young composer was even placed above Chadwick."[12]

Pasmore's overture "Miles Standish" was well received in both Berlin and Leipzig. Although he followed the prudent path of preparing himself for a teaching career, he was one of a small handful of West Coast musicians to be mentioned in an early study of American composers.[13] The most valuable part of his Leipzig experience he could not pass on to his students: "It seems to me," Mr. Pasmore said in an interview in 1931, "I heard there the greatest music I have ever experienced. Brahms occasionally conducted his compositions and Reinecke was leader of the Gewandhaus Orchestra."[14] He studied voice as well as composition in Leipzig, then went to England to study with William Shakespeare, an advocate of the Italian bel canto style of singing.[15] It was in England that he learned how to sing and how to teach singing. Four of Pasmore's own six children became musicians, and he took them to Berlin for their training—an indication of the value he placed on his own European experience as a student.[16]

At first Pasmore worked with Moore to reconstruct the voice that had been damaged in Santa Rosa. "I began . . . the laborious and discouraging task of building back, note by note, the ghost of my former voice" (Moore, pp. 40–41). In two years' time she could report: "By the time I was eighteen [August, 1891] my voice was improving, and I was having more confidence; it seemed that probably my voice would regain its earlier promise. I was studying operatic parts and was prepared in ten roles by the time I was twenty" (Moore, p. 48). She substituted for Mrs. Pasmore, the regular accompanist, when some of the Pasmore children were born. Mr. Pasmore's manner of teaching encouraged her to learn a large repertoire: "My repertoire was large and varied, for at Mr. Pasmore's studio, we not only took our own lessons, but listened to the others. Often I was allowed to accompany, and Mr. Pasmore's own excellent musicianship was an ever-present inspiration" (Moore, p. 48).

If Moore had little to say about Pasmore in her autobiography, she offered even less about Uncle John. Many years later she told an interviewer, "my best work was influenced by my teacher John Haraden Pratt of San Francisco."[17] Pasmore also admired him and offered an insight into his character: "He taught me one of the greatest lessons I have ever learned. . . . His interest and evident pleasure in doing each thing, no matter how small or humble, to the best of his ability, taught me the pleasure that lies in the little things of life."[18] Uncle John had been taught to sing as a boy by his father, Simeon Pratt of Freeport, Maine, whose beautiful tenor voice was legendary in the Pratt family. He found his way to Leipzig in 1879, where he too studied composition with Jadassohn, as well as with Alfred Richter.[19] On his return he became the organist for two churches in the Bay Area in addition to teaching. He was a patient, personally unambitious man who did his best to impart his own rigorous standards to his niece. A song, a wedding gift to Moore, survives in the Moore

Archive, along with some much later variations for violin and piano. They show him to be a fine craftsman writing in a rather conservative style, but they do not illustrate his reputed contrapuntal skill in any obvious way. They do suggest carefully controlled elegance, a control that must have presented a challenge to Moore's facile musical imagination. The only counterpoint exercise by Moore that survives from this period displays a sense of easy discipline, without a sign of the parallel fifths and octaves that had bedeviled her earlier efforts in Santa Rosa.[20]

Moore's handwritten catalog, which she kept from 1889 on Uncle John's advice, shows how easily she turned out short pieces of her own, in addition to the exercises for her teacher. From the "Lullabye" of 1889 that he deemed worthy of being called her first real composition and following numerous but unrecorded practice efforts from previous years, there are one hundred items in thirty-five opus numbers listed for Moore's years in San Francisco. Most are songs and short piano pieces, including marches and dances. Often the songs are settings of her own texts, or texts contributed by her family or their friends. Only a few of the items listed survive. There is also a lost piano trio and an operetta, *The Oracle,* whose music survives. About a dozen of these early songs were eventually published.

Within a year of her arrival in San Francisco, Moore had moved from occasionally accompanying Pasmore's classes to substituting as teacher to organizing her own classes. Her teachers had supported their own study by teaching; now she was highly motivated by her father's financial troubles and her own well-developed sense of duty to follow suit. In 1890 she organized classes of students among her friends in Napa and Santa Rosa, where she had attended school herself. Soon she was making an overnight trip each week to meet them. Gradually she added other students in San Francisco. After her voice became stronger, she took on a regular job as a soprano soloist in the First Baptist Church, a position she held for about five years.

Presently the out-of-town classes dwindled, but having learned from her mistakes, she found herself teaching another group of students, this time in the more distant town of Boulder Creek, near Santa Cruz. Her account of this class is well worth repeating.

The new class was in a thriving little town in the Santa Cruz mountains, and from the outset, it was most satisfactory. Among my pupils were the wife of the hotel-keeper and her grown daughter, the principal of the school, the Presbyterian minister, and other talented residents. My headquarters were at the Morgan Hotel, and nothing was too much trouble for my comfort. The kind-hearted hotel-keeper and his wife and daughter saw to it personally that I had the juiciest steaks, the richest cream, and that the parlor was entirely at my disposal for my lessons.

As I glance through my early scrapbooks and see accounts of the musicales, it takes me back to the warm interest of those sincere people. One account says: "The Drawing Room of the Morgan House was filled with the creme de la creme of Boulder Creek, with here and there a representative from Ben Lomond and Santa Cruz." (Yehudi Menuhin lives at Ben Lomond now.) Mentioning the dignified school principal, the article continues, "He sang 'Love's Sorrow' in his usual happy style." And again—" 'Let Me Love Thee,' as sung by Miss Carr, was immense." During these two years, a number of musicales were given and also one performance of *Penelope*, with the school principal as the "Milkman."[21]

I used to take an early morning ferry from San Francisco on Wednesdays, arriving in Boulder Creek about noon. I would then teach all that afternoon and evening, and the following morning leave for San Francisco at one o'clock, arriving at six. Santa Cruz mountains were noted for their rainfall. The inhabitants used to measure it "by the yard," instead of by inches. Several times, during my period of teaching, the stage met the train at Ben Lomond—and once at Felton, ten miles away—because of washouts. On that trip we had to alight from the stage at several narrow places while some of the men steadied the stage as it crept past a narrow spot, with one wheel over the bank. (Moore, pp. 57–58)

Moore was much more than a voice teacher who commuted. She was the town's cultural and entertainment center, headquartered in the hotel parlor. The experience of teaching and coaching students, most of them older than she, and the staging of skits like *Penelope*, as well as organizing and promoting the musicales, prepared her for much of her later activity. There is a strong similarity between Moore's function in Boulder Creek and the community self-improvement schemes that Sarah was becoming involved in at the same time in Lemoore. For Sarah, though, the musicales and dramatics were means to achieve various community social goals. For Moore, the music was an end in itself.

Moore found time for a very active, though rigidly chaperoned, social life during her San Francisco years. Her autobiography gives more attention to a succession of suitors, starting with a fourteen-year-old farm boy during her first term of school in St. Helena, than it does to her study or her compositions. Her descriptions show how restricted was her independence. By her nineteenth birthday she had made and broken four engagements in San Francisco, all apparently superficial relationships. When one swain wrote to B. O. requesting permission to marry her, B. O. telegraphed his answer (NO!) and dispatched Sarah to the city to break it up. Another suitor was a voice student recruited to play opposite her in a club production of *Penelope* that was given both in San Francisco and Lemoore. He thought her onstage behavior improper and became jealous. This time, Grandfather Pratt provided a sympathetic and supportive ear, helping her to break off the engagement herself. She describes herself as "in love with the idea of love" in those years, hardly a unique situation for a talented, vigorous, and attractive young woman, sheltered or not.

Her relationships with men seem in hindsight to have involved plenty of flirtations but not much in the way of real friendship. Moore's life was quite different from the lives of her suitors, coinciding with theirs mainly when her vocation and their avocation of music brought them together. Yet it was clearly assumed that her career would eventually be superseded by marriage. Sarah had written an essay a few years earlier, perhaps intended to counter Great-aunt Alice Edwards Pratt's example, entitled "Old Maids," which stated the family's priorities:

Then I hail the old maid; give her the first place; let her have all opportunity; let her educate herself, bring out her talent, make as perfect a woman of herself as nature and all the arts, and all sympathy and kindness, can accomplish.
And we mothers, we who know what ecstasy it is, what joy eternal and unspeakable, to nestle the dear little ones to our hearts, to warm them in mother-love, and shelter them in darkness and in light; we who lean upon the strong right arm of the "one man of all the world" for us, let us cherish kindly all among us who know not these joys.[22]

The chaperone situation remained fundamental to her way of life all the same. When she began the teaching trips to Napa, she stayed and taught at the home of family friends. But permission to make this trip of no more than a few hours each way had to be sought, earnestly, in an interview with her father, after her mother had turned her down. At the Bella Vista Hotel, she was supervised every bit as strictly as before:

There could be no tête-à-têtes in a big hotel. I lived the life of a goldfish. It wasn't proper to drive unchaperoned, and San Francisco was not a happy climate for driving. Nor could a nice girl venture into the Park and sit upon a park bench. The actual extent of most love-making in those days was a furtive pressure of the hand or a rare and hasty kiss, snatched at the risk of being observed and "talked about." I am sure there *was* love-making at that era, but it never came under my observation. (Moore, p. 54)

One of her proposals was received in a hotel parlor, and she described the scene. "Of course, as it was in one of the hotel parlors, there was no further 'demonstration.' No 'lady' living in such a hotel would receive any gentleman alone. The bell-boy always brought up a card, and you went down—except, of course, when the family was at home" (Moore, p. 54).

Such a system could not work without making plenty of organized activity available to the young people involved. Carlin, Mary Louise, and other young people living at the Bella Vista and the neighboring Colonial Hotel organized themselves informally for Dutch treat outings to the theater, the beach, and across the Golden Gate to Marin County for hikes. They called themselves the "What's Up" club, "so named because Grandfather would come to the open door between our suite and theirs and say, 'Well, what's up tonight, girls and boys?' No hour was too late for them to be up, joining in, and interested in our fun" (Moore, p. 49). The Progressive Club, organized by one Mrs. Farnham, was a singles group that met regularly at Golden Gate Hall and offered social outings for its members.

Through this group, Moore received her first commission, unpaid, for an operetta that the club's membership could produce. With exuberant self-confidence, she began what was to become a one-woman show.

Mrs. Farnham startled me one day by asking me to write an operetta for the club! I was sure I was unequal to the task—but was intrigued by the idea. I was nearly twenty at the time and busy with my Boulder Creek classes, San Francisco pupils, Church position, and concert engagements. But during the long trips to the mountains [i.e., to her Boulder Creek class], I thought about it more and more. Finally I concocted a silly plot [text lost] about an Irish policeman who left New York and went to Athens, where he re-opened the Oracle at Delphi. He installed his pretty New York bride as high priestess, engaged a lot of Athenian girls and boys as vestal virgins and priests, and himself became the Voice of the Oracle through some ventriloquistic feats, maintaining a great air of mystery and secrecy until his employees were convinced of the authenticity of the "revival." There was a young Athenian heiress whose "rapscallion" of a guardian wanted to marry her (incidentally her fortune), although she was in love with a nice young dry-goods clerk, "out of a job." Her young companion, attending her mistress at Delphi, struck up an acquaintance with a travelling salesman for a wholesale cigar and liquor store in Rome. Altogether, with a combination of misunderstandings and complications, the "plot" was ridiculously funny.[23]

It is not surprising that the lyrics included a rhyme about chaperones, given the situation of its author and the other members of the Progressive Club.

> *Leander*: Oh Doris, strange as it may seem
> To one whose beatific dream,
> Is oysters and vanilla cream,
> Is oysters and ice cream.
>
> It's not "au fait" to go alone,
> And sup on ham or deviled bone,
> Without a proper chaperone,
> Without a chaperone.[24]

Moore's two acts of dialogue for *The Oracle* stand as the only libretto she both wrote and set to music herself. After completing the text, she wrote the musical numbers. The various songs and ensembles borrow from Gilbert and Sullivan, the music hall, and the parlor for their style characteristics. In one preperformance article, she went out of her way to point out that the music was "very unpretentious . . . suited to the popular taste." She found it necessary to apologize for "making the airs catchy," and pointed out that "she expects to do better work."[25]

The music complete, she took charge of preparing the participants, who were her fellow Progressive Club members. Presently she was "chosen" to sing the lead role of the Athenian heiress, which she had written to suit her own voice. Mrs. Farnham prevailed upon E. M. Rosner, director of the Orpheum Theatre orchestra, to conduct, and a pit orchestra was hired. There was one rehearsal with the orchestra, and the novice librettist-composer-director-singer found herself sitting up all night to recopy the bass and clarinet parts, which she had not transposed correctly the first time.

The Oracle was scheduled for two performances at Golden Gate Hall in March, 1894. They became a much-publicized social event. Moore was genuinely shaken by the attention that accrued to her as the result of her achievement, for she had been raised with the idea that, as a lady, she should avoid publicity.

It was an invitation affair, and invitations were at a premium. It had been "front page stuff" in the *Examiner, Chronicle,* and *Call,* for several days, with reporters and photographers at dress rehearsals. As I look back, I am rather amazed at my youthful reaction when I found my own picture on the front page. I went to my room and actually wept, feeling a complete disgrace at being so "public"—as if I were a criminal. Uncle John had supplied my picture, which I had refused the reporter who had come to interview me some days before, saying I did not "care to have my picture in the public prints." (Moore, p. 61)

The reviews were very kind, for such a work from a female member of "society" was definitely a novelty.[26] She sang well, she had prepared the cast well, and "the music, although unpretentious, expresses admirably the situations of the play."[27] No judgment was offered on the book; for such an entertainment, silliness was expected. The San Francisco press would never again make such a fuss over Moore or her work.

In all these vigorous and expanding circles of activity, Moore worked within and took for granted the protected status that went with her position as a member of a privileged family. B. O.'s financial setbacks, which had moved him into a salaried position in the work force, did not disrupt the pattern, which went far beyond the awkwardness of requiring some form of chaperone even when she was working. Family friends provided her with a class of students, a place to stay, and even publicity for the Napa class. There was probably a similar connection to help start the Boulder Creek class as well. Her railroad pass, obtained through Grandfather Pratt, assured that her trips would be the more profitable, since she need pay no fares for her travels. In San Francisco she taught in the ballroom of the Bella Vista Hotel. Her room was paid for by her parents, and she was thus able to negotiate the use of the ballroom in exchange for a monthly free concert, without paying additional rent. Of course, it is likely that many of her students came as the result of Mr. Pasmore's or Uncle John's recommendation, based on her obvious talent and drive, once she had gotten started.

But protection and privilege also brought obligations and problems, thus in some ways limiting her opportunities. Had she been allowed to travel alone, perhaps a way might have been found within the family to send her abroad for part of her training. After all, Great-aunt Alice, some thirteen years Moore's senior, was even then studying in England.

The strong sense of duty she had acquired from B. O. and Sarah led Moore to undertake a teaching schedule that must have limited her own study time. Once she had launched herself as a teacher, she felt that her new obligations should come before any opportunity to travel, even inside the country.

About this time Grandfather decided to take a family party East to visit the Chicago World's Fair [the World Columbian Exposition of 1893] and to tour the Eastern States. We were to go in his private [railroad] car. Of course, he invited me. That was my first difficult decision to make. It was right in the middle of the season. I actually prayed over that problem. If I went, I would have to give up my Church position, and how could I ask my pupils to discontinue their lessons for six weeks or more? But, oh, how I wanted to go! I went to Grandfather and talked it over with him, hoping that he would not think I was silly. I told him that I thought it was my duty to remain, that if I wanted to be a musician, I must expect to make some sacrifice. I know now that he was very proud of my decision. . . . (Moore, pp. 49–50)

The opportunity to travel by private railroad car would disappear with Grandfather Pratt's retirement in 1896. Twenty years would pass before Moore had another chance to visit the East Coast. By missing the World Columbian Exposition, she lost the chance to see such current domestic feminist experiments as the Woman's Building, the Rumford Kitchen, or the Children's Building and the fairgrounds lit with electric lights.[28] She might have attended numerous symphony concerts, of a quality not available in San Francisco, given by the Chicago, New York, or Boston symphonies.[29] She might have met other composers both female and male, including the already prominent Amy Beach,[30] or attended theatrical events that would have influenced her outlook on her art or suggested specific musical approaches or techniques to her. Moore, in placing her duty to short-term professional commitments ahead of her long-term need for personal and professional growth, seems to have been wilfully closing doors when she might have been opening them.

Family ties also bound her closely. Sarah and B. O. had agonized over leaving her in San Francisco to study when necessity took them to Lemoore.

How could these parents leave their daughter in the city? How could they, so far away, sleep at night, not knowing what might be happening to their child? And how could she let them go—the little brother she loved as both a sister and a mother might love? . . . The wise physician who cared for Mary Louise said to her mother, "Your daughter has the constitution and temperament of the singer and the creative musician. She never will be happy away from music and its requirements. You can take her to that remote agricultural locality, so new and poor that for years there will be neither time nor money to build up musical or other artistic surroundings; and with her career halted and nothing to nourish the need of her heart and mind, she probably will become a permanent invalid . . .

Mrs. Carr, do you not believe that Providence can take care of her here as well as in the San Joaquin Valley?" (S. P. Carr, pp. 11–12)

One can imagine that inner conflicts must have been developing within Moore. There were plenty of possible sources: the early frustration of rebuilding her voice and the dashed hope of study abroad; the enormous social pressure toward courtship and marriage, chaperones and all; the potential conflict between an operatic career and that of a composer; the conflict between the social view of music as merely entertainment and her potential as a composer of serious music; the conflict she herself constructed between her almost compulsive teaching and social commitments and the need for study and reflection to develop her powers as a composer. Yet it appears that she could not even acknowledge her dilemmas. Her family had done its best to provide her with suitable training in San Francisco, and she took advantage of her opportunity with admirable diligence. In exchange, she accepted, permanently, the views of society that went with their privileged position.

Once she had been thought too "delicate" to undertake the rigors of regular schooling. Was she now falling back on her earlier "delicacy" when she started to develop debilitating fainting spells? Did they offer a way to sidestep her growing conflicts? Whatever their source: "I was always, it seemed, 'coming to,' and finding myself the center of an excited group, without the slightest memory of having fainted. . . . For years I was subject to these very exasperating occurrences—from over-fatigue, emotional excitement, or from nobody knows what" (Moore, pp. 41–42). Sarah may have suspected as much when she described them as: "a strange physical manifestation. . . . They seemed to be an accompaniment of her intense emotional temperament . . . nature's way of shutting off emotional strain."[31] The fainting spells came on often but at irregular intervals. Sometimes they left her feeling ill for several days. They continued for twenty years or more, until she came to terms with some of these conflicts and began to discover her own strength.

CHAPTER 5

Sarah's Turn

Mary Louise had adjusted to city life in San Francisco quickly, looking no further than her music and her beaux. We have no evidence about how B. O. managed with his new job, but it is clear that the strong-willed and articulate Sarah was not happy. The child of pioneers, she had grown up on ranches in northern California and in the rough settlements of the Mother Lode country as the railroad pushed its way slowly across the Sierra. As a bride, she had been glad to leave Memphis, a far larger and more established city than the Sacramento of her high school days. She had chosen to live across the river from Louisville rather than in the city itself, until young Georgie's death prompted her to seek the comfort of more company. It was her illness and her yearning for rural California that led B. O. to leave Louisville and settle in the Napa Valley. Given this history, it is not surprising that, a decade after their departure from Louisville, Sarah welcomed the business opportunity that took them away from San Francisco to primitive Lemoore in 1891.

From that haven, Sarah expressed her feelings about city and country in an essay, "Give the Country Its Due," which appeared shortly after the San Francisco production of *The Oracle*.

The larger number of writers live in cities and villages, and do not seem to estimate the quality or value of the influence of rural life upon the race. . . .

Population everywhere tends to congestion in town and city. This is not altogether the natural result of the gregarian instinct; it is also the outgrowth of the false estimation of city culture, city manners, city privileges. . . .

There are necessities of urban life. . . . But that they should be preferred for other reasons shows not only moral disease but a lack of the artistic and spiritual elements. . . .

Life in cities breeds selfishness, indifference to suffering, irresponsibility. . . .

39

. . . The large foreign element bears a great part in this condition; probably also, it accounts for the lack of unanimity, of public spirit, and public pride that is remarked by eastern visitors, in San Francisco especially . . . in public enterprises of an intellectual or artistic nature.

There is a neighborliness and heartiness among country people, a quiet patriotism, an ability to wait patiently through bad times for the good times, a willingness to listen to both sides, a strong, true Americanism unknown to foreignized cities.[1]

Though she may have disliked San Francisco and its large foreign-born population heartily, Sarah had not wasted her two years there. In fact, her city experience prepared her for a new career of her own. In Lemoore she blossomed as a social activist in the mold of domestic feminism and what she called "moral uplift."[2] Both were popular aspects of the social reform movements of the 1890s and did not conflict with her distaste for city life. Except for the suffrage movement, which all the Pratt women heartily supported, she was willing to leave the issues of politics and economics to the men. Not for her were the ideas advocated in those years by reformers like Charlotte Perkins Gilman. Although she participated in two women's congresses organized by Gilman in San Francisco and contributed to Gilman's *Impress*, she had no sympathy for Gilman's attacks on the establishment in general and the Southern Pacific Railroad in particular.[3]

Sarah's impetus to activism began with her longstanding interest in religion and philosophy. Sarah had experienced doubts about her Protestant, Baptist religion as early as fifteen years before the move to Lemoore, at the time of Georgie's death. Then, she was engulfed "in a sea of doubt," reading "the dark philosophies of Schopenhauer" (Moore, p. 15). Grandmother Pratt, who had lost several children herself, was probably trying to comfort her daughter when she wrote these verses:

> . . . Though bitter tears be shed
> In secret silence, and the heart be shred
> Of hope apparent;—yet the Power above
> Our doubts and struggles, ever will approve
> The purpose high. . . .
> . . . .
> No more
> Let doubts and fears disturb thine every way,
> But claim the peace, vouchsafed to thee. . . .[4]

Another poem by Grandmother Pratt tells us that some of the family were attending the sermons of the Reverend Horatio Stebbins at the First Unitarian Church in San Francisco in the spring of 1890.

'Twas this he taught. That we should *be*
    All that our inmost hearts believe.
That naught avails, to only *see*,
    And *say*, we do the truth receive.

But hearts must *feel*, and hands must *work*,
    and *live* the truths for other's needs
Nor sacrificial duties shirk,
    But high ideals hold for deeds.

And more he said, but this I draw
    From all his words of wisdom given:
To *live* the higher, holier law
    Of Christ, would make our earth a Heaven.[5]

Stebbins seems to have converted Sarah to social activism as well as to another form of Protestant Christianity. She soon began a course of private study that would lead to missionary work and eventually her ordination.[6]

Meanwhile, Sarah began her public career as a reformer by organizing two women's clubs in Lemoore, the first ones in the state outside San Francisco and Los Angeles. She started with the Alpha Club, intended to provide otherwise unavailable educational advantages to unmarried girls aged sixteen and over: "Book reviews were encouraged as well as programs of recitations, instrumental, and vocal entertainment. . . . The object of this club was the improvement of its members intellectually, socially, and physically.[7] Members could continue to participate after they married, and many did. The Alpha Club had a different purpose from the Lemoore Woman's Club, organized soon after with the motto, "Room for all and work for all." The one was for self-improvement, the other for community service. The clubs acquired a clubhouse and bought a piano. They opened a free reading room and stocked it with periodicals. They arranged to acquire property in the center of town for a park. As soon as the California Federation of Women's Clubs was formed, they joined. They staged musicales, charged admission, and used the proceeds for their program of community improvement.[8] They arranged work parties to plant trees in their new park, then rounded up male volunteers for the heavy labor and served them refreshments.

The first hot lunch program was creatively engineered. The ladies cooked the meals in their homes and transported [them] hot on Chinese laundry carts. They executed a similar feat, when the "smelling committee," whose job it was to inspect livery stables and barns, ditches, and muddy streets, called for a town "cleanup party." Some 200 Lemoore residents turned out for the event and the ladies provided assignments and supper.[9]

One winter Sarah journeyed to a neighboring town several times to deliver a series of lectures under the general heading "My Wife" and then attempted to organize a club similar to the Alpha Club for the moral uplift of young men.[10]

Privately, Sarah described her new situation in terms that leave no doubt about how different it was from cosmopolitan San Francisco, still the only large city on the west coast.

At that time the vast section of country which is now the raisin country of America, was in the first fifteen years of its development. The conditions were primitive, the people, even those rich in land, were living in the most primitive way and toiling hard. Little or no music or books; not a half dozen pianos in the town or roundabout, nothing for culture or entertainment beyond the public schools.[11]

In a dispatch to the *Impress*, Sarah described the new community's accomplishments after a few years of her activism. She mentioned the Lemoore Dramatic Club, which gave performances of her own curtain raiser, *A Couple of Incidents*, at both Lemoore and neighboring Hanford. She spoke with pride of the school buildings in her area, which were equipped for dramatics, and went out of her way to praise the musical life of a third town in the district: "No town of its size in California, and few anywhere can show such a high standard of general excellence in music as Tulare. . . ."

There was a town orchestra, and teachers "who succeed in making their pupils thoroughly enthusiastic. One teacher, a lady, makes musical history, and a deep study of composers, their methods, local conditions and surroundings, and their effect upon music in America and California, as obligatory as the ordinary instrumental and vocal music."[12]

Sarah may have hoped that her whirlwind of activity would make of Lemoore a suitable place for her daughter to continue her career. Perhaps she really believed that the town had become, for its musical activities, "the Boston of the San Joaquin Valley," cr at least culturally self-reliant on Emerson's model.[13] Her achievements in Lemoore were well publicized in San Francisco, for the *Impress* could report in 1895: "Speaking of Women's Clubs, he [Rev. H. W. Haweis, addressing a meeting of the second Woman's Congress in San Francisco] referred with deep feeling to the noble work of Mrs. Sarah Pratt Carr in Lemoore, where she is President of the Woman's Club, and of the new ethical movement in which she is so active, both in Lemoore and Hanford. Mrs. Carr's name was greeted with applause."[14]

Sarah's success with the women's clubs helped build a following that made it possible for her to organize four Unitarian congregations in neighboring towns once she began her missionary work in 1894. The church work seems to have been a logical extension of her club-centered domestic feminist activism. In Hanford, where she began, the congregation consisted almost entirely of women. Rev. Charles W. Wendte, her mentor, describes a missionary trip to her church in Hanford. He was met by a "committee of ladies" and put up at the town's leading hotel, entirely run by women; then he preached to an audience of "one hundred women and two old men."

On our way back to the hotel I asked one of the escort: "Are there then no men in your town, or is it an Adamless Eden?" She laughingly replied: "The men? I will show you some of them," and stepping smartly up to the swinging door of a saloon she pushed it open. There they were, sure enough a score or more of men, lounging, smoking, drinking, and discussing the local affairs and politics, leaving the intellectual and moral life and the social amenities of the community to the women in their homes.[15]

Sarah preached at Hanford until 1897, when the congregation found a full-time minister. In the meantime, she had started a second congregation in Lemoore in 1895 and a third at Visalia in 1896. The following year she began preaching in Fresno as well. She was formally ordained, in the course of these activities, on April 24, 1896, at the Pacific Unitarian Conference. Her own account of her ministry, written a few years later, is very modest.

. . . Your communication asking for my name for the Unitarian Yearbook is at hand. . . . I would rather my name did not appear, as my work was purely missionary work, and circumstances drew me into it rather late in life. . . .

In all of these places except Lemoore, small churches were founded, and two other ministers preached at Hanford, though the church lapsed later. At Fresno I had begun a promising work, where there is now a church, when my husband's health broke; and since that I have been unable to work in the ministry except as an occasional supply here in Seattle and in a little missionary work one summer at a mining camp, during three months, without pay.

Yours truly and with regret that my record is so poor and meager,

Sarah Pratt Carr.[16]

Moore gives another perspective that shows both her own pride in her mother's ministerial work and its unorthodox theological nature, so much in contrast to the orthodoxy of the family's political stance.

My Mother about this time, having studied intensively, was ordained into the ministry and accepted a pulpit in the neighboring town for Sunday mornings, taking the train on Saturdays and returning Sunday after services. Sunday evenings she conducted an informal young people's group in the hall above the bank where Father was cashier. As Mother's denomination was Unitarian, some of the other churches looked upon her (in those days) as almost godless. But before long, she won the warm cooperation of the other ministers, for while they did not approve of her label, they liked her and admitted that she was reaching many who had not been regular church attendants before. (Moore, p. 66)

Wendte admired Sarah's work extravagantly:

excellent work is being done by Mrs. Sarah Pratt Carr in Central California. She has lately established a Unitarian Society at Hanford, the county seat of Tulare County, an exceedingly fertile district, but somewhat notorious as the home of the famous Evans bandits and other desperadoes. Mrs. Carr has done wonders with the place, forming clubs among the girls and mothers and young men and revolutionizing the whole town. She is now holding services twice on Sunday, preaching excellent sermons and organizing church work of every kind. She receives nothing for her services and incurs considerable expense in going to and from Hanford.[17]

In fact, Sarah's life experience had prepared her for her service in newly settled Lemoore far better than Wendte's cosmopolitan background had prepared him to oversee her.

However remarkable her growing success in her new community, Sarah worried about her daughter's welfare. As Moore's career gathered momentum, the fainting spells were becoming more frequent. Earlier Sarah had been persuaded to leave her daughter behind in San Francisco to pursue her career. Now she may have been swayed by the old fear of the potentially harmful effects of study upon Moore's health.

Another cause of mental disease is the excessive exercise of the intellect or feelings. . . . In cases of pupils at school or at college, a diseased state, from over-action, is often manifested by increased clearness of mind and temporary ease and vigor of mental action. In one instance, known to the writer, a most exemplary and industrious pupil . . . first manifested the diseased state of her brain and mind by demands for more studies and a sudden and earnest activity in planning modes of improvement for herself and others. When warned of her danger, she protested that she never was better in her life; . . . that her mind was never before so bright and clear, and study never so easy and delightful. And at this time, she was on the verge of derangement, from which she was saved only by an entire cessation of all intellectual efforts.[18]

Also, Grandfather Pratt was preparing to retire from the railroad, which meant that the Pratts would leave San Francisco and Mary Louise would lose her present living arrangement. Moore had found a room with another of Mr. Pasmore's students for several months on at least one earlier occasion, but her parents felt a need to supervise her social life more carefully than such an arrangement, on a permanent basis, would allow.

In San Francisco, Moore had more students and more concert engagements. As the pressures associated with the production of *The Oracle* grew, she dropped her Boulder Creek class and the position as a church soloist. For the summer of 1894, she secured a position (under an Italian pseudonym) with a small opera company that planned a summer tour. Her roles were to be Marguerita in *Faust,* Rosina in *The Barber of Seville,* and Micaela in *Carmen.* "It happened that I was called to rehearse two operas on one day and three the next. I fainted in my dressing room one evening but was able to keep the matter quiet. The next afternoon I had the bad luck to faint in rehearsal" (Moore, p. 63). The maestro decided that his sub-ninety-pound soprano was too fragile to continue and promised her another try the following summer. Moore, disappointed, struggled through the fall.

When I went home for Christmas vacation, Mother had the family doctor give me a thorough going over. He laid my nervous condition to overwork, and ordered me to rest. So, half glad and half sorry, I returned to "the city," notified my pupils, Mr. Pasmore, and Uncle John, and packed my belongings. Feeling as if I were leaving my second parents, I bade goodbye to Grandfather and Grandmother . . . and went home to Lemoore to REST. . . . I began to think of entering a Convent, feeling that life was quite over for me My career was at an end, and there was nothing else worthwhile except to devote my few remaining months, possibly a year or two, to GOD. . . . (Moore, p. 64)

Leaving her career and her self-confidence behind, Mary Louise now went dutifully home to take her place in Sarah's frontier culture.

CHAPTER 6

Lemoore

"The lovely spring months were my first taste of leisure from teaching, concerts and church choirs since early girlhood" (Moore, p. 66). There was still open space for wildflowers to cover the floor of the broad San Joaquin Valley around Lemoore after the mild winter rains and before the long hot summers. Grizzlies still migrated regularly from the rugged Sierra Nevada east of Lemoore to the coast ranges to the west. Mary Louise tried hard not to be "too citified" in her new surroundings and quickly made friends of the members of Sarah's Alpha Club. Soon there was a round of socials and musicales in which she frequently accompanied her new friend, violinist Lynn Fox, in concertos by Bériot or Wieniawski.[1] She always closed her performances with her own early "Lullabye," which had become popular in Lemoore: "Her 'Lullabye' was sung everywhere; and town people camping in the high Sierras reported the second summer that even at the sheep camps the shepherds were singing it, having caught it from campers of the previous year" (S. P. Carr, p. 12).

Chaperones were irrelevant in rural Lemoore, where life by definition was wholesome. When Sarah scheduled her daughter to sing for her Hanford congregation ten miles away, it was quite acceptable for one of the young men in her social group to drive her there alone. "That she [Sarah] would allow me to drive ten miles unchaperoned with a young man was unbelievable! I shall never forget the shouts of laughter from these country-raised boys and girls over my discomfiture and the downfall of my citified ideas, where such a thing was distinctly improper and never permitted" (Moore, p. 67).

Though the fainting spells continued, by fall Moore was stronger, and she resumed her teaching. One day a week she traveled to nearby Tulare to teach voice at Ada Reed Kruse's Tulare School of Music. From there she went to Visalia for a day, then to Hanford, and finally back to Lemoore where she also met "quite a good class." Sarah was riding circuit to preach in some of the same towns. Moore kept to this itinerant teaching schedule through the winter months during her years in Lemoore, even after her marriage. There were still performances, now unpaid, such as a series of three song recitals, "Evenings with German, French and American Composers," given at Fox and Sweetland's Hall.[2]

There were no more lessons from Uncle John or Mr. Pasmore, and there was very little composing. In San Francisco between 1889 and 1895, there had been about a hundred short piano pieces and songs in addition to *The Oracle*. But between 1895 and 1901, when she left Lemoore, her catalog lists only two anthems for the Lemoore Presbyterian Church, two pieces for violin and piano, two piano pieces, and one song, in addition to music for Charles W. Barrett. Most are lost except some of the Barrett pieces. Charles W. Barrett operated a large hardware business in Fresno and participated in the amateur dramatics that Sarah organized in nearby Lemoore. His friendship with the Carrs continued long after all concerned had left the area. The evidence of the music Moore composed for his lyrics suggests that he was a member of a barbershop quartet with an appetite for topical songs on current events. The songs that were published appeared under his name as author, composer, and publisher. Patriotic songs such as "We'll Never Let Old Glory Fall" and "Parade, Rest" are listed in her catalog. Others, such as "Yankee Dewey Do," promoting the Spanish-American War, or "Maginnis's Billy Goat," are not even listed. These she simply grouped under two opus numbers as "More work for Chas. W. Barrett. Campaign songs—war songs, etc. Have no copies of any of these—(all trash)—mostly published."[3]

The vote for women was a major issue of the day. In 1896 a statewide referendum was called on a suffrage amendment to the California state constitution. Three generations of Pratts and Carrs contributed to the campaign. Mary Louise composed a group of six songs, duets, and quartets for the campaign, of which only "I'm Going to Vote, John" survives. Sarah was among the officers of the State Central Woman's Suffrage Amendment Campaign Committee of California, organized the previous year. She wrote at least one letter to the San Francisco *Examiner* on the issue, denouncing the treatment of women as men's property and championing the right of women to take up teaching or other socially useful activities after their child-bearing years. Grandmother Pratt, by then sixty-seven, became an activist too. She presided over weekly meetings of the Political Equality Club in the Napa town hall or in the local Republican party head-quarters. She undertook to present a paper on the question, "Does the Professional Woman Need the Ballot?," became a delegate to the state convention of the Political Equality Club, and, characteristically, penned a poem for the occasion, "A Lord of Creation's Reverse" (unlocated). In spite of these and similar efforts, the amendment was defeated; suffrage for women remained an issue for another twenty-four years.[4]

Moore's Barrett pieces represent an earnest effort to accommodate her talent to the community, as her mother had done so successfully. They have virtually no stylistic relationship to the songs that survive from her San Francisco years, or to the music she would write later on in Seattle. They do show an easy knack for writing in a current dance-hall style. In fact, some of her "trash" was hard to distinguish from ragtime, which, as a lady, she disdained. To entertain friends and family at home was one thing, but commercial music for the minstrel show or dance hall was quite another. Every fiber of her conditioning prevented her from using this style again in later years, after she had regained her artistic confidence—even when she would have wel-comed a little commercial success.[5]

After the untimely death of her latest San Francisco beau, Mary Louise turned her attention to the young men in Lemoore. John Claude Moore, a young physician, had begun to practice in Lemoore about the time Mary Louise had left San Francisco. The oldest of three brothers, he had contributed to his family's support since his father's death when he was nine. One brother, Fred, a schoolteacher, was also a part of her social circle. Claude continued to support his mother and help his younger brother with his education; he was also paying off his debts from Cooper Medical College (later Stanford). Moore described him as "a sturdy, broad-shouldered farmer-boy, with fair hair and clear blue eyes, strong features, and although not handsome, was very attractive and dependable looking" (Moore, p. 65). At first they were simply part of a group of six young people who often gathered for social activities. But after a time she saw more of Claude.

Back in Lemoore, during the hot summer . . . the "young doctor" took me driving a great deal, and strange to say, Mother did not object, and for the first time, my darling Father was friendly to a young man calling on his "only daughter," and failed to refer to him as a "young cub." My little brother Torrey adored him, as in fact, the whole town and country side had learned to do by then." (Moore, p. 68)

After a year, it was assumed by all that they would marry, and they considered themselves engaged.

Moore's weight had shrunk to eighty-five pounds from her usual ninety-seven as the next hot summer approached. B. O. and Sarah shipped her off to her half-brothers in cooler Washington State for the season. She spent a few wonderful weeks with Thorpe in the mountain village of Leavenworth, where she prepared and presented a recital with a local German pianist. "He was thoroughly familiar with the numbers on my suggested program and happy to play again the familiar German lieder and operatic numbers known to him in his early musical environment" (Moore, p. 70). Well along in the concert, Thorpe's dog, who was her constant companion during those weeks, broke loose from his leash and joined the proceedings. "He marched up the aisle, and with one bound, mounted the platform and laid himself at my feet, just as I concluded the recitative introduction to 'Una voce poco fa.' During the wild applause of the audience for this addition to the concert troupe, I had time to control my giggles and felt more nearly like the mischievous Rosina probably than ever before or since" (Moore, pp. 70–71). The remainder of the summer she spent with Eugene, mostly in a summer tent camp on Lake Washington, from which Eugene and his law partners commuted daily by canoe to their office. Here, too, she felt very comfortable and much among friends. There were only one or two fainting spells through this summer—one as she stood by the evening bonfire and prepared, somewhat reluctantly, to sing for the group. She wrote of the beauty of the summer and the pleasure of her vacation, though she also said she was lonely without Claude.

The season ended with the report of a gold strike in the Klondike, and the Gold Rush of 1897 was on. Both Eugene and Thorpe left their homes and jobs to follow the call of Alaskan adventure, Eugene for the second time. Moore sailed south, instead of north with her brothers, returning to San Francisco and then Lemoore.

As I neared home, I felt more and more depressed. This time it was not: "had I changed my mind," but "had the Doctor become indifferent?" (He was always a most unsatisfactory letter-writer!) However, when he boarded the train at Hanford, having gone over earlier "on business," I was soon encouraged. My affection for him was always that anxious-to-please, easily-crushed sort—so different from my previous experiences. (Moore, p. 73)

Claude's mother objected to her son's marrying but soon became Mary Louise's supporter. Sarah performed the wedding ceremony before a gathering of the western Pratts, Carrs, and Moores in the family parlor, decorated for the occasion with huge bouquets of violets. The date was February 15, 1898, the twenty-sixth anniversary of Sarah's own wedding to B. O. Carr. The couple honeymooned in Los Angeles. Mary Louise, who always identified closely with the roles her father and her uncles had played in the Civil War, thought it appropriate to note in her autobiography that February 15, 1898, also marked the start of the Spanish-American War. Afterward, she resumed her teaching schedule, helping to retire Claude's debts. "It was a happy and a busy time. I was away three days a week at my classes, and always eager to get home. It seemed at the time that Fate persistently sent emergency calls for the Doctor and long confinement cases during my brief stay at home. But it wasn't always so, and we had happy times" (Moore, p. 76). Claude found time to take a role in a park benefit production of *The Little Red Schoolhouse*, along with his mother, B. O., and Mary Louise, who played the melodeon. Probably Sarah directed, since the park was a Woman's Club project.

That summer B. O., who was then sixty-six, suffered an illness described as a sunstroke. Fearful that he might make a serious mistake, he resigned his position at the bank. Sarah gave up her preaching career to look after him. When they could, the Carrs left for a long visit to Seattle, where they presently settled.

By winter the young couple "decided we could afford a baby" (Moore, p. 78). During the pregnancy, which lasted most of the year of 1899, the Moores traveled to the Napa Valley for Grandmother and Grandfather Pratt's fiftieth anniversary. Later they traveled together to Seattle, where Claude considered B. O.'s suggestion that they too relocate in that "wide-awake young city." Moore gave up her out-of-town teaching. Wray Torrey, who had stayed behind in Lemoore to complete the ninth grade, graduated and moved north to join his parents in Seattle. After a scorching summer, the baby finally arrived in September, two weeks late and very large for his tiny mother. Byron Carr Moore was named for the father Mary Louise had always adored. "Of course, I was terribly sick—and, of course, all my life, I have bragged about that twelve pounder. Nowadays, if I get started on the subject, one of my children always interrupts—'Oh yes, Byron was forty pounds at birth, six feet tall, and shaving before he was thirteen!' "[6] Moore was also thoroughly pleased with her ability to provide for her offspring. "As far as food was concerned, I was a good mother. When my baby was only six weeks old, I took in another little fellow of three months (three pounds lighter than my boy) and nursed him through the crisis of his mother's attack of typhoid. . . . It meant turn about—a baby every hour. But God meant me to be a mother, and they did not go hungry" (Moore, pp. 79–80). Not every composer serves a term as a wet nurse.

By young Byron's first birthday, the marriage had been severely shaken. Moore tells in her autobiography of her anxiety over the baby's welfare, Claude's impatience, and Mother Moore's steadfast support. She tells of a beautiful brunette, "Mrs. S.," who moved to Lemoore with husband and son and who began to require extensive medical attention for "some unexplained trouble." "I, who had tried to submerge my urban ideas and conform to the customs so I need never be considered 'citified,' began to feel a certain 'uncertainty' about myself. My baby had exhausted me, and I wasn't up to my usual enthusiasms" (Moore, p. 81).

She gives a melodramatic account of the culmination of her husband's affair: Claude made preparations to elope with "Mrs. S.," that lady's husband threatened to shoot him, and Claude fled to Fresno to avoid the angry husband and reconsider his options. Mary Louise decided to go to her errant husband in Fresno. With a friend of Claude's to help, she drove all night, losing her way in the dense ground fog of the San Joaquin Valley winter before they arrived at seven o'clock. "My husband was expecting us because of a telegram sent earlier, met us, and carried me into the living room. There alone, he took me in his arms and told me if I would forgive him, he would never give me another moment's unhappiness. I not only forgave him, but vowed to myself that I would erase it from my heart and never in the future judge him by the past. (That was a difficult vow to keep.)" (Moore, pp. 86–87).

The couple pulled themselves together, but within days of their reconciliation another disaster struck. In Seattle, her beloved younger brother Wray Torrey, not yet sixteen, drowned in Lake Washington along with a cousin. "For one terrible week they dragged the lake and finally found first Torrey, then Clarkie! My poor mother and father! My poor Uncle Clark and Aunt Grace! My poor brother Eugene who had lent him the canoe! And oh, poor me, who had lost my faith and my darling brother, all in two days!"[7] B. O. and Sarah joined the young family for the winter of 1900–1901; perhaps the bereaved Carrs found some comfort in their new grandson. But from time to time the brunette's husband continued to threaten Claude. The Moores decided it was time to leave Lemoore and move to Seattle.

The house in "the Boston of the San Joaquin Valley" where they had all lived was promptly sold, and the Carrs returned to Seattle. Claude remained behind to wind up his practice, but Mary Louise soon followed her parents with young Byron. After the emotional stress of the months past, the trip exhausted her physically. The baby was by then almost two but couldn't walk because he was sick with malaria.

That trip laid the foundation for years of invalidism for me. My heavy baby was almost two years old, and too heavy to carry and too sick to walk. The many transfers, the scarcity of "Red-caps" in proportion to the travelers, all conspired to exhaust us both. . . .

The weeks and months went by. I lay on a couch, trying to recover from the physical strain of a ninety-five pound mother attempting to carry a thirty-five pound baby for so many weary hours of journeying. (Moore, p. 89)

Her invalidism was not made easier by her disillusionment and uncertainty about Claude. For a time she and the baby lived with her parents at Eugene's home on Lake Washington. It must have seemed an eternity before Claude joined them in January of 1902. By then Sarah had recovered her energy. She rented and managed a large house for her extended family, which, besides B. O. Carr (who was now an old man), Claude, Mary Louise, and young Byron, included Nora, a schoolteacher who had been their friend and boarder in Lemoore, and Virginia Graham, a friend from St. Helena days who had also studied voice with Mr. Pasmore.

CHAPTER 7

Seattle

San Francisco was past the tumultuous growth of its early days in the years Moore studied there. But between the time of her first visit in 1889 and the time she finally left in 1914, Seattle was caught in a phenomenal and continuous boom. In 1893 the Northern Pacific Railroad reached Seattle, giving it a rail connection to the East and expanding potential markets for its lumber, coal, and fish. After the 1897 gold strike in the Yukon Territory, Seattle became the point of departure for innumerable prospectors and adventurers, accelerating its growth even more. The 1890 census had claimed only 42,837 inhabitants. By 1910 its population had soared to 237,194.

The days when Eugene and his law partner had camped in the woods on the shore of Lake Washington in summer and commuted by canoe to work were over by the time the Moores came to stay.[1] The frontier character of the city, with its precarious state of law and order, still prevailed, however. Three years after Moore arrived, a burglar stole the family silver: "Seattle was a very wide open city about that time, and there were many robberies. I was always a light sleeper, and when the Doctor was out, I always had the pistol under my pillow and took it with me when I went to see if Byron needed covering (he always did). But on this night the Doctor was at home, and I slept soundly. In the morning . . . we found there was not even a spoon left for breakfast" (Moore, p. 94). Some months later, the police found the robber and a farmer found the silver. The doctor had taught Moore to shoot, and she was proud of her marksmanship, which won her a prize in a competition. Another time she was quite prepared to fire at a would-be burglar who had broken a cellar window. Hearing the noise, she phoned the police and then sat calmly on the stairs with the gun, waiting for the intruder to emerge from the cellar. Fortunately the arrival of the police scared him away and the broken cellar window was the only damage.

A formal cultural tradition in music scarcely existed in Seattle. The city's first symphony orchestra offered concerts only from 1903, and the orchestra was not firmly established until 1926. A traveling opera company had ventured there in 1877, but opera remained a rarity. Early on, Moore was invited to produce *The Oracle* "for charity" (i.e., as a fund-raiser) for the Ladies' Relief Society. She took the opportunity to expand it to three acts. Once again, she sang the lead herself; Virginia Graham also repeated in the role of Aurora. The second production was well received, as the first one had been.

> While the argument of the play is very humorous the music is so good that it easily takes the leading part. As a composer Mrs. Moore was more successful than as librettist, but was good at both. Her first appearance on the stage was the signal for a round of applause and her splendid work throughout the evening made her a warm favorite with the audience. It was an unusual thing to see the writer and composer of an opera take one of the leading parts. Mrs. Moore is a very clever lady and one whom Seattle has reason to be proud of.[2]

> The beauty of the score of "The Oracle" was a delightful surprise to the listeners. A close criticism, in fact, might find fault with the even rhythm of the music, creating the idea of a sameness of tempo which does not in reality exist. A mingling of stronger colors, a throwing in even of a rougher musical element would make the pretty melodies of "The Oracle" the more charming.

> But the work is one upon which Mrs. Mary Carr Moore may be justly complimented. In solo numbers it is especially strong.[3]

Moore found herself teaching almost as soon as she completed her arduous trip to Seattle: "Fortunately for our finances, I was known to be a musician. Few teachers at that time were available, so I had as many pupils as I could handle. Most of the time I was drawn up before the piano on a steamer chair, playing what I could maneuver of the accompaniments" (Moore, p. 89). She continued teaching until she became pregnant again, late in 1903. At first she had much more work than did Claude.

> It was naturally galling for my husband, whose profession had to grow slowly in a large city, to spend many hours in an empty office those first months. He chafed as any strong man would at the thought of permitting his wife to earn the major part of the income while he found his bank account dwindling. As I

look back on those days, I see more clearly than I could then how restless and discouraged he must have felt. But it was not for long. His own ability and likeable personality very soon won him friends and patients. (Moore, p. 93)

Moore's account of teaching in the raw new city is supplemented by that of Nellie Cornish, a contemporary who began her career in Seattle only the year before Moore.[4] Cornish, a single woman, had neither studio nor her own piano, so she went to her students to give lessons.

Wild nature had not been conquered yet, and dense woods stretched over many places on Capitol Hill and Queen Anne Hill. Where the Civic Auditorium now stands, there was a wood yard, through which I found my way to a pupil's little house. Thus I went all over Seattle, often making my way over dirt piles and potato patches. Manners were wholesome but simple. Often lessons took place after dinner, with "Papa" sitting in the same room in his red woolens and usually in need of a shave, chewing tobacco while reading his evening paper. Children and dogs ran in and out. Telephones (then a novelty) were, like the piano, always in the living room. When the telephone rang, I was expected to halt my lesson and remain silent until the conversation ended.[5]

The two women knew each other, but were never close friends.[6] Their contrasting views of the Holyoke Building, where both rented studio space, suggest the extent of their differences. Moore wrote:

My classes had increased to such an extent that I rented a studio in the old Holyoke Building where at that time all the musicians were "herded"! Some busy days when I was trying to train some light and timid young voice, with a loud pianist on one side and a violinist on the other, all of us in different keys, it seemed a warning of what I might have to endure as permanent punishment if I "failed to be a good girl." It was fatiguing work, and those were difficult days. (Moore, p. 93)

Cornish, whose background was far less cosmopolitan than Moore's, and who had been fending for herself, teaching in small northwestern communities for some years, relished the bustle and excitement of the Holyoke that Moore found so draining. Her most obtrusive neighbor taught acting.

My next-door neighbor was Frank Eagan, who later founded the Eagan Dramatic School in Los Angeles. As I taught my scant class of pupils, I could hear through the open transom Mr. Eagan conducting his flourishing class of embryonic actors, who were gaining momentum and volume by the constant repetition of the famous line, "Fear makes cowards of us all." In my memory I can hear the beams quiver and the doors rattle to the strident voices of his pupils thundering on this line, night and day.

I felt somewhat shy of this aggregation of erudite teachers, most of whom had studied in the East or in Europe. Diffidently I taught with my transom closed and hoped to become a real "Holyoke teacher."[7]

Moore was well aware, as her comment about being a "good girl" shows, that the life of a single music teacher consisted of unremitting work. The Bohemian quality of the Holyoke was not so attractive or glamorous for her as Cornish made it sound. She did not easily identify with single teachers like Cornish who lived as well as taught at the Holyoke.

Presently Moore joined forces with Frederick William Zimmerman and Vaughn Arthur, owners of the Seattle Conservatory of Music. She stayed with them for two years, until she abandoned teaching late in 1903. Cornish includes Arthur among the Holyoke teachers whom she remembered: "Vaughn Arthur, who had received his entire music education in California, was Seattle's outstanding teacher of violin. Slender and not too tall, he wore his grey hair very long but neatly trimmed. Such had been the fashion for artists in his youth, and he kept to that mode. He was always willing to meet his pupils half way financially, and many of his students were given extra lessons without fee."[8]

Moore belonged to several clubs with musical interests. Always a joiner, she was at ease with the social aspect of these clubs as well as with their musical activities, a point which sometimes made other "serious" musicians doubt her own "seriousness." It appears that her club activities increased after Marian's birth, when she had given up teaching and left the Holyoke. There was the Ladies Musical Club, where she read a paper on "Folk Song and Its Influence on the Development of Music," with Norwegian, English, and southern American musical examples. In 1906 and 1907 she chaired the Music Committee of the Woman's Century Club, which sponsored a week of concerts at the State Art Exhibit both years. An evening of Moore's own music was included the first year; a program of music by Seattle composers Arthur Alexander, Kate Gilmore Black, John J. Blackmore, Harry Girard, James Hamilton Howe, Helen Howard Lemmel, Lillian Miller, and Moore, the second. There were also the Schubert Club and the secret, education- and service-oriented PEO Sisterhood, through which she organized the Chaminade Quartet of women's voices. The quartet was active for about five years. None of the numerous arrangements she made for them survives.

In the spring of 1909, a chapter of Arthur Farwell's new nation-wide American Music Society was organized in Seattle with Moore as its first president. According to a newspaper clipping, the center was "open to any and all persons interested in establishing a higher standard of art life in America and especially a higher standard of creative work among our American musicians." Late in August, Farwell himself visited the Seattle center. The new group moved quickly to put together three concerts for American Music Day at the Alaska-Yukon-Pacific Exposition on September 25. A concert honoring American composer Dudley Buck followed in December. In 1910 and again in 1911 the Seattle center sponsored a composition contest, with the winning numbers performed at a "manuscript" concert. Works by Moore appeared on both of these programs.

Moore had begun to compose again as soon as they were settled in Seattle. Between the time she moved to Seattle and the start of *Narcissa* in 1909, there were about seventy short works, mostly songs and short choral pieces. All were intended for local parlor, club, or church use. Often they were performed by her own Chaminade Quartet at the Unitarian Church where the Moores and Carrs were members and Sarah sometimes preached. More than a third of these are lost, but those that survive suggest a struggle for renewed technical competence and stylistic growth. She soon regained her skill, although the sunny, straightforward energy of pre-Lemoore days had disappeared. Witmark published a number of songs and choral pieces in these years. "Summer Passes" from 1906 appeared in print three decades later. Moore thought highly enough of "Brahma" to orchestrate it in 1915.[9]

In its length (some thirteen minutes), choice of subject, and structural features, "The Quest of Sigurd" reflects both Moore's gathering artistic resolve and her personal conflict at the time it was written, around 1905. It is the only surviving work of any length at all from the years preceding the grand opera *Narcissa*. Moore drew her text from *Sigurd the Volsung,* William Morris's popular retelling of the Norse saga of the Nibelungs. Morris's aesthetic ideas must have appealed to both Moore and her mother, as they had to Arthur Farwell.[10] His view that creativity is universal, and that inspiration and genius are nothing more than craftsmanship, supported the aspira-

Pages from "The Quest of Sigurd," op. 59. (Reprinted, by permission, from the composer's 1905 manuscript score, Mary Carr Moore Archive, Music Library, UCLA.)

tions of these western domestic feminists, intent as they still were on creating their own homegrown culture.

Moore chose one short section from the book-length epic as her text: "How Sigurd Met Brynhild in Lymdale," from book 3.[11] In it, Sigurd, led by the flight of his falcon, rides into a castle and finds the widow Brynhild, whom he has not seen before. She is weaving in golden thread the early events of the Volsung saga, including the stories of Sigmund, Fafnir, and the forging of Sigurd's own sword, Wrath. The two fall in love at once and live happily together. Presently this idyll is interrupted; Sigurd takes up his sword and rides "forth to the night" and another hundred pages or so of adventures.

Moore set only about a third of the lines of this section. Her cuts, together with two changes of tense, alter the sense of the story to resemble a scenario she desperately wanted for her own life. In her version, Sigurd has chosen to return to Brynhild, and their pledges of love are renewals of past commitments rather than something new. Further, Moore ends her setting with:

> All the earthly exaltation, till their pomp of life should be passed,
> And soft on the bosom of God, their love should be laid at last.

Her Sigurd never rides off into the night, but remains at home with Brynhild, forever happy and faithful.

Although this cantata was Moore's most extended single number to date, its scale remains small. It was obviously designed for performing forces readily at hand. A San Francisco reviewer put his finger on the inherent weakness of so modest a treatment of so heroic a subject after a 1916 performance: "She too can weave an attractive skein of music. But I think she makes a mistake, at least in the present stage of her artistic development, when she essays to wield the hammer of Thor. She has the vision of beauty; but it is in dainty snatches and I felt the lack of a sense of heroic continuity. At the same time, the charm and the spontaneity of her music are unmistakable."[12]

"The Quest of Sigurd" has the simple seriousness and integrity characteristic of Moore's better songs. Its primitive ingenuousness is not inappropriate for a setting of Morris's poetry, in spite of its small scale. Apart from its personal meaning for her, it is important because it represents Moore's only technical preparation for the novel and extended work that was soon to come. There are no compositions even faintly dramatic and only a couple of slightly extended choral pieces between "Sigurd" and the four-act grand opera *Narcissa*. By the time she set "The Quest of Sigurd" it had already occurred to her that the Whitman Massacre of 1847 would be a good subject for an American opera, but it had not occurred to her that she would be the one to compose it. For the time being, she was fully occupied with her young children, her club activities, various short compositions, and her unhappy marriage.

CHAPTER 8

Turning Point

Though she was entering her thirties and had a growing family of her own, Moore was still very close to her parents. She lived with them for a time in Seattle and continued to see them frequently after she moved into the Denny Way home that she had designed and a distant Carr relative had built. She adored her father, but it was her mother, Sarah, who continued to have a strong and immediate influence on her. The crisis through which Moore passed near the midpoint of her Seattle years is glimpsed most easily through Sarah's writing in the same period.

Moore's mother had not outgrown her compulsion to teach, preach, and organize. B. O. was now retired, drawing a veteran's pension in consideration of his age and general disability.[1] Out of deference to him, the much younger Sarah had already abandoned her career as a full-time minister, but she gave no sign of retiring herself. If it was no longer convenient for her to organize congregations, she could still preach occasionally. She frequently directed her own plays in amateur productions.[2] In addition, she could give more time to writing. She published six novels and at least one short story between 1907 and 1913.[3] In the course of her own writing she organized two writers' clubs in Seattle, thus continuing her longstanding urge to teach and to engage in what she later called "moral uplift," even while pursuing an essentially solitary art.[4]

Sarah's earlier social activism had provided a working example for Moore of how a woman might fulfill her domestic obligations while undertaking a vigorous and altruistic career of community betterment and creative activity. Now, under changed circumstances, Sarah had found another outlet for her energy. Her very practical, down-to-earth, here-and-now approach to her writing contrasts sharply with the isolated-Romantic-genius theory of creativity that is often associated with the musical and literary giants of nineteenth-century Europe.

The settings and characters of Sarah's novels bear very close resemblance to the locations and lives of the Pratts, Carrs, and Moores. For instance, the hero of her children's books, Billy To-Morrow, is modeled after Moore's first son, Byron Carr Moore. And her didactic novel "Waters of Eden" has a California setting that strongly resembles her beloved Napa Valley and St. Helena of the 1880s. Thus the moral messages in her books about the separate roles of men and women, as well as about patriotism and the place of art in everyday life, must have seemed pointed indeed to Moore, who was more torn by her personal conflicts than ever.

Was Moore struggling to be a wife and mother, a homemaker and hostess and family entertainer, while still hoping for a way to become a composer of serious art music in those years? Sarah's feminism placed definite limits upon such aspirations. She made it clear in *The Iron Way* that music was primarily a social grace, desirable for a gentleman: "his polish, his music . . . won women," but essential for a lady.[5] For a young man like Wash Dooboy in "Waters of Eden," professional music study offered the salvation of a career: "He was another being, erect, his eyes glowing with a new-found purpose. 'I know now what I got ter do. It's music! I'll work, I'll starve, quit cussin', do anything I haf ter, for to learn—what—what I heard last night, what I'm a-hearin' yet. . . .' "[6] But for a woman, a professional commitment to the arts constituted a profound moral challenge: "Honora looked down on her with troubled eyes. . . . A public dancer! Would all that love and money could give end in such a career?" Old Mrs. Garrison presently replied: " 'Face the fact. . . . If there's nothing high about it now, put your effort into lifting it, against the time when this child comes to her own. Educate her to all good things, divert her if you can, but be prepared to let her live her own life.' "[7] If undertaken at all, a creative career in the arts should be centered in one's own country. When pursuit of the good and beautiful in American life was governed by the profit motive, it achieved a saving practicality, according to this speech by Ward Browne.

"I've never been abroad,—been too busy; but I can't see why these Americans who run away from America's crudeness and vulgarity don't stay at home a part of the time and shine up their own premises. . . . I'd teach them

that heathered Scotland, rose-decked England, not even the terraced, leg-
ended hills of Attica are more beautiful, more truly romance's own than this
rich, opalescent Arvilla Valley with its cerulean skies and its Spanish story. . . .
It would pay, you know! Pay big dividends. In five years the whole earth
would know,—we know it now,—that this is the most beautiful spot on earth;
and the world would come here."8

Common prejudices of the time and place appear also. Sarah sang
the praises of the clean and uncomplaining Chinese workers who had
helped build the railroad, while taking a dim view of immigrant Italian laborers whom she felt were not properly Americanized until the
second generation: "these hot-headed Latins [i.e., Italians] that live in
America, but not *of* it till a second generation binds them to the soil."9
Such a view harks back to B. O.'s unsuccessful campaign for the
California State Legislature in the 1880s, and to Eugene's action in
defending the Seattle Chinese community from mob violence, as well
as the jingoism of the Barrett songs about the Spanish-American War
from Lemoore days. It also helps explain why the Carrs preferred
Seattle to San Francisco with its far more heterogeneous popula-
tion.10 It must have contributed to Moore's firm resolve (years later)
to make "native American birth" a requirement for membership in a
composers' society.

Would Moore's obsession with music attract her to the city? Sarah
sang anew the virtues of the American countryside, again through
Ward Browne: "Whenever a race or a community is divorced from
the land degeneration sets in. Earth is the mother of us all; if we stray
far from her we are soon hungry."11 Culture and the arts did not
require the city in order to thrive: "In many vineyard homesteads she
[Honora] found comfort and luxury . . . tastefully blended. . . . In
humble homes she met a courtesy as fine as her own; good books;
large information modestly used; some talent blossoming; some art
pursued under difficulty, made possible by joint family sacrifice."
"'What have you more in the city? A little more embroidery, less
health; nature corseted into a simpering dame. . . .'"12 Moore followed Sarah's lead in shrugging off the primacy of the city, at least of
the musical capitals of the East Coast. Like her mother, she learned to
draw her artistic strength from the provincial surroundings that both
nurtured her and gave her opportunity.

While Moore agonized over her husband's infidelities, Sarah
slammed the door on all thought of divorce. Again in "Waters of

Eden," she created a heroine in Honora who remained fiercely loyal
to an unconsummated marriage and a spouse who had disappeared
years earlier.

"I could never contemplate divorce for myself. . . . I was reared by a
slender code of three articles, the virtue of courage, the necessity of honor,
and the wickedness of divorce. I promised my mother that whatever terrible
trials marriage might bring me, I would bear it till death."[13]

Ward Browne, Honora's suitor, discussed divorce further with wise
old Mrs. Garrison.

"What of the woman who silently endures the marriage relation when it
galls? . . . Should she fight instead, seek freedom?" . . .
"To endure silently . . . that's the best fighting I know. People pretend to
vow 'for better, for worse;' and at the first little cloud over matrimonial waters
put their craft about. Shirking they are; just plain coward, half of them."
"Then you don't believe in divorce?" . . .
"Oh it's a good thing sometimes, when a brute beats his wife, for instance,
and the children; she ought to have a divorce in that case, unless—unless she
began it first. But oftenest, . . . divorce is a cheap and easy repudiation of
responsibility,—a brutal way of defrauding children who are innocent."[14]

Through her novels, Sarah expressed a restrictive code of conduct
and a narrow view of the American woman as creative artist that were
impossibly limiting for her daughter. Yet her influence was far from
being all bad, for Sarah had written some years earlier of the rights of
women, especially their right to blossom after their years of childrear-
ing were done: "After the family has been reared and trained there
remains a third or a fourth of life; it should be the best part. Shall a
woman, any more than a man, be condemned to piecing quilts or
absorbing only such knowledge as can be gained within the home?
Even that knowledge cannot become fully her own until she gives it
out again in some form of teaching or action. . . ."[15] Not only did
Sarah write about this prospect, she showed her daughter the way
through that most telling route, personal example.

One cannot discuss Sarah's influence upon Moore in these years
without touching on her comments about America as a nation and her
pride in its shaping. Moore embraced this aspect of her mother's (and
her whole family's) teaching and through it presently found a route to
artistic salvation. Sarah presented her conception of the institutional

pillars of American society in a description of summer camping on the islands of Puget Sound, within sight of the skyline of booming young Seattle: "Court-house, school-house, and cathedral,—these nobly crowned the higher hills, voicing the three virtues for which American civilization stands—justice, learning, and religion."[16] She wove a romance of love and adventure around her childhood memories of the building of the Central Pacific Railroad across the Sierra Nevada, an achievement that helped tie the nation together. One reads in *The Iron Way* of the heroism, patriotism, and personal loyalty of all those who helped, and of the evil deeds perpetrated by the railroad's opponents.

It is unclear whether Sarah's articulation of these positions on divorce and the role of music in life, at the very moment her daughter's conflicting feelings about them reached a climax, was undertaken as her direct response to her daughter's obvious travail or whether it was a summation of her own life struggles. Whatever the case, Sarah's writings express deep and long-held family values, which had a continuing and powerful influence on Moore. In fact, they almost destroyed her.

By the time Moore's second child, Marian, made her appearance on April 3, 1904, the new mother seemed more relaxed. The baby arrived on Easter, missing her grandfather's seventy-second birthday by a few hours. The doctor was prospering at last; Moore did not resume teaching after Marian's birth. The couple shared an active social life: "Seattle was a very gay place in those days; receptions, teas, dancing and theatre parties gave me a side of life for which I had never had time, before. I still kept up my music, did some singing, and quite a lot of composing."[17]

About a year after Marian's birth, Moore miscarried and was by her own account quite ill. Soon she realized that her husband was paying court to another woman, this time a member of the Moores' social circle. His behavior, her discouragement and poor health, and the latent conflicts between her own ambitions and the values her mother was even then articulating in print all contributed to bring about a crisis. "For awhile, I tried to carry on—but with my recent illness and my grief over my inability to make myself beloved by my husband, I brooded too much. I kept thinking of the children's future—if I took them away with me—as a 'divorced woman'" (Moore, p. 96). So distasteful was the idea of divorce to her, so rigid her commitment to the sanctity of marriage, that she had even avoided meeting divorced women socially.

No one can imagine, nowadays, the effect of that phrase, upon many of us in those days; particularly, I was prejudiced—and loathed the idea for myself. Yet I could not ruin my husband's life by clinging to him. I began to reason, that the beauty and culture of this really lovely girl, would make her a better companion for my children than I could be, grieving, delicate in health, and looking forward to a life of bitter loneliness. (Moore, p. 96)

She kept strychnine tablets at hand for the fainting spells which still plagued her. On a night when the doctor was at the hospital and she suffered from a blinding headache, she deliberately overdosed on the pills: "There was no excuse for me, whatever—except that I thought sincerely, it was better for the happiness of all, that I should go."

Moore was in convulsions when the doctor returned. The death of his hospital patient before he could be operated on made it possible for Claude to come to his wife's rescue: "I was, of course, terribly remorseful—also ashamed that I had made such an attempt and had been unsuccessful. The final result was a very real reunion between the Doctor and myself, which lasted longer than I could have dared to hope, and the friend left for a long visit in the East" (Moore, p. 97). She later spoke of her suicide attempt as a crime, but the experience led her to be much more tolerant of others' sufferings.

When I have dear young friends, nowadays, who come to me with their troubles, I can only know from experience, how bitterly they suffer; and my only explanation of the ordeals through which the majority of human beings must pass—one way or another, is the thought that without these growing pains, we would be like jellyfish; it takes "trial by fire" to develop that spinal column which enables us to stand erect. (Moore, p. 97)

Moore's physical health was restored during a year passed near rural North Bend, where Claude ran a hospital along the right-of-way of the Chicago, Milwaukee, St. Paul and Pacific Railroad, then under construction. The Moores often rode horseback together. The children, too, prospered in the outdoor environment. Moore found, as she later said, "much inspiration for composition" in the rugged, wild country. John Wesley Moore, the last of the Moores' three children and tangible evidence of their "very real reunion," was born August 2, 1907.

The path Moore followed away from her emotional dead end and the strictures of Sarah's aesthetic approach is not so obvious, though it may be guessed. After the years of artistic temporizing and periodic ill health that had followed *The Oracle,* she now began to commit herself more fully to developing her talent as a composer. Her gathering creative impetus may be inferred from the greater number of compositions from the Seattle years, in marked contrast to the Lemoore period just before. "The Quest of Sigurd" was a milestone in her emotional and artistic progress.[18] However tentatively, it represents the first clear statement of her growing seriousness of purpose. Some years later, at another moment of self-questioning as she pursued her quixotic calling, she wrote in her datebook, "I believe God gave me the gift—to use."[19] Her efforts to implement her new commitment to art music without completely rebelling against her family's value system would continue for the rest of her life. She had to find the strength to disentangle herself from her mother's aesthetic domination, develop her own compositional language and aesthetic imperative, and still salvage what she could from her family life. The laborious process of internal reconciliation between the conflicting values of family and creativity was now under way. Her ability to mend herself provides the only possible explanation for the monumental achievement of *Narcissa* that followed.

CHAPTER 9

Narcissa

Principle is the first question in our national music today. . . . Our composers owe it to their countrymen to take thought of the new meaning of this nation among nations, and to examine their work in the light of that meaning. Their responsibility to the American people is identical in force with that of the authors of the Declaration of Independence and the Constitution, in the respective spheres of artistic and democratic evolution. Both are spiritual matters at base, and are closely related. A national music is to a nation what a song is to the singer who conceives it, a trustworthy expression of the quality and strength of his spirit.[1]

It is a measure of the extent to which European music dominated American concert life that the very concept of an American art music was not seriously and continuously discussed or implemented until after 1895.[2] Arthur Farwell founded the Wa Wan Press in Boston to publish the music of Americans in 1901, the year Moore moved to Seattle.[3] Then he traveled and proselytized extensively in behalf of American music, encouraging the organization of American Music Centers in the cities he visited, including Seattle.

Moore was by no means the only composer who was moved to try her hand at an opera on an American subject as a result of this movement, nor was she the only one to portray Indians or aspects of Indian culture.[4] But Moore seems to have been the only one who chose to use a historical event from the Pacific Northwest as the subject for a serious American opera. Survivors of the 1847 massacre of missionaries Marcus and Narcissa Whitman near Walla Walla still lived, and there was continued public discussion of the event.

When I first settled in the North, my attention was called to the many thrilling episodes in the development of the Northwest. The stirring romance and martyrdom of the Whitmans, Marcus and Narcissa, as well as the staunch loyalty to principle and the cause of humanity, of Dr. John McLaughlin of the

Hudson Bay Company interested me beyond measure. It seemed that someone should commemorate the lives of these noble patriots.[5]

The jump from a modest effort like "The Quest of Sigurd" or *The
Oracle* to a major opera was enormous. Moore had doubts about trying it and urged both Farwell and Henry Hadley to take it up before
she decided to try it herself.[6] The first major challenge was the
libretto. There were published accounts of the incident, as well as a
biography of Marcus Whitman, but the materials were diffuse and
contradictory.[7] It was necessary to develop a coherent outline of the
story and present it in a few scenes, using a minimum number of solo
voices and singable English. For this project Moore turned to her
mother, the most formidable literary talent close at hand.

The subject must have been a compelling one for both of them. As
Sarah wrote, "missionary passion is the theme of the opera, with
patriotism as a second motive scarcely less powerful. . . ."[8] Sarah's
own ministry had been missionary in nature. She had considerable
literary experience; she even had some practice in treating historical
materials, though not on the scale required by this project.[9] Farwell's
call for an American national music struck a responsive chord with
Moore, for it invited her to attempt great, important, patriotic things
in her art, as her father, grandfather, and uncles had done in their
military service and working careers. The concept that her art could
so directly serve her own western American culture was a revelation.
Later the whole undertaking was carefully identified by Moore as a
"labor of love," implying the high-minded idealism of the venture as
well as its entirely noncommercial nature.

Narcissa is Moore's first major work and her largest opera. It is
central to an understanding of her subsequent career as a composer.
Further, its three productions in 1912, 1925, and 1945, mark major
turning points in her life. Hence more attention is given here to its
genesis, content, and critical reception than to any other of her works.

Both women agreed that the libretto should concentrate on historical fact and that they would not introduce the invented romantic
entanglements characteristic of most operas. The text was not to be
rhymed: Moore called on her mother for rhythmical prose, as in the
Psalms of the King James Version, a style suitable to their noble
conception of their subject. Their title for the work, *The Cost of Empire*,

is a far better indication of their aspirations than *Narcissa,* the one substituted by their publisher. Sarah succeeded in reducing the complex web of historical detail to a few dramatic scenes while remaining true to the overall story. She apologized for the changes she made: "the requirements of the drama make it impossible to be exactly correct historically owing to the necessity for compressing years into hours, and for picturing the incidents of many places as taking place in one spot."[10]

Like the other composers of Indianist operas, Moore attempted to prepare herself to represent the Indians as sensitively as she could. Sarah wrote in the foreword to the published score:

An effort has been made to give the Indian sympathetic treatment. Misunderstood, defrauded, outraged, his relations with Americans make that chapter in our history one of growing shame. No plea of the "destiny of the white race" can ever wipe out the infamy. The Whitmans least of all people deserved their martyrdom; yet according to Indian ethics—probably as good as any in the sight of God—their lives paid only a just debt.

Moore traveled to the site of the Whitman Mission and attended exhibitions of songs and dances presented by tribes in the vicinity. She borrowed a cylinder recording of other Indian music but later explained: "The Indian 'Pow Wow' closing Act 2 is not an attempt to write a real authentic Indian chorus. . . . I tried to represent the spirit of the chorus, without thought of authenticity. The main impression on my mind was a jumble of syllables, and the frequently reappearing step of an unexpected major 3rd."[11] For the massacre scene she tried to recreate sounds remembered from childhood, when she had witnessed a sham battle on a visit to Uncle Eugene's military post in New Mexico and "heard the blood-curdling Apache war-whoops" (Moore, p. 33). At first she hoped to compete for the ten thousand dollar prize for an American opera that the Met had announced in December, 1908, but she could not come close to the deadline of September, 1910. She began the music late in 1909, after Sarah had already worked for more than a year on the libretto. The full score was not finished until July, 1911; the orchestration had taken about as long as the initial composition.[12]

The characters are, then, historical figures. Marcus Whitman was a medical doctor and Presbyterian church elder who, like others of his time, was inspired to become a missionary by the report that Indian tribes of the Far West had sent emissaries to St. Louis to seek the white man's "Book of God." In pursuit of her own missionary vocation, Narcissa Prentiss married Marcus Whitman in 1836, and soon became the first white woman to cross the North American continent. She is described in contemporary sources as refined and well educated; it was said that her gregarious nature suffered, as did her health, in the isolated circumstances of the mission. Narcissa is reputed to have had a beautiful singing voice, which held the attention of whites and Indians alike. In the opera hers is the character developed most fully and sympathetically. While both Marcus and Narcissa are eloquent advocates of their mission, it is through her that the personal suffering that is the consequence of their actions is portrayed.

Dr. John McLoughlin was chief factor for the Hudson's Bay Company at Fort Vancouver. His unfailing kindness toward the American missionaries and the settlers coming from the United States eventually cost him his position with the British company. Those Indians who were friendly toward the Whitmans and their mission are represented by Chief Yellow Serpent, his son Elijah, and Elijah's sweetheart Siskadee. The two most colorful character roles in the opera belong to unfriendly Indians. Waskema was an ancient Indian woman whose prophecies were believed to be the result of special powers. Throughout the opera she warns that the Indian is doomed by the arrival of so many "Boston Men," as the settlers were called. Tom Hill, or Delaware Tom as he is known in the opera, had left the mission area by the time of the massacre, but Sarah bent the facts enough to bring him into the action.

The opera opens in the village church of Rushville, in upstate New York. The congregation is singing "By the Waters of Babylon." Marcus, who has just returned from the British-claimed Oregon Territory, appears with two Indians and asks the congregation to support his missionary work. He is reluctant to ask Narcissa, his betrothed, to share the hardships and dangers of such a life, but she insists on accompanying him. She dedicates herself to their mission in a love duet with Marcus, and they are married on the spot. Act I concludes with a hymn that was commonly used to bid farewell to missionaries in the 1830s, Samuel F. Smith's "Yes, My Native Land I Love Thee." The self-sufficient, cantatalike nature of this act, together with its declarations of religious fervor and patriotism, make it suitable for

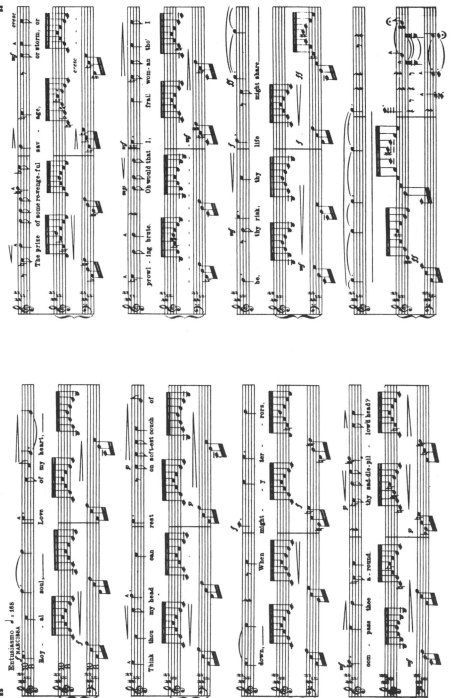

Pages from "Royal Soul," *Narcissa*, Act I. (Reprinted from the piano-vocal score [New York: Witmark, 1912].)

separate concert performance; there were several such performances over the years, often in church settings.

In Act II the audience is transported to Fort Vancouver, the Hudson's Bay Company's opulent station on the Columbia River in the Oregon Territory. Dr. McLoughlin, the factor in charge of the station, arrives from England by sea and the Whitman party appears from the opposite direction. The Whitmans are heartily welcomed by McLoughlin; Yellow Serpent invites Whitman to settle among his people. A wild song and dance by the Indians at the fort concludes the festivities.

Five years have passed when Act III opens at the Whitman Mission, which had been built near the site of present-day Walla Walla, Washington. A settler's orphan occupies the cradle left empty by the death of the Whitmans' own child. Narcissa's opening soliloquy about the hardship and loneliness of her life, followed by a prayer and a lullabye, is one of the opera's most poignant scenes. Delaware Tom urges the Indians, who are dismayed by the arrival of settlers from the States in growing numbers, to rebellion. Yellow Serpent, Elijah, and Siskadee remain loyal to the missionaries; Narcissa's beautiful voice weaves a spell that quiets the other Indians. Elijah proposes to lead the braves on an expedition to California in order to avoid a confrontation. In the sentimental ballad, "When the Camas Blooms Again," he promises to return in the spring and make Siskadee his bride.

Although it is midwinter, Marcus decides that he must leave for Washington, D.C., right away, for he believes that the United States is preparing to cede its claim to the Oregon Territory to Britain.[13] A brilliant final chorus of fifteen parts expresses the gathering conflicts. "The Star Spangled Banner" is heard in the orchestra, as the immigrants sing "Our country's flag, the glory of the Lord." Simultaneously, the Indians chant "Woe, the Indian's fate is sealed"; Dr. McLoughlin sings "My doom comes with the morrow, my state is gone"; Narcissa wishes Marcus "Godspeed"; and Marcus sets forth to "Joy only must you borrow for prize soon won."[14]

The massacre takes place in Act IV. Marcus has returned successful from his trip. The Indian braves are expected home and a chorus of Indian maidens welcomes the return of spring in song. Soon a grief-stricken Yellow Serpent rushes in with the news that his son Elijah was murdered in California by a cowardly American. When he leaves to mourn his son, Delaware Tom incites the remaining Indians to massacre. Marcus and Narcissa and other inhabitants of the mission are slain before Dr. McLoughlin arrives. Yellow Serpent returns and swears vengeance on the murderers. Siskadee's lament for Elijah and the death wails of the Indian women bring the opera to a somber close.

Narcissa's composer and librettist had often been involved with amateur productions, but *Narcissa* was not for amateurs. It was conceived on a grand scale. To get it produced Moore turned for help to John Cort, for twenty-four years one of the leading theater managers and operators on the West Coast. He had moved east from Seattle in 1911 as Moore was finishing the opera. From his New York office Cort advised Moore to bring her new work to that city and put it before the producers there. Cort had planned to show her opera to Henry Savage, whose successful productions ranged from spoken comedy to grand opera. When Moore arrived in the fall of 1911, Savage was struggling to survive the very recent failure of several road companies. Apart from the financial plight of Savage and other producers, there was probably some truth in the observation that "New York managers looked upon a Westerner and a woman who had composed a grand opera in the light of a joke and refused her a satisfactory hearing."[15]

The trip was not entirely in vain, for Moore did find a publisher. An enthusiastic recommendation from Arthur Farwell persuaded Witmark to issue the piano-vocal score. Moore's work was the first grand opera published in the United States by that firm, which changed the original title, *The Cost of Empire,* to the more romantic *Narcissa.* Meanwhile, John Cort had decided to put his name, but not his money, behind a premiere of *Narcissa* in Seattle at his Moore Theatre there. The composer returned home with instructions to raise a chorus and select minor parts and understudies from local talent. Cort took responsibility for engaging prominent singers for the roles of Marcus and Narcissa and arranging for an experienced stage director. The production was to be financed mainly by the composer's husband, who eventually covered a three-thousand dollar deficit on an overall budget of ten thousand dollars.

The fact that the opera included eleven solo roles requiring eight

Pages from ensemble finale, *Narcissa*, Act III. (Reprinted, by permission, from the composer's 1947 copy of the 1911 score, Mary Carr Moore Archive, Music Library, UCLA.)

principals in addition to some smaller solo parts did not seem to bother Moore at the start, but she later recognized it as an impediment.

It is not a simple project. Mr. Temple (our first producer, long with the Met) said that the only opera he could recall with so many "bit parts" was *Meistersinger*. But, the story could not be told properly without local color, and certain allusions were (at the time I wrote it) very important to those who gave me the material. It will work out, but requires a real interest on the parts of performers and producers. And, of course, many rehearsals.[16]

The composer intended that the several minor roles included for historical effect be taken by members of the chorus: "'Narcissa' was so hampered by the many chorus lines, and I dimly realized it at the time, but not until we began to pick out chorus men and women to do those unimportant parts; as it was a labor of love, and as we had better voices than the average chorus, it was possible."[17]

Both Moore and her mother were unstinting in their praise of the stage director sent by Cort. Edward P. Temple had acquired his considerable qualifications as stage and production manager for *Narcissa* by staging operas for Henry Savage, at the Metropolitan Opera, and at the Hippodrome in New York. Arriving just four weeks before the first performance, he molded the largely amateur cast, including a chorus of some sixty-five young singers, into a professional-looking production. The press remarked on the unexpected smoothness of the opening night. The excellent staging was complemented by authentic Indian costumes and props, which heightened the sense of historical authenticity in the events portrayed.[18]

Drilling the chorus was to have been the extent of Moore's conducting responsibility, but an experienced and willing conductor for the overall production seemed to be unavailable, perhaps because of the composer's gender. By default, Moore found herself on the podium, baton in hand. Marcus Whitman was sung by Charles Hargreaves from the Metropolitan Opera, and Luella Chilson-Ohrman from Chicago was Narcissa. Anna Ruzena Sprotte, a former member of the Royal Opera Company of Berlin who had recently arrived in Seattle, created the role of the Indian prophetess Waskema. The other principals were local singers, and the substantial chorus was composed of students of Seattle voice teachers.[19]

People came from all over the Northwest to hear *Narcissa*, which was hailed as "the most ambitious musical work ever attempted in this part of the country."[20] A survivor of the massacre was in the opening night audience. The Seattle premiere of this grand opera was a source of great civic pride. The preview for sponsors was followed by a premiere on April 22, 1912, that was a triumph for the composer and her mother, who took bow after bow as the stage was strewn with flowers. Four generations of the composer's family witnessed her achievement, for the Pratts had come from Santa Monica to join the Carrs and the Moores in the audience. Three more equally successful performances followed.

Critical response to the opera was thoroughly favorable. The New York–based *Musical America* gave it most of a page, including a photo of the set, with inserts of Marcus and Narcissa. After introducing it as a triumph and giving a summary of the plot, the review continued:

Considered, however, in the light of a narration well told, ably constructed and given an adequate musical setting, the opera fills its purpose entirely. Regarding the music itself there can scarcely be a difference of opinion. The score is rich in free, spontaneous melody given excellent treatment and at no time forced. In using the original Indian melodies Mrs. Moore has shown wonderful skill. In the manner used they give a most vivid coloring and obtain a fine effect.

The reviewer singled out three numbers for special praise: "Royal Soul," Narcissa's lullabye from Act III, and "When the Camas Blooms Again." These, along with "the handling of the chorus and the effectiveness of the ensemble show the composer to possess creative ability of the highest order."[21] Seattle critics were likewise complimentary.

"Narcissa" . . . is strikingly original and in some places startlingly so. It is a poem set to music; unlike the standard opera blood does not flow, or at least visibly, the tragedies occur unseen and are merely the topic of musical narration.

There is a solemnity and dignity pervading the whole which never loses its grip, and in this many will find fault, for there is not a single moment of relaxation from beginning to end.

Strangely enough, there is not a single incident in the action of the play worthy of the name, until the climax; the whole fabric is supported solely by pleasing melodies and magnificent stage pictures. There is little scope for acting. . . .

In "Narcissa" has been struck a note that is absolutely untouched. There does not come to mind any opera in the history of music which has very much in common with this one. Certainly it is American grand opera, and the only one worthy the name.[22]

The absence of any romantic complication in the plot was noted by many commentators, though none offered much in the way of perceptive observations on the romantic view of patriotism and duty on which the work is based. One local critic went so far as to suggest how the plot could be altered to make a bona fide "melodrama" out of the story.

There is just one thing in which Narcissa seems to fall short, and that is its entire lack of a conflict of passion. Of course, Narcissa bears Whitman the intensest love possible; but there is no particular obstacle to heighten its development, such as out of which really great drama—music or otherwise, grows. If the Indian prophetess Waskema had only been infatuated with Whitman and then driven to jealousy when he brings back Narcissa, such an element might have been provided. But of course that would have been taking liberties with history, and Mrs. Carr and Moore have sought to stick to facts.[23]

Others were quite willing to accept the opera's content, however: "I have twice witnessed the Passion Play in Oberammergau, and this opera, 'Narcissa,' or 'The Cost of Empire,' approaches nearer to that than anything else I have ever witnessed."[24]

Moore's gender was duly noted by the critics, then and later. One critic simply observed, "'Narcissa' stands alone in this country, and is the work of a woman."[25] Others hastened to assure the readers of Moore's feminine qualities, despite the magnitude of her achievement: "the composer is not a man-hating suffragette of solitary habits and masculine qualities."[26] "Not the least pleasing characteristic of Mrs. Moore is her modesty. Her achievements she regards as merely the result of years of training and hard work, and she declares that anyone could do what she has done if they would but apply themselves."[27] One noted that Moore had made a breakthrough: "she has broken down the traditional idea that profound operatic composition (and its production) belongs preeminently to men."[28] Others found it necessary to put Narcissa in proper perspective: "Were one impetuous, he might say that Mrs. Moore frequently exhibits a musicianly genius. But it is safe to say that she has written with great tact, approaching in cleverness some of the best tone-painters of the day."[29]

Critical discussion of one aspect of Moore's work—her handling of the orchestra—became entangled in the commotion caused by the fact that it was a woman, even a lady, who had composed and conducted a grand opera so successfully: "It has generally been conceded that women are successful in composing melodious and artistic songs and smaller choral works, but so far few women have ventured into the orchestral field. It has been a matter of comment that Mrs. Moore's work is rich in its orchestral effects."[30] The idea that women's compositional abilities were generally not suited to orchestration persisted. A critic reviewing the 1925 performance in San Francisco observed: "Mrs. Moore excels orchestrally; her instrumentation caused not only admiration but surprise on the part of critical musicians who had not dared to expect so much of a woman."[31] The *Musical America* critic pointed out that "the score is at times extremely thin and at other times overbalanced." Two Seattle critics joined in this harsh judgment, saying "the entire orchestration of the opera obviously needs revision,"[32] and noting "periods of emptiness and lack of substance in the orchestration of the work."[33]

Moore's score called for an orchestra of forty. In fact, she had fewer than thirty musicians in the pit, leaving several essential parts uncovered. The entire orchestra was present for only one of the five orchestral rehearsals, resulting in even more problems during the performances. Sarah used this fact to defend her daughter's orchestration: "It is said that no one on our newspaper force is able to read a conductor's grand opera score. This accounts for the fact that they could not distinguish between a thin orchestra and a thin orchestration."[34] Why the orchestra was understaffed is not clear, but the error was repeated in later productions. It was particularly easy to ascribe shortcomings in the orchestration to a provincial novice such as Moore, since orchestras, customarily dominated by non-English-speaking musicians, were something of a mystery to American listeners. The omission is regrettable, for it gave critics a handle with which to denigrate the whole opera. It seems clear enough now that the scoring is competent, if not the most compelling aspect of this very impressive opera.

It was frequently said that *Narcissa* was the first grand opera to be composed, orchestrated, and conducted by a woman. But it was not recognized that the point of view from which its story is told is really the most unique and original thing about *Narcissa*. Here, after all, is a grand opera in which the winning of the American West is seen through the sensibility of a female protagonist sympathetically and accurately portrayed in her historical role. This revolutionary conception was never fully recognized either in the opera's three productions or in the superficial critical commentary the work received. Its implications were not acknowledged, and perhaps they were scarcely recognized by Moore herself, who simply composed the libretto as she believed it should be set. Both composer and librettist began, it is true, with the idea of celebrating Marcus Whitman's heroic exploits. Missionary passion and patriotism were their stated themes. But it was the idea of Narcissa as a full participant in the Whitmans' common mission to which they were both drawn. Moore's richest and most insightful musical portrayal is reserved for Narcissa, the character both librettist and composer understood best. It is Narcissa who is the most human and compelling character in the opera, and thus it is her view of the events portrayed that inevitably colors the unfolding of the drama. Whether the other characters in the opera are sufficiently developed in Moore's realization remains a question that can only be answered in a production that attempts to clarify and exploit the point of view brought to the opera by its creators.

In *Narcissa*, Moore objectified her painfully acquired view of duty and her patriotism, turning them at last to serve her creative imperative. Involving her mother so deeply in her first major opera yielded results of great significance to her personal and professional future. First, Moore made Sarah her accomplice in an enterprise that, with its aspirations for national attention and major professional productions, went far beyond Sarah's previously expressed ideas about the proper sphere for creative work by women. Second, by involving Sarah in a project in which Moore, as the composer, had to make the final decisions about what was needed in the libretto and what must be cut, Moore established herself as the dominant creative personality. Thus she achieved a measure of both aesthetic and psychological independence. In other words, with *Narcissa* Moore achieved emotional and creative maturity. But the comments about the composer's sex that figure in the published stories about the opera suggest that she still would have to deal with external barriers of prejudice if the opera were to have more productions and continuing recognition.

Narcissa retained, in spite of her many later achievements, a very special place in Moore's estimate of her own music; the years of effort she expended in getting further productions testifies to that. There had been nothing in her previous work that even began to suggest she was capable of such a major achievement. From a writer of songs and one slight operetta came, with that flash of creative energy that always defies explanation, a major, if misunderstood and imperfect, American opera.

CHAPTER 10

After *Narcissa*

By now a matron approaching her fortieth birthday, Moore went to New York early in 1913. She took with her the two younger children, the score of *Narcissa,* and her record of provincial successes.[1] Her disappointment there may be inferred from the relative scarcity of information about her stay. Certainly her six-month sojourn in the East turned out to be unproductive as far as her career was concerned.

What did Moore find in New York? The tides of musical and artistic change of the early twentieth century ran far more powerfully there than in frontier Seattle, though not nearly so strongly as in Europe. While Moore was there, for instance, the artistic novelties of the Armory Show attracted crowds from all walks of life. Viewers saw the works of impressionist and cubist painters for the first time; Duchamp's futuristic "Nude Descending a Staircase" formed the centerpiece of the controversial show. Moore's friend and supporter Arthur Farwell dismissed "Nude Descending a Staircase" in print as "the greatest artistic joke in many years." He concluded that cubism in art had no analogue in music, that ultra-modernism had already appeared in music in the form of Debussy's excessively refined subjectivity and that it would presently trigger a reaction.[2] Moore was definitely interested in Debussy's harmonic experiments, but it is doubtful whether she was much influenced by the Armory Show. She may even have sympathized with commentators even less responsive than Farwell, some of whom spoke of the dangers of alien "Ellis Island Art" as similar to the risks of imported anarchism to the established political order.[3]

In music, Mussorgsky's *Boris Godunov,* later understood as an important source for certain twentieth-century musical innovations, had its first American performance at the Met in early 1913.[4] Schoenberg's atonal *Pierrot Lunaire* and Stravinsky's primitivistic *Rite of Spring* had not achieved American performances, though *Pierrot Lunaire* was attracting attention in print from American critics traveling abroad. Moore probably saw James Huneker's column, which appeared in both the *New York Times* and *Musical America* under the heading: "Schoenberg Makes Huneker Writhe: A Hearing by the Famous American Critic of the Nerve-Shattering 'Lieder des Pierrot Lunaire'—'Evil, Be Thou My Good' the Schoenberg Motto."[5] Russolo's futurist manifesto, advocating "noise music" that was to consist of explosions, murmurs, and the like, was being dismissed as coming from a "Milanese crank."[6] Ragtime, surreptitiously tried and abandoned by Moore fifteen years earlier, was finally being suggested as a legitimate source for American art music.[7] Moore's exact contemporary, Charles Ives, was known only as a retiring but successful idea man in New York's insurance industry and was probably quite unknown to Moore at that time.[8]

Moore was more likely to have encountered the younger Claire Reis, organizer of the People's Music League and later executive director of the League of Composers. Reis had been deflected by prevailing sex stereotypes from a career as a musician to one as a music patron, a path followed by many women but rejected by Moore.[9] Innovators in the arts were often associated with radicalism in politics, always a problem for Moore, however creative and innovative she herself might be. She would not have sought out the colony of rebellious and reformist painters, poets, and writers in Greenwich Village, and she must have detested socialists and anarchists like Emma Goldman, who was active in New York at that time and had recently written, about the political party of Moore's family, "Republicanism stands for vested rights, for imperialism, for graft, for the annihilation of every semblance of liberty. Its ideal is the oily, creepy respectability of a McKinley, and the brutal arrogance of a Roosevelt."[10]

Victor Herbert's very popular operettas would have been more to Moore's liking than the work of Ives or the European innovators. Herbert's serious opera *Natoma*, on a California mission subject, had been premiered two years earlier; she may have had a chance to hear the Philadelphia-Chicago Opera Company production of it in New York. By 1913, Herbert, who met and encouraged Moore, had established himself as an important supporter of American art music and was helping found the American Society of Composers, Authors and

Publishers (ASCAP). She might also have heard and seen shows by Rudolph Friml or Jerome Kern, both just getting started in their careers.[11]

Oscar Sonneck may have excoriated the Metropolitan Opera, in addressing a woman's club in 1913, as "a huge incubator of antiquities in music," but there were operatic novelties in town.[12] Among them were Kienzl's *Le Ranz des vaches*, Goldmark's *Cricket on the Hearth*, Zandonai's *Conchita*, Damrosch's *Cyrano*, D'Erlanger's *Noël*, and an operetta by John Philip Sousa, *The American Maid, or The Glassblowers*, produced by John Cort, who had been so helpful with the Seattle production of *Narcissa*.

Other musicians and composers with whom Moore later worked were drawing some attention. Olga Steeb was performing on the West Coast; the Pasmore Trio concertized in Kansas and Iowa. Charles Wakefield Cadman proposed a prize for a new American opera for the projected Panama-Pacific International Exposition in San Francisco. Ethel Leginska, Modest Altschuler, Andrès de Segurola, and Ellen Beach Yaw, all later based in Los Angeles, were active in New York in 1913. A few woman composers were drawing attention, within limits. Charlotte Lund's recital of songs by no less than twenty-two American composers, nine of them women, was considered very unusual, even among New York's very numerous concerts.[13] Two women, Harriet Ware and Celeste D. Hecksher, were able to arrange public concerts of their own music while Moore was in New York. Ware mustered a large chorus of women's voices and several vocal soloists for a performance of her cantata "Sir Oluf" in Carnegie Hall. Hecksher enlisted the New York Symphony under Alexander Saslavsky and violinist Efrem Zimbalist, among others, for "the first orchestral concert ever given in this city by an American woman composer."[14] Both women were portrayed as aristocratic ladies and their music received as suitably feminine and "melodic."

Moore set to work to promote her own music in these new surroundings. A few clippings from her scrapbooks give some idea of her progress. The hometown paper sounded optimistic at first:

warm reception accorded Mrs. Mary Carr Moore in New York . . . one of the guests at the 21st annual dinner of American dramatists and composers, on which occasion Victor Herbert was the guest of honor. The guest of honor was at Table A and at Table B Mrs. Moore was seated with Mrs. Alice Harriman, the well-known publisher and author, also of Seattle. Mrs. Harriman, in a letter to Miss Stella G. Webster of Seattle, pays tribute to the impression made by Mrs. Moore, who was handsomely gowned and whose delightful personality found many responses there.

Among those who showed a close interest in Mrs. Moore's work was John Philip Sousa, who was there with his wife and daughter. . . .

No one can help admiring Mrs. Moore's courage and it is kind news to hear that she is finding a happy welcome in the city from which recognition must come.[15]

Her work was featured at another such event shortly afterward:

A session of the Theatre Club of New York, devoted to grand opera, was held at the Hotel Astor, January 28, and was attended by about 500 women. Mary Carr Moore of Seattle gave an informal talk on "Narcissa," an historical music drama, of which she is the composer. Scenes from this opera, which was produced last Spring at Seattle, were given by Edith Hallet, Frank and Roy Williams.[16]

Alice Harriman, the publisher who had started as a newspaperwoman in Seattle, helped her make these connections. But these meetings did not automatically bring the business associations she now required. To be sure, someone, perhaps Richard Hageman, then an assistant conductor at the Met, helped arrange for her to sit in a forward box where she might observe conductor and orchestra in great detail.[17] But the evidence of another clipping indicates that she was quickly categorized as a nonprofessional, society woman composer along with Ware and Hecksher and given this kind of coverage: "Neglect of your family, under certain conditions, will not harm the family. . . . This startling observation is from Mary Carr Moore, only woman composer of America who has written, scored and conducted a grand opera for a series of public performances." The report of the interview, which points out that Moore was clearly not "a strident amazon, advocating housework for husbands or solitude for babies," is accompanied by a separate box with selected quotations from the composer.

Neglect your family a little if genius clamors in your soul. Women have not made artistic history because they feared to neglect their homes. A woman can take care of home, babies and talent if she lives twenty-four hours a day. American women have the temperament to be great composers. They have rich history to draw from. But they fear to step out of their homes. Being wives and mothers should not deter women from being great artists. It should stimulate such ambition.[18]

Moore wrote in the margin of her scrapbook that the story was "funny," that she was "mad" at being misquoted and accused of neglecting her children. She did not say, but she must have known, that such a story also meant that she had not managed to break down the barrier of gender, any more than Ware or Hecksher had. Because of her sex and her status as a married, middle-class woman, she would not be regarded simply as another composer seeking a hearing for a new opera.

Six months in New York did nothing to further Moore's career as a composer. Any hope for a New York production of *Narcissa* had disappeared, seemingly before she arrived. Her experience there strengthened her sense of alienation from the coming tide of modernism. It also caused her to give up further attempts to gain recognition on the East Coast. She met in New York a wall of sex discrimination far higher than had existed in Seattle, one she could not breach. She was glad enough to leave with some promises that her songs might be sung in the future and that "The Quest of Sigurd" would be performed by the Rubinstein Club of Women.[19] She produced four short pieces in those months, a small output for her. Of these, only the "Barcarolle" for piano, in 5/8 time, was much performed.[20] Her search to develop her musical language further had already begun in Seattle; its direction bore little relationship to the novelties she might have discovered in New York. The professional rebuff she suffered there may even have contributed to the partial aesthetic retrenchment of the next few years.

By June 1 Moore was back in Seattle. The separation from her husband had not improved her marriage. Claude's actions were a continuing affront, for which she continued to accept the blame. She still avoided divorce as a way to deal with his infidelities, but it was only a few weeks before a different kind of incident changed her mind. The morning after July 4, Moore looked out to see her nine-year-old daughter enveloped in flames and running toward the house. She put out the fire by rolling Marian in a rug, but despite her quick reaction, the child was deeply burned on her arms, legs, back, and breast. For a time the parents feared for Marian's life.

Moore never ceased to blame her husband for this accident, for Claude was to have taken Marian along on his Sunday house calls that morning. He took a lady friend instead, leaving Marian to play with the neighbor child who had produced the nearly fatal leftover sparklers that caused the fire. Later Moore spoke of this incident as the last straw. After that it no longer made sense to remain in the marriage for the children's sake. For the rest of 1913 and all of 1914, Moore lived at several Seattle addresses other than the Denny Way house.[21]

More blows followed quickly. On November 1 her beloved father, who had been failing for some time, died at Valle Vista, the home he had once owned so proudly in the Napa Valley.[22] Perhaps his death permitted her to start the formal divorce proceedings. These, however, must have been slowed by the death of her attorney brother Eugene the following January. Eugene, then in his midfifties, had been very supportive over the years; his widow Alice remained a staunch friend.

There is no direct evidence of Moore's reaction to these personal blows, but in the period of separation that preceded the divorce, her music took on a schizophrenic quality. Even before going to New York, she had begun to look for a newer style to follow that of *Narcissa*. Sarah registered three "dramatic sketches" with the Copyright Office in 1912. If they were intended for her daughter to set, all three were rejected, as was her attempt to reconstruct the text of *The Oracle*. *The Leper*, a one-act "tabloid grand opera" with a libretto by Seattle writer Dudley Burrows, which Moore chose to compose next, reflects a letdown after her thirty months of intense work to bring *Narcissa* to performance. It also reveals her unshaken and hopelessly unrealistic idealism about marriage. Its two characters seek only mutual self-sacrifice on the altar of their romantic attachment. The harmonic language is transparently imitative of Puccini's *Madama Butterfly*, in a way that is unique among her works. No wonder she later dismissed it as "meller-drammer," though she stopped short of destroying the manuscript. With *The Leper*, she had entered a period of musical as well as personal uncertainty. Other private expressions of personal loss such as the bathetic song "Finis" contrast wildly with some would-be commercial ventures in the world of vaudeville.

Her practice at being the life of the party, her quickness at composition, and her long experience with extemporized theatricals must have suggested that she give vaudeville a try now that she must support herself, and Seattle was the headquarters of at least one circuit of vaudeville theaters. In *Memories*, librettist Charles E. Banks had Robert Burns, Omar Khayyám, and Thomas Moore reminisce about their lost loves.[23] Moore conducted an inadequate production of this twenty-minute sketch at the Seattle Orpheum in 1914; later it was used on the Keith-Orpheum vaudeville circuit for a year.[24] *The Firemen of the Wissahickon Inn, or, How the Chief Fell off the Waterwagon,* unacknowledged in her catalog, is pure slapstick.

Chief! Now, how would you save a woman from a sixth story window?

Fireman: Get a bar of soap and a pail of water, then make a lather and tell her to climb down.[25]

For this one, Moore simply selected and "adapted" tunes that seemed appropriate. Two other vaudeville sketches, *Potato Salad à l'Opéra* and *Three and a Pool,* date from the next year or two.[26]

By contrast, the very serious "Mysterious Power," one of Moore's most important songs, is also from this period. Marian was probably still hospitalized and the composer was attempting to deal with the new reality of her broken marriage when she wrote the text and music.

> Oh, thou who strangely hast the pow'r
> To move my very being to its depths
> Whose ev'ry breath and thought
> Stirs answ'ring impulse, leaping forth to meet
> All it longs to find, yet fears to know
> Enslaving me
> Yet lending my soul wings
> With which more eagerly to cleave
> The bright clear heights, wherein thou dwellst.
> Ah, were this all of life for me,
> Then life would deeply satisfy.
> Oh, thou, who strangely hast the pow'r.

"Mysterious Power" is the most important early exception to the artistic retrenchment that accompanied the radical personal step of the divorce. It is a particularly fine example of Moore's willingness to experiment with new harmonic ideas and to explore new usages, but not to abandon her basically Romantic aesthetic heritage. It shows her continuing to shun the stance of musical rebelliousness, just as she shunned political or social rebellion. At the same time, it reveals her search to establish her own emotional balance and to find a musical language that might yield some overall integrity of expression in terms that suited her view of the world. The text's restraint and resultant ambiguity allowed it to be used as a sacred song in churches in Los Angeles in later years.

The divorce became final in December, 1914. She was not emotionally prepared to stand on her own feet, either personally or artistically, when it came. Her emotional scars remained raw. Only later would it be confirmed that Moore had at last achieved maturity as a creative artist. In January she departed from the Seattle that had grown up around her.

CHAPTER 11

San Francisco, 1915–26

Moore and the children spent several months with relatives, now scattered in Los Angeles and San Diego as well as the Bay Area, before taking up residence in San Francisco. The city to which she returned after an absence of twenty years had changed as dramatically as had Seattle. Most obviously, the great earthquake and fire of 1906 had destroyed most of the city. New buildings and empty lots replaced many of the structures she remembered. A new Tivoli Opera House had opened its doors in 1913 to Mary Garden's Chicago Opera Company and then had become a silent movie palace. A site had been reserved for a civic opera house, near the ruins of City Hall, in what would eventually become the Civic Center. The San Francisco Symphony, conducted so far by her friend Henry Hadley, was but four years old. Her teachers, John Haraden Pratt and Henry Bickford Pasmore, were still vigorously at work; Pasmore's daughters, returned from their European successes, had joined him. Establishment of the San Francisco Conservatory was still a few years away, though its eventual founder, Ada Clement, was already teaching.[1] The great Panama-Pacific International Exposition, intended to celebrate the opening of the Panama Canal as well as the rebuilding of the city, was about to open.

Once there had been talk of producing *Narcissa* for the Exposition; now Moore had to content herself with a program of songs and vocal trios in the Washington State Building, a performance of "My Dream" on a concert designed as a fund-raiser to preserve the Exposition Art Palace,[2] and a chance to conduct her own song "Brahma" on a concert of orchestral music by San Francisco composers. "Brahma" was particularly well received: "One of the features of the programme was Mary Carr Moore's song, 'Brahma,' which is a lyric with a thrill in it and thrillingly sung by Harald Pracht. . . ."[3] "The 'Brahma' of Mrs. Mary

Carr Moore, with its impressive monody for baritone, sung by Harald Pracht, its creepy drum rhythm and sighing strings, struck me as distinctly the best work of hers that I have heard."[4] The orchestra of eighty was both larger and perhaps better than other groups conducted by Moore during her career, for this is one of the rare favorable comments on her orchestration.

Her old friends rallied around her. She developed a class of private students and soon found a receptive club public for her music. In October, 1915, alone, there were programs of her songs and vocal trios for the Forum Club, the Pacific Coast Women's Press Association, and the Channing Auxiliary of the First Unitarian Church. Harriet Pasmore, better known as Radiana Pazmor, was a member of the trio on all three occasions and on at least one occasion sang "Finis" and "The Tryst." Among other activities, Moore spoke on Massenet's *Thaïs* for the Twentieth Century Club and helped organize the San Francisco Music Study Club at Mme. Vincent's studio. She traveled to Pasadena to accompany her cousin, soprano Ellen Beach Yaw, at a concert that included at least one of her songs.[5]

Still she mourned her divorce. She could not bring herself to set the lyrics of despair she wrote in the blank pages of the red leather journal she had given her father a few years earlier.

> There comes a moment in this surging life
> When all of strength, and all of self-control
> Gives way; and the dead past, in bitterness,
> Resistless, overwhelms my tired soul!

or,

> Shall Life, forever mock at all the soul's desires?
> Shall Love, forever be an empty name?[6]

A short, unnamed libretto from the same period by Sarah portrays a couple about to divorce. The "other woman" nobly rejects the husband and sends him back to his wife after contemplating the couple's sleeping child. Moore sent it to her mother with the comment that it was "too personal" to use.

The simple passage of time, the work of teaching, and the friendship of Lillian Quinn Stark, all helped toward a recovery.[7] "O Wondrous Soul," a jewel-like setting of Moore's own text, perhaps her most perfect song, expresses her gratitude to this friend who encouraged her to resume composing:

> O wondrous soul,
> With what deep insight art endowed,
> To play upon the heartstrings vibrantly,
> And stir to quivering life long silent tones,
> Not yet inured to voiceless agony.

And who helped her express her grief:

> Yet more, to ease the tense unrest,
> And send upon this arid waste of time,
> The blessed dew of tears.[8]

Moore also wrote a suite of incidental music for a reading of Robert Browning's "Saul" to be given by Stark. The healing power of David's music and his love for Saul must have seemed an apt topic in the spring and summer of 1916, as Moore regained her emotional balance. Then too, "Saul" had been a much-loved poem in Moore's own family, as Grandmother Pratt's poem attests.

> We had planned an evening with Browning,
> For we were alone, we three;
> And longed for the inspiration
> That Browning's poems would be. . . .
>
> But hush! Holy ground we're approaching,
> Read we now of David and Saul.
> Through the darkened "Tent" thrilled sweet music,
> We listened, and heard it, *all*.
>
> While the words from the lips of David
> Like the fabled "Apples of Gold,"
> Seemed benedictions falling *on us*
> In blessings manifold.[9]

Moore shortened the text of Browning's poem, but did not change its meaning. The suite's six movements form an unusual shape, reflecting the stages of the healing process through which Browning takes David and Saul in the poem.

Saul was to have been premiered at the Overseas Club on November 9, but Stark's death earlier in the day forced a cancellation. She had read it in public once, a month earlier. For several more Bay Area performances, George Churchill Paterson, a longtime friend with an enthusiasm for dramatics and a connection with the Southern Pacific Railroad, took over capably. Often *Saul* was done with the reader in costume and the three musicians (piano, violin, cello) offstage or out of sight. The music was much admired: "You have today listened to a genius worthy of comparison with the great modern composers."[10] "There cannot be any question regarding the fact that this is among the better of Mrs. Moore's work, indeed it may well be regarded as one of her biggest and most ambitious musical compositions."[11] "The incidental music was excellent and effective, and the program carried those present into a unique realm of music."[12] "Miss Moore manifests her remarkable gift for truly creative composition in this utterance of the harp of David; the various themes serve to show most convincingly that musical composition is not the sole prerogative of men."[13] In reporting a performance of Moore's music at the Cora Williams Institute, Berkeley, on November 10, 1922, a reviewer wrote:

Mary Carr Moore is too well known to need much reviewing, but certain qualities in her work should be stressed again and again. There is a seriousness, a decided musical sense, and, anon, an atmospheric quality, refreshing to hear. . . . In her incidental music, Mrs. Moore reached the climax of the afternoon's work. The prelude is an effective bit of atmospheric writing that would stand alone, as a trio, as well as an introduction to the poem. As the latter, it quite prepared one for the varying emotions soon to be expressed in speech, and lends a certain mystic, Oriental charm, which ranges through a gentle playfulness, to dignity and grandeur at the end . . . [and], at the close, a breathless hush.[14]

By 1923 Moore had arranged the music as an instrumental suite of five movements for piano and string quartet. Later performances, of which there were many, were often in this quintet version. Sometimes she dispensed with the reader, for the music stands very well on its own without Browning's text.

One cannot help but speculate on the effect of Stark's death on Moore. In the short period of their acquaintance, Moore produced two of her best works, *Saul* and "O Wondrous Soul," both dedicated to Stark. But after her death, which was not unexpected, the rush of other events continued. In the fall of 1916 Moore began teaching music in two public high schools.

Arriving at the Mission [High] School at 8 AM (no hour for a musician to be abroad, unless returning homeward) I taught, during the week, five recitations in Harmony; two classes in Boys' Choral, two for girls, and one for mixed; two orchestral practices a week and some music history, to keep us out of mischief, until 12 noon. Then, by street-car, I went across town [to Girls' High School], and if possible had a cup of coffee, and taught a large class in Harmony; also choral work, orchestral rehearsals, and music history. I recall that I had something like 480 harmony slips a week to correct, when, and how, I could.[15]

She had probably finished *Saul* before the school year began, but the club performances and some private teaching went on concurrently. And at the end of the school year the students at Mission High School put on *Harmony*, a "musical farce" she had contrived for their benefit. The dialogue was a spoof on music teaching, and the music she borrowed for the occasion ranged from "O sole mio" through her own students to Chopin, ending with her own "We'll Never Let Old Glory Fall," still attributed to Charlie Barrett. The cast included "Ino Moore, a Lady Composer." Two years later, when *Harmony* was repeated for the annual Pacific Music Society Jinks, Alfred Metzger called the evening "one of the most enjoyable and entertaining affairs ever given in San Francisco."[16] "Miss Ino Moore" also appeared on that program as a "Lady Conductor." Under the label "Miss Alexandria Sassylafsky," she conducted an orchestra of socialites in a performance of Leopold Mozart's *Toy* symphony.

Before the school year was out in 1917, Moore met and married Arthur De Celles dit Duclos. Arthur worked for Sherman Clay, a rapidly expanding music business in San Francisco. He played the piano and was younger than she. He introduced her to Wesley Webster, who soon became her principal publisher.[17] He also helped her obtain a large new Steinway piano to replace the old Chickering that her parents had gotten for her years before.

The divorce and remarriage may have seemed regrettable to the Pratt clan, though Moore's divorce was no longer unique. Aunt Harriet Pratt Sherman had soon followed her example. At the family party for the Pratts' sixty-eighth anniversary in April, 1917, Harriet's very recent remarriage was celebrated as well. Moore took the moment to announce her own second marriage: "just as dinner was announced, [Mary Louise] appeared and laughingly introduced the gentleman with her as her husband, Mr. Arthur Duclos of San Francisco.[18] Two years later, the Pratts gave an interview to the press on the occasion of their seventieth wedding anniversary. Louisa was past ninety and Robert Henry was a lively ninety-five. Louisa had supported the suffrage movement (still not successful) and the women's club movement, but she was not quite sure where it would all end: "The woman of a generation ago was of necessity too much isolated. It was necessary that she should make her way out into the world to become the companion and not the servant of men. Now that she is out I see some danger of getting too far out. The home should be a woman's first duty and her greatest pleasure."[19] If there was disapproval of Moore's divorce and remarriage, nothing survives beyond this most gentle reproach. As for Sarah, who was now living in southern California most of the time, the record suggests that she kept her own counsel on the subject of divorce after "Waters of Eden" and lent her daughter what emotional support she could.[20]

The new bride opened the Mary Carr Moore School of Music in the fall of 1917; the building at 1334 Page Street doubled as the Duclos residence. Its faculty consisted of Mary Carr Moore (voice, harmony, orchestration), John Haraden Pratt (pipe organ, counterpoint, musical form), Naomi Weaver Gannon (piano), Ruth Collyer (piano, primary and intermediate), Arthur Argiewicz (violin), and Stanislas Bem (cello). On the fourth Saturday of each month there were practice recitals, which were open to the public. On the first and third Saturdays Moore and Gannon gave lectures on opera that were open to the students, and to the public for fifty cents; on Mondays from four to five Moore lectured on music history, open to visitors for twenty-five cents. Both Marian and Wesley made modest debuts at one of the practice recitals.[21] Illness, unspecified, is given as the reason Moore gave up the conservatory after a year.

Around 1922 the couple moved across the Golden Gate to a cottage in Corte Madera near Overmarsh, where the Pratts had spent their last years. Marian had recovered well from her burns and blossomed into a teenage beauty, as her mother had once been. She reports that her mother was very happy in those days, and that mother and daughter had many happy times together during Marian's high school years. Moore seemed particularly pleased to be living quietly on the hill at Chapman Park (part of Corte Madera), where she could compose freely. She took her new domesticity seriously, giving up her teaching and even learning at long last how to cook. She taught her new household skills to Marian, who would have nothing to do with music. The club performances and musicales continued, occasionally including selections from *Narcissa*. One musicale at the Duclos home honored the visiting Mrs. H. H. A. Beach, the best-known American woman composer of Moore's generation.[22]

The marriage to Arthur and very likely a share of her grand-parents' estate gave her some financial security and liberated her from her heavy teaching responsibilities. She took the opportunity to experiment with new harmonic techniques and compositional devices. Her experiments, many of them songs, are suited to the confines of her renewed domesticity. They appear to have been written to sing in private, at home, with Arthur at the piano. "Your Hand on Mine, at Eventide" is dedicated to her husband, and its melody is based on his initials, *A*rthur *De Ce*lles *d*it *Du*clos. This initial motive is played twice in the introduction over a series of descending chords that include eleven of the twelve possible chromatic notes.

For Christmas 1923, for Arthur, she wrote a modest piano piece, "Rêvons," an experiment with an impressionist texture. Some hint of her uncertain view of herself as a composer in those years is indicated by her choice of "Rêvons" to orchestrate and submit, along with "A Chinese Legend," to Alfred Hertz, then conductor of the San Francisco Symphony.[23] The correspondence between Moore and Hertz survives.

My Dear Mr. Hertz:
    I am leaving, for you—these two scores—"Rêvons"—and "A Chinese Legend." The latter has not all the stands completed but I could make the balance of them in two or three days, if you should consider it. . . .
    I expect I could do better work—if I were able to devote more time—but the music *must* come second to the family.
    However, the "future is long" and I like to work.
    Thanking you for your great kindness in consenting to look them over, I am most gratefully yours—
                                                    Mary Carr Moore
    (Mrs. A. D. Duclos)

Hertz did not respond at once, so Moore prompted him.

                                                    Feb. 2nd, '25
My dear Mr. Hertz:
    I have been wondering if you have found either of my small sketches for orchestra—"A Chinese Legend"—or "Rêvons"—available?

Page from "Your Hand on Mine, at Eventide," op. 81, no. 7. (Reprinted, by permission, from the composer's 1919 manuscript score, Mary Carr Moore Archive, Music Library, UCLA.)

After Mr. Eichheim's charming and authentic "Oriental Sketches"—I imagine my Chinese number might not find welcome. But perhaps the shorter number might be "tucked in" on some program. It is quite unnecessary to tell you how much I would appreciate having it done. If there is any possibility, I would be glad to know—and will bring over the parts.

Most sincerely yours—

Mary Carr Moore

Hertz's reply, when it finally came, was negative.

February 5, 1925

My dear Mrs. Moore:
I am very sorry to say that I will not be able to find a place for your sketches in this season's program.
There are manyfold reasons for this which I will be glad to talk over occasionally when I will have the pleasure of meeting you personally.

Very sincerely yours,
Alfred Hertz[24]

Moore's tentativeness came both from the knowledge that she "could do better work," and from her awareness of the systematically uncooperative treatment of American composers by European-born conductors working in the United States.[25] The correspondence with Hertz took place in 1925, some six months after Marian had married and left home. Byron had long been on his own, and Wesley must also have been away, preparing for medical school. Her immediate family responsibilities had shrunk only to her home with Arthur. "Music *must* come second to the family" looks like a smokescreen, sent up to hide the ambivalence that had cost her so much over the years. She still earnestly wanted the conventional life of a middle-class American woman of her time and place, and she was doing her best to live it. She was also a creative artist of considerable gifts. Her experience with Claude had demonstrated the incompatibility, for her, of her chosen life-style and her professional calling. But she was not yet able to accept that lesson. She needed to satisfy herself that she was capable of a successful marriage. Hence Arthur, and her renewed attempt to trivialize her talent.

In spite of all this, Moore produced, in addition to *Saul*, two important longer works in this her second San Francisco period, as well as securing a revival of *Narcissa*. *The Flaming Arrow*, a one-act opera, was completed by March, 1920. The libretto, the second and last from

Sarah Pratt Carr actually set by Moore, carries a story line entirely different from that of *Narcissa:* Hopi and Zuni pray and dance to competing gods for rain, resulting in the union of a young Hopi chief with his childhood friend, the daughter of a Zuni chief. At first there were three characters, but a few years later she added two more and renamed it *The Shaft of Ku'pish-ta-ya.*

The Flaming Arrow was received even more enthusiastically than *Saul* had been.

To hear a rendition of this musical gem, which was directed by the composer, is forever to refute the theory that woman possesses no creative genius. Mary Carr Moore (Mrs. Arthur Duclos) is one of the really talented women of the West.[26]

Mrs. Duclos has written not only in appropriate terms of descriptiveness, but with musicianship throughout. The tribal idiom is presented without being oppressive, and cries, prayers and festal occasions are clothed in true melodiousness.[27]

On hearing Mary Carr Moore's "The Flaming Arrow" last Thursday evening, many capable musicians were faced with the fact that a "resident composer" may be far bigger than the classification implies. . . .
Mrs. Moore has applied the five-tone scale as a basis, but she has mellowed [it] with an Anglo-Saxon touch that makes for a certain American wholesomeness pertinent to and consistent with the subject. There is a continuity of beautiful melody throughout, which is dominated by spontaneity and never trite; moreover, the truest dignity is maintained. . . .
That the occasion was a "jinks" may have alienated many minds from the possibility of serious features, but "The Flaming Arrow" made serious impression on its first hearing.[28]

The Flaming Arrow represented a high tide of critical acclaim for Moore. It also had more productions than any other of her operas. There were two, with different casts, for San Francisco clubs in 1922; productions in Yakima, Washington, in 1926, 1927, and 1934; and at least seven more between 1926 and 1934 in the Los Angeles area. The catalog bears the notation, "Many subsequent performances." Moore conducted most of these productions herself.

Beyond These Hills, completed in 1923–24, uses a different harmonic language than either *Saul* or *The Flaming Arrow.* It is something of a curiosity in its attempt to fuse elements of her concurrent sentimental song style and harmonic experiments with her more "serious" usages as found in *Saul* and *The Flaming Arrow*. A suggestion of Mahler, whose work had recently been introduced in San Francisco, is found in the instrumental interlude at the midpoint of the piece.[29] Her work is a cycle of solo and part-songs, calling for a quartet of mixed solo voices with piano. As with *Saul*, the text was of personal interest to Moore, as this letter to Sarah indicates:

There are XX different stanzas or rather poems, of varying length, from six lines to 27 (odd alignment) each with a different thought along the same line: that is, the impossibility of reaching a "goal," which removes itself to greater heights as we approach; the lack of, often, the "listeners," sometimes the loss of the one "listener," "my soul." But never mind, "for we must sing, or else we die," . . . "and God will hear!"

Isn't it a lovely thought? I have used all but four, feeling there was too much of the discouragement and sadness, and wishing to get quicker to the Optimism.[30]

Gilbert Moyle had asked her to set his poetry to music after hearing *Saul*.[31] *Beyond These Hills* had its premiere on radio station KPO in San Francisco, at a time when network radio had not yet developed. George Paterson, who had read *Saul* frequently, read the poems first. Flora Howell Bruner, the soprano who took one of the parts, was also the station program director who had arranged for the performance. Moore herself played the piano. This, too, was well received, although there were not, apparently, as many performances. "The music is modern in feeling, but despite occasional complicated harmonies, is melodious enough to hold the interest of all music-lovers who have safely passed the jazz-stage. . . . A sombre instrumental prelude ushers in the impressive quartet at the opening [and] the work proceeds through the whole gamut of the emotions.[32] The straightforward optimism of *Beyond These Hills*, along with its unashamed eclecticism, makes it an attractive and challenging ensemble work for solo voices.

Moore needed all the optimism she could muster to achieve a San Francisco revival of *Narcissa* and to survive the public controversy, the personal obstacles, and the financial problems that came with it. She had programmed selections from the opera for Bay Area audiences perhaps ten times since her move to San Francisco in 1915, but it was not until she was living in Corte Madera in 1924 that she began purposefully enlisting local support for a production. The approaching Diamond Jubilee for San Francisco, an improved personal financial situation, and increasing confidence that she had accumulated a strong following through the successes of *Saul, The Flaming Arrow,* and *Beyond These Hills* all probably helped persuade her that the time was ripe.

In October, 1924, as plans were forming to present at least two performances of the opera the following May, Moore offered a program of excerpts at the Paul Elder Gallery. A promotional leaflet outlining the purpose of the "Narcissa Project" followed within weeks. An advisory board listed on the back of the leaflet included the music critics for the major San Francisco journals and newspapers, directors of the San Francisco Conservatory, presidents of many of the city's music clubs and music teachers' associations, and members of the board of supervisors (the city's governing body). It was chaired by Moore's old friend and publisher from Lemoore days, Charles W. Barrett, by now a San Francisco resident.

In spite of the impressive roster of supporters, the "Narcissa Project" did not approach its goal. The production was planned for May, then postponed until fall, and the number of performances increased from one to nine. Multiple casts of local singers would take the leading roles, a change from the previously announced plan to bring in guest artists: "the change to resident artists as principals was brought about by general request because of the large number of fine voices at hand."[33] About the same time, the Casiglia Opera Company spoke of adding *Narcissa* to its repertory in January, 1926, but this, like the loan fund, turned out to be only talk.[34]

Women's clubs, always important to Moore's career, were involved in the planning. The San Francisco Women's Press Club, which had earlier made her an honorary member, offered to sponsor *Narcissa* for 50 percent of the gross proceeds. Its support lasted only about three months, ending in a squabble that is puzzling because it is so out of character for Moore. One Martial Davoust, business manager of the club and publisher of a San Francisco weekly, claimed that he had acted as Moore's agent in arranging for the production and that she had taken his plans and negotiated behind his back with the Wilkes Theatre. Two days before the opening, he sued Moore and the Wilkes Theatre for fifteen hundred dollars.[35] The suit did not interfere with the September opening and seems to have carried only nuisance value, but it succeeded in alienating Moore from the Press Club's membership.

Two widely known singers joined the local cast after all. Alice

Gentle, a favorite with San Francisco audiences, sang the role of Narcissa at the opening. Anna Ruzena Sprotte came from Los Angeles to sing four performances as Waskema. Mme. Sprotte, the original Waskema in Seattle, had recently been responsible for a concert of excerpts from the opera before the Los Angeles Opera and Fine Arts Club. The chorus numbered forty-seven; the orchestra, an understaffed twenty-five.[36]

The production was an artistic success but, as operas regularly are, a financial failure. "The performance went off with an aplomb that must have indeed been gratifying to the woman who has spent so many tireless nights in the training of her people. Certainly it was gratifying to the audience assembled, who showed their appreciation to the composer and to the singers by curtain call after curtain call and a stage literally banked with flowers."[37] As before, there was disagreement about its dramatic impact stemming from the critics' failure to grasp all of the opera's underlying themes. "They attempted so much that the story is like a series of historical events, linked in continuity it is true, but without the high dramatic tension that is now an essential in the stories of modern operas. That is why it would seem as if 'Narcissa' is destined to be featured in historical pageants, instead of becoming a part of popular operatic repertoire."[38] "Faithful as her book was to history, picturesque as it was with its colonial and Indian types, it was lacking in the qualities that persistently held attention. If it were to be compared with a really thrilling book like the one used by Bizet in 'Carmen,' its lack of dramatic incident and of variety would be made plain."[39] Some critics found it convincing even so. "The story is well told and the drama portrayal markedly vivid."[40]

The dramatic structure of the work is firm and coherent, and each act has its minor and major climaxes. . . .
    The lyric beauty of the score . . . impresses one at the first hearing. Excluding some recitative passages which convey essential parts of the narrative, the flow of melody is abundant, and its character follows faithfully the emotional vicissitudes of the drama. . . . Most important of all in opera, the music has atmosphere and emotional sincerity. There is nothing of empty theatricality about it, but each situation is set forth with a directness of mood that convinces the mind and appeals to the sympathies.[41]

After the gala opening night, the theater was never more than half-full. It was Moore who ended up paying the bills.[42]

In addition to the challenges of preparing several casts, generating enough funds to open the production, and dealing with Davoust's nuisance suit and the misunderstanding with the Women's Press Club, Moore had to face two major personal problems that summer and fall. She responded with a display of character that is hard to believe in a woman who half her life earlier had escaped from the conflicting demands of family life and career aspirations through a flurry of fainting spells and headaches. First there was her unhappy experience as a new grandparent, retold here, sentimentally, in a radio interview many years later.

I think the most difficult moment of my life was when, in San Francisco, in 1925, during the orchestral rehearsal of *Narcissa* (before its week's run during the Diamond Jubilee) the management concealed from me that my dear daughter had gone to the hospital for her first baby. Of course, I took a taxi to the hospital immediately after, but found her very ill, and the baby not likely to live. The dear little baby died the next day, and during that long week of nine performances . . . I could only be with my daughter between times, instead of being the help, and comfort, which it was my right, and duty, to be.[43]

Second, Moore's second marriage was in trouble. Arthur had begun to drink heavily and was rapidly going downhill. There is only speculation to explain his sudden deterioration; a veil of silence covers what must have been a series of unpleasant scenes. Had he found it too difficult to fill the role of "Mr. Mary Carr Moore" after so many performances and successes? Had her need for dependence gradually evaporated in the last few years of their marriage? Later, Moore was very reticent about Arthur, even concealing her second marriage entirely from her Los Angeles students. Whatever financial assets had accumulated in the marriage disappeared in his illness and in the *Narcissa* production.[44]

For a time, Moore moved in with Marian and her husband Clyde. Then she spent several months with Adelyn and Orley See across the Bay in Oakland. While there, she wrote a string quartet for Orley, a violinist and a founder of the Oakland Symphony. By fall she was ready to move to Los Angeles, where Olga Steeb had invited her to teach.

CHAPTER 12

The First Los Angeles School

Moore left her second marriage with profound regret over the manner of its ending, but without the debilitating, bitter despair of her divorce from Claude. Only a few years before, she had thought it proper to write to Alfred Hertz that her family "must come first." Now, with children grown and marriages dissolved, family responsibilities were clearly secondary. She was more free than she had ever been. Free to struggle to earn her own living, it is true; but free also from the conflicts that had beset her so sorely over the years. Their scars would always be with her, influencing personal and artistic decisions alike. For the first season she would live with her mother again out of convenience, but now her situation was different. In Los Angeles she experienced a burst of creative energy that lasted a full decade before it began to wane in the face of relentless economic pressure and renewed family obligations. Her catalog shows a corresponding shift of interest, from songs to operas and longer instrumental works, an indication of heightened aspirations and a singleness of purpose that no longer wavered. The exuberance with which she exploited her new opportunities as composer, teacher, performer, organizer, and promoter belies the notion that she had ever been delicate or suffered from invalidism. From Moore's career in Los Angeles one begins to understand just how heavily the claims of duty and family had weighed on her over the years.

The city where Moore now lived was still relatively provincial. It acknowledged, perhaps mistakenly, the cultural hegemony of longer-established San Francisco although it had already outdistanced both Seattle and San Francisco in population. Its growth showed no sign of stopping in the 1920s.[1] The various cities of the basin, such as Glendale, Hollywood, and Pasadena, were still separated from one another by orange groves and connected by a system of electrified interurban rail lines. Souvenir photos from the period tend to show modest frame farmhouses set amid groves of orange trees that extend for miles to snowcapped mountains in the background, a reminder of the great physical beauty as well as the semirural quality of the Los Angeles basin as it was when Moore made her move south. Spanish-speaking missionaries had arrived in 1781, but the city in the 1920s was as Anglo-dominated as Seattle and counted far fewer members of minority groups than did San Francisco.

A promotional pamphlet published in 1927 outlines the city's art music activities. Its writers saw their city as partaking of a spirit of freedom and cultural enterprise unique to the West, particularly Los Angeles.

There is a spirit abroad throughout the entire western slope of the United States which is peculiarly favorable to a strong native art development. People, who come west from eastern cities and farms, undergo a subtle spiritual change of which they are scarcely conscious until they return to their old place of residence. Then they discover a lack of freedom, a sense of being cramped, a feeling that there are things impossible of attainment, and find themselves in a state of mind from which the Pacific slope with its vast distances, cheerful living conditions, natural, rather than traditional, mode of life, had entirely released them.[2]

The pamphlet enumerates the city's achievements in painting, sculpture, and architecture before getting around to music. Its list of musical institutions begins with the Philharmonic, founded in 1919 after several earlier attempts and subsidized for some years by William Andrews Clark; the Hollywood Bowl, a summer home for the Philharmonic, founded in 1922; Adolph Tandler's Little Symphony, a remnant of one of the Philharmonic's forerunners; the Women's Symphony, the oldest of its kind in the United States, dating back to 1893; and community orchestras in Hollywood, Long Beach, and Glendale. These groups were supplemented by various school, church, theater, and even industrial orchestras.[3] Opera had first come to Los Angeles almost a half-century after its arrival in San Francisco, with the first U.S. production of Puccini's *La Bohème* in 1897, only a year after its European premiere. By 1927 the touring San Carlo Opera Company visited for three weeks every year, and the San Francisco Opera for one, but the ever-hopeful Los Angeles Grand Opera Association and similar organizations were still empty-handed, as they have since for the most part remained.[4] Regular concert series of visiting virtuosi such as the Auditorium Artists Series and the Behymer Philharmonic Course received much public attention.[5] There were chamber music ensembles such as the Zoellner Quartet, which toured widely in the early 1920s.[6] Not far away were the Ojai Valley Chamber Music Festival, which numbered Elizabeth Sprague Coolidge among its principal sponsors, and the Alice Coleman Batchelder chamber music series in Pasadena.[7] Network radio was in its infancy, but local radio stations were already offering live performances.

The popularity of music study is clear from the number of music conservatories. USC already had a large music school which offered both bachelor's and master's degrees. UCLA was still the Southern Branch of the University of California and had its campus in downtown Los Angeles.[8] In music it offered only a normal program for prospective music teachers through its Teachers College. The Hollywood Conservatory, Olga Steeb Piano School, Zoellner Conservatory, Institute of Musical Art, Los Angeles Music School Settlement, Los Angeles Conservatory, South West College, and fourteen more private schools offered various kinds of music programs to students of all ages, as did any number of individual teachers working from their own studios. There were nine schools of drama and dancing as well.

Music clubs included oratorio and choral groups, opera study clubs, church choirs, industrial choruses, and school choruses. Some of these sponsored their own series of public concerts. The Wa Wan Club claimed to be the largest of the music clubs and was probably one of the oldest, at nineteen, in 1926. The Woman's Lyric Club acknowledged 130 members in a 1927 program. The Euterpe Opera Reading Club, which concentrated on low-budget readings of operas using local singers and piano accompaniments, was able to expand its membership from 23 at its inception in 1925 to 956 after only five years of activity. The Gamut Club for men and the Dominant Club for women were working together as early as 1911 to develop civic support and hospitality for L. E. Behymer's visiting artists.[9] No fewer than 178 women's clubs are included in the list of cultural resources mentioned in the 1927 pamphlet. Moore belonged to as many as 19 clubs, not all of them music groups or women's clubs, by 1930.[10]

The Los Angeles Department of Playground and Recreation under Glenn M. Tindall started a music program in 1927, probably at the behest of the various music clubs and of such prominent resident composers and musicians as Charles Wakefield Cadman. Its playground programs included choruses and glee clubs as well as harmonica bands, ukelele orchestras, and "toy symphonies" for children "too young to understand or participate in a more advanced type of musical activity." The enormous popularity of do-it-yourself musicmaking among Los Angelinos is reflected in statistics from this program, however exaggerated they may be: in February, 1927, 762 participants; twenty-eight months later, 613,463 participants—an eight hundredfold increase.[11]

A sizeable group of composers, including many women, was already active in Los Angeles by 1926. Many wrote, or had written, for local churches, schools, and clubs; some were established as teachers, patrons, or performers. A few had wider reputations. A 1919 photo of the founders of the California Federation of Music Clubs includes composer–club performer–lecturer Charles Wakefield Cadman; composer-singer-publisher Carrie Jacobs Bond; patron-clubwoman-composers Abbie Norton Jamison, Bessie Bartlett Frankel, Gertrude Ross, and Grace W. Mabee; professor-composer George Stewart McManus; and singer-clubwoman Anna Ruzena Sprotte, all of them among the southern California delegation to the state federation's first convention.[12] Fourteen years later, a *Who's Who in Music and Dance in Southern California,* designed to celebrate the area's achievements and opportunities, lists many composers, a third of them women, among its 520 names. By far the most prominent among them was Charles Wakefield Cadman. Gertrude Ross and Fannie Dillon were also frequently recognized.[13] By 1930, Moore was attracting considerable local coverage herself.

The Civic Bureau's brochure and the content of scrapbooks assembled in the years between the two world wars at the Los Angeles Public Library reflect the same pecking order for the art music establishment. The Philharmonic, with its foreign-born conductors, all-male membership, and mostly international visiting soloists, stood as the central feature. Adulatory star-status was conferred on such traveling virtuosi as Heifitz, Piatigorsky, and Rubinstein, who commanded large fees in return for their trouble in traveling so far to perform. Plenty of space, with fewer pictures and smaller headlines, was reserved in the press for the far less well rewarded activities of local performers, organizations, music patrons, and teachers, as well as the "resident" composers. The populous music clubs, with many women among their members, provided the basic audience for all these activities, as well as many students for the classes of the music teachers, Moore among them. One periodical, the *Pacific Coast Musician*, was well established as the reporter of local music activities. In line with this pecking order, its front pages described the activities of the famous. But most of its space was devoted to reporting the doings of local musicians.[14]

It is often stated that Los Angeles was without art music of any interest at all until the émigrés from Nazism began arriving in the mid-1930s.[15] In fact, there was a very active and vital indigenous musical life in Los Angeles, which claimed, based on the 1910 census, more musicians per unit population than any other U.S. city.[16] Its resident composers were producing a surprising amount of music, whose quality is probably far higher than might be supposed from its present obscurity. They wrote for an unusually large audience.[17] They were more conservative in their musical tastes and their politics than were the better-known American "ultra-modernists" of the period between the two world wars. This pre-émigré culture, which always included a number of foreign-born musicians and was always cognizant of its resident composers, turned out to be sufficiently stimulating to Moore that she never moved away from Los Angeles. It stimulated and attracted other composers as well. Taken collectively, this indigenous musical activity is sufficiently important to be called the "First Los Angeles School." It deserves more attention than it has attracted so far.[18]

Several composers of the First Los Angeles School, some already mentioned, reappear at later points in Moore's story. Two other members of the local music establishment had wide influence in the community and were closely associated with Moore at this time. Each contributed to this now-unknown Los Angeles musical culture in a distinctive way. One is the music patron Mrs. Cecil Frankel, who used her own name, Bessie Bartlett Frankel, as a composer. The other is the pianist and teacher Olga Steeb.

Mrs. Frankel was one of Moore's composition students. A prominent and imaginative supporter of the Philharmonic, as well as of chamber music in Los Angeles, she made several attempts to extend her considerable influence as a music patron in Moore's direction. She was close to Moore in age and in aesthetic and social outlook. Frankel was the daughter of A. G. Bartlett, who had begun as a cornetist and who had prospered as president of the Bartlett Music Company from the time he organized it in the late 1870s. He helped start the School of Music at USC and, as a member of the school board, got the first music program started in the local school system. His wife was a "fine contralto singer and pianist but not a professional."[19] Frankel, too, was a contralto, trained in the local Cumnock School of Expression as well as in the public schools. As a talented daughter of prosperous parents, she was sent to study voice in New York, Naples, and London. She performed as both singer and "dramatic narrator" in various cities before she married Cecil Frankel in 1911. A collection of her own music shows that she was interested in new works for narrator and various instruments ("melodramas") in the period 1900–1910.

After her marriage Frankel continued her father's tradition of strong support for civic music activities but abandoned her performing career. She organized the California Federation of Music Clubs in 1918 and served as its president, and as a vice-president of the national federation. In 1924 she became president of the Women's Committee of the Philharmonic, a position she used over the years to develop and administer a series of concerts in the public schools by the orchestra. In her father's memory, and presumably because she shared her husband's enthusiasm for chamber music, Frankel founded the Bartlett-Frankel Quartet, the first resident professional string quartet in southern California. The quartet, whose members were always the principal string players in the Philharmonic, was established in 1929 and lasted for seven years.[20] She guaranteed the members' salaries and arranged a Candlelight Concert series for them, as well as concerts at local schools and colleges. Her personal subsidies ran from a high of $8,050 in 1929 down to $3,293 in 1934 to simply a guarantee that their salaries would total $3,600 in their final season, 1935. Thereafter, as president of the Los Angeles Chamber Music Society, she underwrote the appearance of touring quartets in various concert series and colleges in the area. The Frankels built an elegant home, "La Casa Sogno," on the beach at Santa Monica, where they entertained frequently. They were regularly "at home" to a large circle of musicians and friends, including Moore, following the Philharmonic's Thursday evening concerts. (As late as 1940, Moore had a long conversation with Stravinsky at one of Frankel's parties.)

The level of Frankel's support for Moore never compared with her generous subsidies of the Bartlett-Frankel Quartet or the Philharmonic. But it was in line with the going custom that foreign-born artists, such as the quartet's members, commanded far higher fees than did native artists, male or female. Mrs. Frankel clearly felt some constraints about what it was appropriate to do for a woman who had to support herself but was as much a lady as she.

Frankel profited personally from Moore's encouragement of her creative abilities, subordinated since her marriage to her role as music patron. By 1930 Frankel was going to Moore regularly for composition lessons; these continued for some years. She found time to take part, alongside many younger composers, in the Mary Carr Moore Manuscript Club. One result of her study was a program of her own compositions, given at the Ebell Club in 1933. Another result was a small but steady additional source of income for Moore in those lean years; Frankel apparently paid Moore's going rate, five dollars an hour, in cash, for each lesson.[21]

Most important to Moore was Frankel's longstanding support for her as a composer. Moore was regularly invited to the Frankels' home; it was very likely through Frankel that she was able to arrange for the conductor Pierre Monteux to hear a two-piano performance of her new piano concerto in January, 1935, at the Steeb School. Frankel also arranged for conductor Artur Rodzinski to hear some excerpts from *David Rizzio*. Frankel furnished the hall for the California Composers Society festivals in which Moore was heavily involved, in 1937 and 1938. And Frankel did her best to get her friend a teaching position at UCLA, writing to its president in 1932:

At present I am writing to draw to your attention Mrs. Mary Carr Moore whom I consider one of the best teachers of harmony, theory and composition one can find anywhere. I have seen her work in classes and have had the privilege of studying with her myself for several years. . . . In her own creative work she has received recognition which few women and even men received. . . .

I understand that Mr. Gantvoort is retiring this year and I bespeak your attention in her behalf. Mrs. Moore is well qualified as she has a background for the work which few have, and has kept abreast of the times in her work which is very necessary, as you know.[22]

Her effort was unsuccessful in this case. But, with Mrs. Irish, she saw to it that Moore's *Narcissa* finally received a Los Angeles production in 1945.[23]

Sarah Pratt Carr and
Col. Byron Oscar Carr,
San Francisco, 1872

Mary Louise Carr at age
five, 1878

Mary Louise Carr at age
twenty, as composer of *The
Oracle*, San Francisco, 1894

Mary Carr Moore at age twenty-eight, at the
time of the second production of *The Oracle*,
Seattle, 1902

Moore's children Marian
Hall Moore and Byron Carr
Moore, Seattle, ca. 1909

John Wesley Moore, Moore's
youngest child, Seattle,
ca. 1909

Moore at age thirty-eight, as composer of *Narcissa*, Seattle, 1912

Illustrated review of *Narcissa*. (Reprinted, by permission, from *Musical America*, May 11, 1912.)

HISTORICAL OPERA OF THE NORTHWEST

Mary Carr Moore's "Narcissa" Has Successful Première in Seattle.

SEATTLE, April 27.—The anxiously awaited *première* of Mary Carr Moore's opera, "Narcissa," was given last Monday evening under the most favorable conditions. A brilliant audience tendered the composer, who occupied the conductor's desk, applause that amounted to a triumph.

"Narcissa," a historical music drama, the libretto written by Sarah Pratt Carr, the composer's mother, deals with one of the most notable events in the history of the Northwest. The familiar story of Marcus Whitman, his bravery, patriotism and untimely end, forms the basis for the opera. The story follows history almost exactly, departing from it only in the compressing of events, to fit the necessities of stage portrayal.

Act I opens during the Sabbath morning service in the church of Marcus Whitman's native town in Rushville, N. Y. The service is interrupted by the arrival of *Whitman*, accompanied by two Indians, after a long absence in the Northwest. He has come to plead for help to carry the gospel to the Indians in the far West. *Narcissa Prentiss*, his betrothed, begs to return with him. *Marcus*, though fearing for her safety, finally yields, his own desire supplementing hers. They are united and sped on their westward journey amid the prayers of the congregation.

The scene of Act II is laid at old Fort Vancouver, stronghold of the Hudson Bay Company, where *Dr. John McLaughlin*, the factor, commands in baronial splendor. He is expected home from his historic trip to England, and arrives laden with gifts. Amid the general rejoicing the signal gun is heard and all is commotion and terror. The song of the approaching missionaries reassures the fort people, and the missionaries are welcomed in a royal manner. *Yellow Serpent*, chief of the allied tribes, invites *Marcus* to install his mission at Waillaptu, promising him support and the friendship of the tribes.

In Act III, five years later, the *Whitmans* are installed at Waillaptu. An orphaned child of a settler lies in the cradle of *Narcissa's* dead baby. The coming of immigrants, destroying pastures and driving away game, has made the Indians sullen and resentful. *Delaware Tom*, a renegade half-breed Delaware Indian, incites them to open rebellion. This is furthered by the Indian prophetess, *Waakema*, who, in the moments of greatest rejoicing, has predicted woe for the Indian. The *Whitmans* are upheld by *Yellow Serpent*, *Elijah*, his son, and *Sisbadee*, his betrothed. An outbreak is impending, but *Narcissa*, with her beautiful voice, weaves a spell about the superstitious Indians, subduing them for a time. *Dr. McLaughlin* comes to the Mission and new promises are made. The arrival of immigrants rekindles the anger of the Indians, and *Elijah*, to avert open rupture, plans an expedition to California, promising *Sisbadee* to return in the Spring and make her his bride. *Marcus* discovers that Congress proposes to let England have the Northwest and starts upon his terrible and historic mid-Winter overland journey to save the Northwest to the United States.

The fourth act opens in the Spring of the following year. *Marcus* has returned successful. Indian maidens in gala attire go out to meet the returning braves. *Waakema*, the Indian prophetess, foretells impending catastrophe. *Narcissa* is apprehensive. The Indian discontent grows and soon the death wail is heard. The braves return, many horses riderless. *Yellow Serpent*, stricken with grief, relates the cowardly murder by a white man of *Elijah* while on his knees at prayer at Sutter's Fort. The Indians are enraged. While *Yellow Serpent* goes to his lodge *Delaware Tom* incites the friendly Indians, the Cayuses, to massacre the immigrants. In the absence of the latter the stranger tribes, hostiles, guided by *Tom*, batter down the Mission House door and kill the inmates, including *Marcus* and *Narcissa*, their "golden singing bird." *Dr. McLaughlin* arrives, but too late. *Yellow Serpent* is summoned and swears vengeance on all who participated in the massacre. On the hillside *Sisbadee* mourns her lover; and through all wails the death chant of the Indian women.

From the fact that the librettist was limited to historical events, for her material and adhered so closely to those events, the opera is peculiar in lacking the very element that forms the chief feature of nearly every opera. Save for the devotion of *Narcissa* to *Marcus* and the simple romance of *Sisbadee* and *Elijah*, the love element, as usually associated with operatic form, plays no part. Considered, however, in the light of a narration, well told, ably constructed and given an adequate musical setting, the opera fills its purpose entirely. Regarding the music itself there can scarcely be a difference of opinion. The score is rich in free, spontaneous melody given excellent treatment and at no time forced. In using the original Indian melodies Mrs. Moore has shown wonderful skill. In the manner used they give a most vivid coloring and obtain a fine effect. While Mrs. Moore generally shows skill in her handling of the orchestra the score is at times extremely thin and at other times overbalanced. This, however, is a remediable matter and should in no way stand in the light of other merits. *Narcissa's* solo in the first act, "Royal Soul," as well as the duet that follows it; *Elijah's* solo in the third act, "When the Camas Blooms"; *Narcissa's* lullaby; the handling of the chorus and the effectiveness of the ensemble show the composer to possess creative ability of the highest order.

The title rôle of "Narcissa" was happily suited to Mme. Luella Chilson Ohrman's voice, which is a high soprano of exceptional range and power. Her conception of the rôle was admirable in every respect and her portrayal of a noble and loyal woman most successful. Charles Hargreaves, who sang the part of *Marcus Whitman*, proved himself to possess a tenor voice very pure in quality and gave the part a most praiseworthy interpretation. He was at his best, probably, in his scene in the third act when he takes leave of *Narcissa* to depart on his journey. The credit for another splendid characterization goes to Charles Darbyshire, who sang the part of *Delaware Tom*. His rich baritone, which he used with splendid control, well suited the part. Equally successful was Mme. Hess-Sprotte, as *Waakema*, giving the rôle the dramatic interpretation it calls for. Henry Hanlin sang the part of *Dr. McLaughlin* in a convincing manner. Frederick Graham, as *Yellow Serpent*, Alfred A. Owen, as *Elijah*, and Romayn Jensen, as *Sisbadee*, demand mention for able work. The several minor parts were taken by Walter F. Paul, James Valentine, Hicks Taylor, Carl W. Harrell, John H. Armin, Davies Lacear, Lottie Meeker Kessler, Ethel Hostrower, E. Louise Norton and Florence Moore.

The cast for all four performances was unchanged with the exception of the Wednesday matinee, when the parts of *Narcissa* and *Marcus Whitman* were sung by Maude Conley Hopper and Neal Begley. Both singers achieved success and received much well-merited applause. Edward Temple, of New York, who, in a short period had prepared the staging of the performance, deserves a word of special praise. The excellent staging, elaborate costumes and completeness in detail contributed no small part in making the opera, as a whole, a success.

CARL PAIGLEY.

Charles Hargreaves as "Marcus Whitman"; Oval Inset: Luella Chilson Ohrman as "Narcissa" and Scene from Act 1, Interior of Church in Rushville, N. Y.

Moore as Mrs. Arthur De Celles dit Duclos, Corte Madera, California, 1922. On the piano is "Dweller in My Dreams," published in 1922.

The California Society of Composers, Los Angeles, 1937 or 1938. Standing, from left: Frank Colby (editor of the *Pacific Coast Musician*), Zhar Bickford, Baruch Klein, Hugo Davise, Homer Grunn, Ernest Douglas. Seated, from left: Scott Bradley, Mabel Woodworth, Vernon Leftwich, Moore, Frances Marion Ralston, Arthur Carr (no relation). On floor: Ethel Dofflemyer. (Courtesy of Celeste Grunn Feliciano.)

Moore, Los Angeles,
ca. 1945

Four generations:
Moore with daughter,
granddaughter-in-law,
and great-grandchildren,
Los Angeles, 1952

Frankel and Moore saw eye to eye in their aesthetic judgments about the experimental, "ultra-modern" music of the day. When, as a member and sponsor of the local Pro Musica chapter, Frankel was invited in 1928 to meet Béla Bartók, she sent a letter resigning from Pro Musica "at once."[24] Moore's comment on hearing Bartók play his own music: "ouch." Frankel and Moore remained friends and allies in the various artistic and personal disputes of the day. Her patronage and friendship extended to others, including Moore's colleague Olga Steeb.

Olga Steeb and Moore had met at least a decade before Moore left San Francisco in 1926 to join the faculty of the Olga Steeb Piano School in Los Angeles, but there is no record of their having culti-vated their acquaintance in the interim. Steeb's school was the largest and most consistently successful of the many private conservatories that operated in Los Angeles during the 1920s and 1930s. In training pianists and studio piano teachers, it certainly dominated. Olga, her two sisters, and her father all had a hand in running the school, which by 1934 had its own building, complete with studios, an auditorium, and living quarters for some of the teachers, at 3839 Wilshire Boule-vard.[25] The school was built around Olga's remarkable talent as a pianist and took its character from her personal qualities.

Born June 14, 1892, in Los Angeles, Olga was the oldest child of musical German-born parents, from whom she received her earliest musical training. When she quickly outstripped them, they sent her to Thilo Becker, a Leipzig-trained Australian, with whom she remained for eleven or twelve years.[26] Though Becker did not push her into public performances, there were notices in the Los Angeles papers that hinted at her unusual talent from the time she was ten. Touring pianists Teresa Carreño and Ignace Paderewski heard her play dur-ing her student days and gave her encouragement. In 1909 she went with her mother to Berlin, where she created a sensation. The English-language *Continental Times* wrote: "Besides being the pos-sessor of an enormous repertoire Miss Steeb is the possessor of a perfect technic, is not surpassed by any pianist in variety of tone color, has the rarely heard 'grand tone' and is wonderfully poetic in her readings, has absolutely no mannerisms and in gradation of power in crescendos and diminuendos no living artist surpasses if anyone equals her."[27] On her home side of the Atlantic, a front-page "Berlin Letter" in *Musical America* reported: "Miss Steeb is the biggest living genius that I know of. I look for her to be recognized within five years

as the greatest piano genius since Liszt."[28] German-language newspapers were equally complimentary, calling her "ein Unikum, ein
klavierspielendes Wunder."[29] Her repertoire was widely reported as
including all the compositions of J. S. Bach and four hundred other
works in addition. Two years after these initial stories, she played nine
concertos in the space of two weeks with the Berlin Philharmonic.[30]
There were other successes in Germany, but by 1915 she was at home
in southern California, as head of the piano department at the University of Redlands. In 1919 she moved to USC; four years later she
opened her own school. She traveled to Europe at least once more
after World War I. She performed frequently up and down the West
Coast for the rest of her life.

Los Angeles gained much from Steeb's residence there. There was
her series, Historic Recitals, surveying the piano repertoire with unprecedented breadth. There were frequent chamber recitals with
members of the Philharmonic. And there were her very numerous
appearances—more than a dozen—as soloist with the Los Angeles
Philharmonic, each time with a different concerto. She regularly drew
reviews such as this one, which covers her playing of a piano concerto
by Respighi:

It was given a superb performance by Olga Steeb, whose playing and musicianship on this occasion easily measured up to world's standards. The mental
grasp, poise, phantasy, rhythmic and tonal balance plus technical equipment
disclosed by Miss Steeb in this performance, justly gives her a place among the
few really great women pianists of the day. Hers was an achievement the
memory of which, we can store away together with those of Carreño, Esipoff,
Samaroff, and the young Lubka Kolessa.[31]

Olga Steeb's extraordinary memory and technical command were
also recognized by her peers. On one occasion, the Russian pianist
Mischa Levitsky was to play a piano concerto by Saint-Saëns with the
Philharmonic. He canceled his appearance at 6:30 P.M., the evening
of his performance. Olga was called at seven. She went on after intermission, playing the concerto as if she had rehearsed it thoroughly
and planned to perform it long in advance of the event. For this feat,
both the orchestra musicians and the audience gave her a standing
ovation; the *Times* reported it on the front page.

At her school, Steeb required all the diploma students to attend
regular master classes that she herself gave, to take Norma Steeb's

music history course, and to take Moore's classes in theory and composition. She wanted students who could think about the music they were learning to play. By the time Moore joined the faculty, there were as many as two dozen teachers at the school and its branches, most of them piano teachers in the preparatory (high school) division, in addition to the apprentice teachers in the normal course for studio piano teachers. There were always plenty of students, working in a pleasant and, for a conservatory, relaxed atmosphere, as long as Olga was there.

The school was sufficiently prosperous that, in the early thirties, the Steebs were able to build a large, rustic house on Mulholland Drive, at the top of the Hollywood Hills. The high-ceilinged living room, easily able to accommodate two grand pianos and an assemblage of students, colleagues, and guests, has a view of the San Fernando Valley; the front of the house faces Los Angeles and the Pacific Ocean. Even now, the house is often above the smog. Steeb and her husband, Charles Hubach, shared the house with her parents; her sister Norma; Creighton Pasmore, one of her teachers and a duo-piano partner of Victor Trerice; Ted Gilbert, who taught violin at the school; and occasionally others.[32] Charles Wakefield Cadman loved to visit, talking with Olga in his gentle way or playing chess with Olga's father.[33] Privileged students were often allowed to spend the night curled up in the generous window seats.[34] Moore probably visited the spacious house from time to time, though her life-style was quite different from Steeb's. Once, she visited the Steebs' summer cabin at Lake Elsinore for a weekend. She used the time to write "Murmur of Pines," a piano piece she dedicated to Olga, rather than join the outdoor activities. Nor did Moore join the party of Steeb family and teachers that annually took horses and pack mules for several weeks of fishing and hiking in the Sierra Nevada, in what are now Kings Canyon and Sequoia national parks.

Steeb gave Moore strong and continuing support as a teacher, paying her well for her two days a week at the school through the difficult years of the Great Depression. She respected her as well for her continuing productivity as a composer in the face of the heavy teaching obligations Moore took on outside the Steeb School. On the other hand, Steeb, who was two decades younger than Moore, had more eclectic tastes in music, cherishing a strong interest in the current "ultra-moderns." She attended the first classes given by Schoenberg in Los Angeles, for example. Steeb guaranteed one thousand dollars toward a planned production of *Narcissa* for Los Angeles in 1930, but it has been reported that Moore's later piano concerto, which was dedicated to Steeb, was something of an embarrassment to her.[35]

Late in December, 1941, a few weeks after the United States entered World War II, Steeb died of cancer. Within a year, the school, which had been organized entirely around Olga's talent and strength of character, had virtually disappeared.[36] It had provided Moore with a modest but steady and relatively undemanding source of income for more than fifteen years, as well as with a continuing flow of talented students.

Steeb's present obscurity is as remarkable as Moore's own, though the reasons for it are slightly different. The most obvious is her failure to make recordings. All that survives of her art as a concert pianist is two or three short Duo-Art mechanical piano rolls. Beyond that, there was the bad luck of poor timing. World War I broke out as she launched her career, and she was forced to return home, where a wave of anti-German feeling associated with the war worked against her.[37] Later, it seemed to her associates that her tightly knit family circle had suffocated her. They saw her parents, with whom she had continued to live, as rigid and domineering. "She should have stayed in Berlin," remarked one of them. She "didn't do enough for herself," said another. "What a cruel fate she has had—all along," Moore wrote after Steeb's funeral.[38]

Members of the First Los Angeles School labored in isolation from the rest of the country, although like Americans in other places, they worked in the shadow of the domination of American art music by Europeans. They rarely received top billing, even in their own region. But opportunities were greater, especially for the women among them, in this rapidly growing young city than in more established centers like San Francisco or New York. They worked in an imperfect, obscure Eden, but a fertile one nonetheless. From 1926 on, Moore was one of them.

CHAPTER 13

Teaching

Moore quickly set out to supplement her income from the Steeb School. She promoted herself in several ways, but the focus of her activity was teaching. She no longer offered voice lessons, as she had in earlier years. Instead, she took on the challenging job of finding private students in music theory and composition. Over the years, her salesmanship was successful enough that she was reported to be "the most active harmony teacher in the city, judging by the number of affiliations she has and the number of pupil's compositions which are heard here and there."[1] The modern character of her teaching approach is emphasized, along with its suitability for teachers, in a Steeb School summer announcement.

Course of 20 Lessons in Harmony and Composition with special attention given to modern Form and Analysis of the whole tone scale and its chord progressions, designed for teachers and advanced students who desire to review theoretical principles, or to acquire a broader understanding of their application.

Also, a Course of 20 Lessons in Sight Reading and Ear Training with assistance in conducting of school orchestras and chorals, and care of the unchanged voice, designed for public school teachers.

These classes will be under the personal supervision of Mary Carr Moore, Head of the Theory of Music Department.[2]

Her datebooks show a steady stream of private students over the years.[3] There was a series of smaller conservatory affiliations in the early years. Right away she added a class at the Philip Tronitz Studio. In 1927 she added another class at the Hollywood Conservatory and, some time later, one at the Los Angeles Music School Settlement. She also served on the board of the settlement, a charitable enterprise: "Imagine getting individual training from a famous composer like

Mary Carr Moore for 12-1/2 cents or 25 cents or 50 cents a lesson, and you get the idea of the school."[4]

The following year, she joined the faculty of the newly formed Musart Conservatory, an ambitious attempt to combine the teaching of music, dance, and theater.[5] This association was short-lived, but another one made the same year turned out to be her most reward-ing, longest, most time-consuming, and most aggravating teaching association. It eventually displaced all her conservatory connections except for the Steeb School. California Christian College (which changed its name to Chapman College in 1934), founded in the early 1920s, was located on Vermont Avenue opposite the Southern Branch of the University of California. Its students took some of their humanities classes on the public campus in the college's first years. Perhaps CCC's decision to augment its music program sharply re-sulted from the scarcity of music classes across the street as well as the realization that the college would have to offer a complete program of its own as soon as the Southern Branch moved to its new campus in Westwood. Moore was one of three people invited to join its faculty in 1928. She was to teach two classes weekly in harmony and counter-point at first; more classes would be added as the department grew. The position "would pay about a hundred dollars a month, if not immediately—soon." The possibility of a school-sponsored produc-tion of *Narcissa* was discussed as an added inducement.[6]

She considered the offer for some days. The college had nothing of the prestige that the Steeb School could offer to a musician. Probably she was already piecing together sufficient income for her needs. Still, the idea of being a professor in a four-year college and developing its curriculum had its attractions, including greater stability than her array of conservatory affiliations. Moore held no degree or diploma, a deficiency that limited her options for a teaching position and made this offer more appealing. The Christian orientation of the college, whose graduates tended to become ministers in the Disciples of Christ denomination as well as teachers and social workers, was not difficult for her to accept, though she herself had not gone to church regularly since her childhood. She would still have nothing to do with her mother's continuing theological explorations and discussions, but she retained her generalized, optimistic attitude toward organized religion.

March 1, 1931. No creed for me. All creeds. I find myself so in sympathy with thought behind any sincere expression of religion, that I do not want to "bound my horizon;" many tongues, many racial experiences dictate the manner of expressing the spiritual emanations of my brothers of this world. I cannot side with one against the other, but find it in my heart to agree with all, since all are striving to bear witness for a Great, Eternal Truth, that enfolds us all.[7]

Her enthusiasm for teaching and her idealism won the day; she accepted.

There were never more than a few hundred students at the California Christian College.[8] But Moore's teaching load grew quickly, and enrollments rose steadily as well. She began with eleven students in two classes, Advanced Harmony and Music History and Appreciation. Soon the history and appreciation class was required of all students in the college. Two years after she started, she was meeting six courses twice a week. In the mornings she taught Advanced Harmony, Counterpoint, and Canon and Fugue; after lunch Harmony I, Orchestration, and History and Appreciation. This schedule continued as long as she taught at Chapman, but after 1936 she added a class on opera and regularly supervised one or two students taking graduate work in composition.

Student recollections describe Moore's very successful teaching style, as well as her manner.

She was a tireless worker, and she carefully corrected and edited our work. She said that she did it late at night in bed. . . . She illustrated problems in vocal music, either with the scores produced by students in the class or with moderately well known works in English such as *Martha* or songs by her friends (in particular, Richard Hageman). One thing she did have was a singer's sense of music, and she was forever after us to make things effective for singers. She was far more interested in our vocal music than in anything else.[9]

She used to tell me, well doggone it, you shouldn't let your talents go to waste, you should develop them. . . . As I remember her, she always had time for you. You know, always willing to chat. On the other hand, she was always busy, she always had a million things to do. Always tearing around, and yet as I say she had plenty of time if you wanted to chat with her, that's fine. But after that, zoom. Very energetic. . . . [10]

She taught every individual in the class as if they were the only one. . . . She would never put them down. . . . She would extract something good from the weakest example. Would get the person enthused, show them how to fix it, but she never did the fixing herself. One girl I thought was really hopeless. By the third week she had written a song to the text, "O Captain, My Captain." She built people up, extracted better work from them than they thought they could do. I was greatly inspired by her.[11]

She had white hair, but so much animation. She was ageless. She had that childlike quality that great people have. There was a sensitivity, a trusting quality about her. Love radiated from her. She never said a harsh thing to a student. A real lady. . . . [12]

They commented frequently about her energy and enthusiasm, which never seemed to flag. They thought her perhaps a decade younger than her actual age. Small in stature, buxom, with tiny feet, she wore thick glasses and held the music close to her eyes to read it; her bad vision made it necessary for students to play the musical examples that required sight-reading. Unlike many musicians, she did not indulge in fits of temperament. Though she rarely asserted herself outside the classroom, she was generally regarded as one of Chapman's outstanding faculty members. "There was a joke that she *was* the whole department there."[13]

The faculty lunched together in an atmosphere of collegiality that is remembered nostalgically. For convenience, four right-handed faculty women sat opposite four left-handed faculty men. Paul Delp, a philosopher, sat opposite Moore. With the small student body and the small faculty, the conversation often revolved around the progress of their students, as well as the faculty's own triumphs and sorrows. "She was a delightful, white-haired, fussy, genteel lady, terribly interested in music, not pushy, quiet and sweet, quite talented in her own way."[14] The college administration expressed its appreciation of her quality, and perhaps attempted to compensate for her low pay, by awarding her an honorary doctor of music degree in 1936. The following year, the student body dedicated its 1937 yearbook, the *CEER*, to "our revered mentor, Dr. Mary Carr Moore, [to whom] we, her musical charges, hopefully and appreciatively . . . wish to express our gratitude, [for the part] that Dr. Moore has had in our college."

There were many concerts at Chapman, given by both faculty and students. One program of compositions by Moore's students took place under especially trying circumstances and shows how seriously all concerned took their work.

At 5:52 P.M. had very serious shock of earthquake, followed shortly by another, then two faint shocks. We were all frightened. I was in the kitchen and ran out into the yard. Bits of slate from adjoining apartment roof fell on my head, ground shook under my feet. At seven, having dressed between shocks, went to California Christian College for rehearsal. Found the main building unsafe, concert transferred to small hall. Audience kept arriving so it seemed best to go on with concert. *Four* heavy shocks during program. All very courageous. After the two songs by Mary Halsey (sacred) we all repeated the Lord's Prayer together. So many colored people in audience owing to Mr. Wilkins' numbers—all very brave. . . . [15]

Moore's teaching of harmony and counterpoint was thorough. One student still has his English translation of Richter's *Harmony*, the same text Uncle John Haraden Pratt had followed with Moore forty years earlier, from her class. Another, who took the same class at the Steeb School, has a notebook filled with carefully corrected counterpoint exercises and statements of the appropriate rules. Moore's papers include a chart with examples of Romantic and post-Romantic cadences taken from Schumann, Wagner, Debussy, and Puccini. To these are added one by Mascagni and several by Americans, including Horatio Parker, her friends Fannie Dillon and Henry Hadley, and some from her own music. There is also a neatly constructed wall chart with ranges and transpositions of the orchestral instruments, handy for her orchestration students. She wrote detailed letters of instruction to one student concerning counterpoint exercises, carefully copying out an assigned fugue subject and explaining her corrections. Her students responded well. The men went out to careers in radio, films, and arranging; both men and women became teachers. Some were later able to give music scholarships so that Moore might recruit more students for Chapman.

Moore kept a record of her enrollments and teaching assignments, as well as her salary, between 1928 and 1942. In that time, her total student enrollment rose fivefold, from 22 to 113. The pay record, given here in edited form, does not reflect the growth of her responsibilities or her success as a teacher. Instead, it reflects the impact of the Great Depression as well as the financial hardship suffered by Chapman when its erstwhile neighbor UCLA moved to the new Westwood campus.

1928–29	$ 766.73	two courses each semester: "less than $100 per month, but as the classes were so small, I felt that the fee was ample"
1929–30	1,033.27	probably four courses taught each semester
1930–31	900.00	six courses per semester from here on
1931–32	775.00	method of calculating salary changed to percentage basis second semester
1932–33	279.50	percentage lowered; some payments late
1933–34	238.00	
1934–35	556.75	
1935–36	766.37	
1936–37	857.29	one or two master's candidates from here on
1937–38	1,200.57	
1938–39	1,017.90	
1939–40	1,085.35	opera course added here
1940–41	1,075.62	
1941–42	1,200.00	some payments late[16]

For the sake of comparison, Moore recorded that in 1933–34 the Steebs had paid her half again as much, for much less teaching. The following year, when she was paid $766.37, the far more famous Arnold Schoenberg was receiving $4,500 for his similar position on the new UCLA campus.[17] It is clear that Moore would have been much better off financially if Mrs. Frankel had succeeded in getting her a position there, even had she been paid considerably less than Schoenberg. Low salaries were, apparently, the lot of all who taught at Chapman in those years; another faculty member reports "room, board, and $25 a month" as his reward.[18] When the college closed its doors in 1942 and moved its few remaining students to Whittier College for the duration, leaving those faculty who were not in the military unemployed, Moore wrote to Chapman's president:

It has been a difficulty for all members of the Faculty; probably less so for me, as I always had some outside resources, in the way of private pupils. You will know by now, that I could never have subsisted, (with my family and responsibilities) upon the very meagre salary that Chapman paid. I always thought I should be put in a higher bracket, since the Music Bachelor, and the Music Master degrees, could not have been offered, except for my own technical equipment, without employing several more teachers, in that department; but realizing how beset with debts, Chapman College has been, and the noble work it is doing, I put aside my personal needs, and made up the budget by working harder, on the outside.[19]

There was talk in the leanest year (1934) that Moore would become dean of a new integrated conservatory of the arts such as Musart had aspired to be and as the Cornish School had become in Seattle. Exploratory discussions included a diverse group from the community, according to a few entries in the datebooks.[20] Times had grown too difficult, however, and the necessary financial backing to pursue the project was not available.

Two students have offered comparisons of Moore's teaching with that of her better-paid counterpart at UCLA, Arnold Schoenberg. Jack Blake, who later worked for the San Diego public schools, worked with Schoenberg when he first taught at USC and followed him to UCLA, where Blake became increasingly dissatisfied as the classes grew larger and more impersonal. Though unapproachable, Schoenberg was a fine teacher who paced the floor nervously, chain-smoking as he developed his point, then wrote furiously at the blackboard, coming out with four or eight bars of four-part, vertically written score. When Blake transferred to Chapman, he found Moore's teaching "a whole different thing." Classes were small, with far superior, intimate student-teacher relationships. Blake, who wanted to be a musically trained sound technician in the film industry, found Moore inspiring and learned a lot from her.[21]

Constance Shirley is a splendid pianist who pursued a career as a teacher and composer. She became the first student to receive the master of music degree in composition under Moore, and then she went off to UCLA to work with Schoenberg. She speaks, as do the other students, of Moore's remarkable ability to encourage virtually everyone who came under her influence to compose and to coax a lot of work from them.[22] Schoenberg, by contrast, encouraged her to be more self-critical. As she put it: "He taught me taste." Moore had a knack for finding and nurturing talent and a willingness to work with inexperienced students. On at least one occasion, she swallowed her pride to act in a student's interest. When it was time for Albert Harris, a student who worked with her privately in the early 1940s, to go on to another teacher, she sent him to Eugene Zador. Zador had recently been critical of her own score for *Legende Provençale,* but she rightly judged that he could help Harris in several ways.[23]

As soon as she started teaching at CCC, Moore sought to give her composition students and other young composers more exposure. As often as she could, she took students to play their own compositions for various club audiences.[24] That wasn't enough, so she organized her own club for student composers. First she simply called it a "composer's club" and invited her students from the Steeb School, from CCC, and from her own studio to bring their music to play for one another. Other teachers sent their students as well. Before long, the students responded to her encouragement by organizing themselves into what they insisted on calling the Mary Carr Moore Manuscript Club. There were only nine members at first. Stiles Johnson, a CCC student, was the first president.[25] "It was a very, very productive time, not like today," one longtime member commented.[26] After ten years of activity, the club could claim to have had 170 members active at various times over that period.[27] There were occasional programs to which the public was invited. The third of these, in 1931, featured music by twelve composers, including Mrs. Frankel and Richard Drake Saunders, later a critic for the *Hollywood Citizen-News.*

The club settled into a routine of monthly meetings during the school year, usually at Moore's home. In 1932, annual competitions started, and public concerts consisted of works that had won or placed in any of a variety of categories. J. Charles McNeil, who later earned a master's degree under Moore, donated a trophy; Charles Wakefield Cadman followed suit; and soon there were a variety of such prizes for winning songs, piano pieces, instrumental works, and chamber music. By 1935 two concerts were required in order to give all the winners a hearing. Active members were expected to present at least two new compositions a year at club meetings. There was also a group of assisting members, who sang and played the composers' works.

After the first ten years, the club began to print yearbooks; the first of these listed thirty-two publishers who had issued music by fifty-four members, including Moore. A brochure assembled after fifteen years lists the same composers plus several others.[28] While Moore's old friend Wesley Webster was responsible for most of the publications, other compositions were taken by G. Schirmer, Carl Fischer, and even more distant publishers such as Novello and Boosey and Hawkes.[29] Presently the Manuscript Club became a provider of programs by young composers for other clubs; the pay was slim, "often enough for gas money and a hairdo."[30]

The club was very popular with its members. Often forty or fifty members and guests would crowd into Moore's living room for meetings. Elaborate festivities marked its tenth, fifteenth, twentieth, and even fiftieth anniversaries, since the club continued after Moore's death.[31] From the start, it had good press.

A woman, a musician with a big heart, has started a movement here to help young musicians. Her efforts have been tireless and her methods have been so unique and original that people from other cities have come to learn how in so short a time she has been able to do so much and develop such genuine talent. She prophesies that Los Angeles in a very short time will be the musical center of the world.[32]

Its aspirations were broad: "It has been the wish of the founder, Mary Carr Moore, that, in this club, the one tie would be that of the Universal Language, MUSIC, and that all division of religion, politics, or custom might be forgotten, and all work together in the cause of HARMONY."[33]

In the 1930s, as Moore's reputation as a teacher continued to grow, critics of her music tended to think of her as old-fashioned, a change from their perception during her earliest years in Los Angeles. Some, who knew her only by hearsay or at a distance, thought of her as unpleasantly aristocratic. Yet in her teaching, as in her activities in behalf of younger composers who came under her influence even remotely, there is a strong egalitarian sense. Wherever she happened to be, good students blossomed, whether they had sought her out or whether she found them and caused them to flower through the force of her personality. Many years earlier, Sarah had written in "Waters of Eden" that "genius is all about you, waiting to be discovered." As a teacher, Moore practiced what her mother had preached.

CHAPTER 14

Promoting and Surviving

Moore formed her many teaching connections in Los Angeles mainly to support herself. At the same time, she was eager to develop audiences and promote performances of her music. She put together brochures offering her services: "American Composer / Interpretative Recitals / Opera Lectures / Story-Songs for Children / Program Plans Available for Clubs and Schools"; inside them were excerpts from published criticism of *Narcissa* and a list of her works published by Witmark, G. Schirmer, and Wesley Webster. Like many other musicians of the First Los Angeles School, she placed advertisements in the *Pacific Coast Musician* to announce her availability. That journal's *Year Book* for 1926–27 carried an advertisement offering club and recital programs from her works, informal lecture-recitals, or formal recitals with soprano, baritone, or violinist. Many other musicians also advertised. Frances Marion Ralston took a full page advertisement as "Composer-Pianist"; Elinor Remick Warren likewise announced her availability for both solo programs and as accompanist. Olga Steeb was, through the Hans Thorston Concert Management, available "for your course or club." Other advertisers with whom Moore was associated at various times included Mme. Anna Ruzena Sprotte, the first "Waskema" from the Seattle production of *Narcissa,* who initiated Moore's early association with the Los Angeles Opera and Fine Arts Club; Ann Thompson McDowell, a pianist who specialized in programs of American music and who often accompanied visiting artists; Marguerite LeGrand, who would teach with Moore at California Christian College; Homer Grunn, an Indianist composer who also taught at CCC; and Charles E. Pemberton of the USC faculty. The *Pacific Coast Musician* was read in San Francisco too, and H. B. Pasmore, her old teacher, listed some of his recent compositions.[1]

The target of all those ads was the many thriving music clubs, which provided the main performance opportunity for most of the resident composers. Moore, who was very gregarious and an inveterate joiner, felt at home with these clubs, as she always had. She attended meetings of social, fraternal, and patriotic clubs as time permitted, in addition to the music clubs to which she belonged. Since she also reviewed concerts for *Music and Musicians* and attended concerts for her own pleasure, her evenings were busy.

In her first Los Angeles season, club performances of Moore's works were relatively rare, but even so her music drew attention. The Los Angeles Opera and Fine Arts Club, which had given an abridged reading of *Narcissa* two years earlier, gave her an entire program in October, 1926. She filled it with songs, some choral pieces, and a reading of *Beyond These Hills*. A review was favorable:

it is complimentary to the composer that this one-composer program so escaped the tiresomeness that usually attends concerts of that character. . . . We were led to expect [a lot from the composer of *Narcissa*.] Nor was there any disappointment. . . .

Beyond These Hills leaned strongly to the so-called "modern" expression, not forgetting the whole-tone scale, effectively used. . . . No more interesting number was on the program than the beautiful quartet cycle and it was admirably sung by Miss Hill, Mme. Sprotte, William Pilcher, and Gage Christopher.[2]

That first June, she offered a program at her rented home on West 8th Street of pieces by her composition students; a similar program at the Steeb School by her students there; a program of her own compositions for the Poetry and Music Club; and two groups of her own songs, sung by herself, for the Music Teachers Association convention, which drew this comment: "These compositions attested to those present that in Mrs. Moore, Los Angeles possesses an exceptional creative talent. Her music shows dramatic force, invention and beauty, as well as musical craftsmanship of a high order."[3]

She found an appreciative and expanding audience, as this list of performances over the next year or two indicates.

- *The Flaming Arrow* was produced for the Los Angeles Opera and Fine Arts Club. It had won the club's Sanger-Moore-House prize in a competition the previous year.[4] Moore supervised the production: "Richly harmonized and sung by a well-chosen cast, the compact work was charming in its presentation, the musical as well as the dramatic interest being well sustained throughout the performance, and the emotional content of the opera allowing for many effective and colorful contrasts in the interpretation."[5]

- *Saul,* in the quintet version and without a narrator, was the featured work on a program at the Hollywood Conservatory: "Of particular interest was the rendition of three movements from the orchestral suite, 'Saul.' . . . Heard to advantage in two groups of songs, of which the 'Dweller in My Dreams,' 'Sunset,' 'Mysterious Power,' and 'Shadows' were particularly significant. . . . Versatility was the keynote."[6]

- Moore joined Alice Barnett and Mrs. M. Hennion Robinson as the featured composers at the Wa Wan Club's annual "resident composers' day." Béla Bartók, visiting Los Angeles as a Pro Musica artist, was listed among the guests.

- A program of "native music" at the California State Federation of Music Clubs convention in San Diego included music by ten men and eight women, Moore among them.[7]

- An hour of Moore's music was broadcast live over KEJK in March, 1928, the first of many such broadcasts.

- Moore brought out her "Mother Goose Revue" for the Woman's Twentieth Century Club at Eagle Rock, where her cousin, the retired singer Ellen Beach Yaw, lived.

- The Pacific Southwest Exposition in Long Beach declared July 28, 1928, "Mary Carr Moore Day."

- A program of her music, given at the University of the West, included the violin sonata, *Saul,* several songs, and the aria, "Sola, abbandonata," from her newest opera, *David Rizzio.* A few days earlier, Moore herself had played a piano reduction of the "Intermezzo" from the same opera for a private gathering for the first time.

- For the Cadman Creative Club at the Ambassador Hotel, a Moore program included the quintet version of *Saul;* two pieces for violin and piano ("Reverie" and "Message to One Absent"); "Romanza" for cello and piano; some songs; and a scene for soprano and tenor from the new opera.

- Moore played her own "Barcarolle" and "Rêvons" for piano and then accompanied Emilie Hardy in a group of her songs for "writers' night" at the MacDowell Club of Allied Arts.

- *Narcissa* got a reading (almost certainly abridged) at the Euterpe Opera Reading Club in June, 1929. The following year a program of excerpts was given at the Cadman Creative Club, and Mrs. Tefft, the program chairman, announced plans for a staged production at the California Christian College for the next fall.[8]
- Moore traveled to Oakland for a presentation of *David Rizzio* to the Opera Lecture Club in April, 1929. The San Francisco Pen Women planned a literary tour of Europe for 1930, timed to end in Venice for the projected production of *David Rizzio* there.[9]
- Mrs. Frankel arranged an informal reading of *Rizzio* at her home; the guests included the conductor Artur Rodzinski, who was reported to be "so favorably impressed that he asked to see the complete orchestral score."[10]
- In a space of five weeks, between October 10 and November 17, 1931, Moore's music was performed at eighteen separate events.[11]

With performances such as these, Moore quickly established herself among the leading composers of the First Los Angeles School, just as she had established herself as a strong teacher and champion of younger composers. The flow of local club performances would continue unabated for twenty years and beyond. Her efforts to secure wider recognition for her music, which went on concurrently, are described in later chapters.

On Mondays and Wednesdays Moore spent the day at Chapman College teaching her six courses, all requiring preparation and generating papers to grade. On Tuesdays and Fridays she went to the Steeb School, usually for a shorter period. Sometimes she followed her day at Chapman with an evening class at the Los Angeles Music School Settlement. At home there were private students. There were singers to coach and rehearsals for her various performances. There were requests for her music, which sometimes demanded hours of copying unpublished parts by hand. There was organizational work in behalf of her own music and that of fellow composers, some her students. There were concerts, club programs, and social events. When she first arrived in Los Angeles, Aunt Mary Magwire Carr, the widow of General Carr, still lived there. Her mother and many of the younger Pratts also lived in southern California, and so there were family gatherings as well.

Her early conditioning as the daughter of an aristocratic family set her apart from others in her musical circles. She is remembered as always neatly coiffed and well though conservatively dressed: "lacy" rather than "chic." She was ever the gracious hostess, and her students and guests were seldom aware of the shaky state of her finances. She had not learned to cook until her second marriage, and now she had left her brief domestic phase. She preferred to teach more hours and arrange for household help when she could. She noted it as a rarity when she cooked dinner herself on New Year's Day, 1940, for a sizeable family group. The following year, she remarked that she hung out a wash for the "first time since Corte Madera days (1922–25)."

For all her independence, she actually did not live alone very much of the time. At first she lived with Sarah. Then for a time she shared a house with Emilie Hardy and her mother. Hardy was the young singer who first tried out the music for Mary, Queen of Scots, from *David Rizzio*.[12] Wesley spent some time with her during his medical training, before he took up practice in Quincy, California. And Marian and her two sons lived with her for some eight years, starting in the fall of 1933. Still, she prized her new independence, imperfect as it was. At least once she expressed impatience with her very heavy workload.

March 21, 1931. It is the "little things" that take so much out of one—to answer piles of *unnecessary* letters, when I want to write to my children; to write my monthly columns for "Music and Musicians" so I may attend concerts I could not otherwise afford; to correct *endless* exercises, when I ache to get at my composing. It seems rather a waste—but who am I to judge? It may be the only way I can "justify my existence."[13]

But she did find time to compose. When? Generally between midnight and 2:00 or 3:00 A.M., to judge from the datebook entries. The old nocturnal habit she had early acquired from her parents and grandparents persisted. Only now she had to get up early to meet her classes in the mornings. In Los Angeles, Moore did not sleep much.

Did she regret her marriages? Each of her former husbands reappeared briefly after her move to Los Angeles. Claude was a member of the family party for Christmas, 1928, when all the children and their parents gathered at Marian's home in San Francisco for the holiday. Neither Claude nor Mary Louise was married just then, and their children attempted to reunite them. Moore's notes about the family gathering are noncommittal and other reports conflict. On Christmas Eve: "Lovely reunion, all of us happy! . . . First reunion of all the family since 1911!" After Christmas dinner, the children took care to leave their parents alone in the evening: "Claude and I had a nice long talk while the children drove up to Twin Peaks to see the enormous Xmas tree."[14] One more dinner gathering of all the family two days later, and they went their separate ways. At the time Moore was bubbling with optimism about her newly completed Italian opera, *David Rizzio,* and contemplating two further opera projects.[15] She anticipated that *Rizzio*'s success would liberate her from her heavy teaching commitments. Many years later Claude told his daughter-in-law about this meeting, saying that Moore "talked of nothing but her music" and that he "couldn't stand it."[16] Another equally late report has it that Claude apologized for the divorce, blaming the breakup on his own lack of sense.[17] Moore simply told her daughter "they had a very nice visit and talked over old times." Marian added, from the perspective of half a century, "It was nice of them to be so gracious about our invitation."[18] Five years later, Moore noted their thirty-fifth anniversary in her datebook with no further comment.

A few years later Arthur turned up, under entirely different circumstances. A business contact in late June, 1931, seems to have been their first meeting in five years. "He looks well," she commented at first.[19] Later, he caused a different reaction.

Friday, July 10, 1931. Arthur Duclos called. . . .[He came] (it transpired later) to look over the piano, hoping I would allow him to borrow money on it! That was an unfortunate thing! To think, after all these years he has not been able to support himself *alone!* Has not helped me at all, after the first few months. He must have forgotten that my Chickering piano was the means of getting this Steinway; and a "lien" on the piano would of course result in my losing this one! Sorry I was not able financially to make him a loan. But I feel he should have asked someone else, rather than come to me under the circumstances! Was rather inconsiderate.

February 27, 1932. Arthur Duclos phoned.

February 28, 1932. Arthur Duclos called, took me down to call on his mother. She was not at home??? I wonder if he knew it? Took me to Mrs. Peery's for tea at 5, left me there.

February 29, 1932. Arthur Duclos telephoned to borrow money! Now, I see. Said he would call, so I phoned Mary and Luther [Hoobyar] to come over. They stayed until 11; I served chocolate, but Arthur outstayed them— remained until 2! Old habits! Nice visit, but I'm afraid it was all for the loan. I gave him $10.00. Idiot! I guess he needs it badly.

April 30, 1932. Found from information from music store, that Arthur had forged my name to a check. Poor boy! I am as sorry as I am shocked!

Arthur never reappeared. Moore later would speak of her first marriage to her students, but they did not know about the second. She would advise a student some years later, "don't love too deeply."[20] At last she accepted the unsuitability of marriage in her own case: "September 7, 1931. I am glad these worries don't affect me as they used to! Guess, not having a husband to be bothered is easier. Men *are* rather queer! Can't depend on them—except a few! Papa!!" Perhaps she finally understood that no other human could come close to the idealized image of B. O. that was her model.

Her relationships with her children could not be put away so conveniently. Byron's difficulties with his first wife led to many arguments and left her convinced at one point that she would have to make a home for Richard, their son. That did not happen, but the breakup of another marriage brought a permanent change in her life. Marian announced in 1933 that before long she and her two young sons would arrive in Los Angeles to live with her. Where family responsibilities were concerned, Moore was very much of the stiff-upper-lip school, but for once a crack in her determined mask of gracious good humor and gentility is briefly visible. She confided to a student that she was not sure how she could live with this new development. But when the student wrote expressing concern, Moore replied, "I didn't mean to convey the idea that we are not happy; Marian has about gotten over her shock and trouble; and after all—it is simply heavenly to have her here. And—if money is scarce, that is a very small matter; and most people are in the same situation. It will surely be better soon; in fact I find it is better now, and am feeling less anxious."[21] In her datebook she wrote: "August 17, 1933. My last night alone. Tomorrow Marian and the dear boys (*darling* Marian) will be here." "August 18, 1933. . . . Darling Marian looks tired. It has been hard on her! Poor little thing; as if I hadn't suffered enough—so my children might be spared! I feel sorry for Clyde too, poor boy. Wish it needn't have happened. It is good to have Marian with me again, hope I can make her happy." To welcome her daughter properly, she invited about three hundred people to tea.

Within a month of Marian's arrival, they moved the now-frail but still very alert Sarah in with them, a necessary step which they all tried to manage as graciously as possible. A last vignette of Sarah is supplied by a student who lived with them one summer:

Her mother was a tiny little lady. Very old school in the way she dressed. Just darling, with high collars, and, just, ruffled, like a little old-fashioned lady. But she used to write at night; she said she'd gotten that habit many years before. Living in the city was too noisy in the daytime. So she would sleep every morning till eleven or so. Before I went to work (I was working at the college), I would take orange juice and something upstairs for her. . . . She'd have a lunch, you know, later on in the evening. She'd be awake every night. If I'd go out on a date or anything and come home I'd always go in and have a long talk with her and she was always awake at two o'clock or so.[22]

Marian, too, loved her late-night talks with her grandmother. Sarah continued to pursue her theological interests. She was working on a writing project about the early conquests of the Sierra Nevada (lost) and making notes on her daughter's early life. She contributed all she could from her Civil War widow's pension to help run the household. She died very suddenly, on Christmas Eve in 1935. "How I wish I could have done more to make her happy," Moore noted the following day.

Sarah had helped her buy her first car, a Chevrolet, in 1931. At age fifty-eight, hopelessly nearsighted, Moore learned to drive. Much later, a student remarked about her driving that "she must have had a guardian angel." Some datebook entries suggest her problems with automobiles.

Dec. 14 and 15, 1931. Driving lessons from Wesley.
Jan. 2, 1932. Lonely. Went out in my car; bumped a lady on Wilshire Blvd. Bumped a lady's car, and she was lovely about it.
Jan. 8, 1932. Mother came over. We both think I am too nervous to drive.
Dec. 26, 1937. Marian and I went to church to hear our boys. It had rained hard and was muddy. I ran off driveway and got the car stuck in the mud! Had to send for a "wrecker" to get out. Cost $3.00 plus 50¢ for church. Expensive luxury!
May 17, 1946. . . . Took too short a turn on Santa Monica [Boulevard], and drove a block on the ties between the tracks!! Luckily, no car either way, until I "escaped" at the next crossing.

In 1933 she drove all the way to Detroit, spent some time with Byron there, and stopped in Chicago for a performance of her music at a Pen Women convention. But she occasionally managed to get hopelessly lost in Los Angeles and sometimes took the wrong roads on her drives to and from Quincy, in northern California, going far out of her way. Students spoke of her driving as "maniacal," or simply called her "the world's worst driver." Still, the car helped her keep her appointments all over town.

If learning to drive was a challenge, the hard times of the Great Depression were a heavy and relentless burden.

Jan. 5, 1932. CCC is obliged to cut all salaries 20%. Pretty hard—and the hours of extra time I've given. Everyone is suffering.
Jan. 6, 1933. Back to Steebs' at 1, to meet Mr. Spaulding. He needed to borrow money. How terrible to have to refuse him, but when I pay the movers, and the rent, I'll be down to nothing. And my dear children helping me at that, and Lucy too! What difficult times I've seen (and others, too, of course, worse off than I) for the past six months.
Oct. 3, 1936. I keep feeling frightened about finances, wonder how we can get through. May be better—Chapman, *large* classes, but little money.
Oct. 5, 1936. Teaching is difficult this year. I can't seem to get over feeling tired. It worries me. I should not keep such long hours, but what else can I do?
May 27, 1937. Federal Music Project Audition, 12 noon. Heard 23 applicants, many of them excellent. I was tired, and distinguished myself by dissolving in tears over some of the necessary decisions! When will I learn to control my emotions? But oh, the poor people, hungry and frightened. One poor man, 57, who sang "When You and I were Young, Maggie," but of course, couldn't be passed. It was the widow of Brahm Vandenberg, with four dependents who, thank God, sang beautifully and earned an A, who caused my tears! How much tragedy and sorrow lies behind all this![23]

Meanwhile, she continued to put in her long hours of teaching. She took on extra jobs, such as helping her eye doctor compose a piano concerto and then orchestrating it for him.[24] Marian did her best to keep her grammar-school-age boys out of Moore's hair and took over much of the responsibility for running the household. She also started a night school program soon after her arrival and presently was able to contribute to the household through a secretarial job. But after 1935, the accumulated pressures of work and finances brought about a steady decline in the amount of creative work Moore could manage. In the late 1930s, Moore's attention quietly shifted from composing new works to arranging, editing, and copying the many unpublished older ones. Her wide round of club activity shifted toward a greater focus on American music. She became involved in the Federal Music

Project and spent more time attending performances of her own orchestral and chamber music, several times appearing as conductor.

Alice Preston Carr, her half-brother Eugene's widow, died late in 1936. Her legacy may have been the only substantial sum Moore ever had at her disposal.[25] When her newly acquired "means" (about sixty-eight hundred dollars) became available early in 1938, she purchased a house large enough for herself, Marian, and the boys, finally bringing to an end her almost annual moves from one rented house to another. In addition, she retired some accumulated debts, though she herself went on working without pause.[26] She had weathered the worst years of the Depression. She still had her independence, and the accumulated fatigue that went with it.

CHAPTER 15

The Los Angeles Operas:
David Rizzio and *Legende Provençale*

In the decade following her second divorce and the move to Los Angeles, Moore composed more fluently than at any other time. The list of major works from this period of maturity is truly impressive:

- 1926: String Quartet in G Minor. Written in July, the month before her move.
- 1927–28: *David Rizzio,* opera in two acts. Vocal score started in September, completed April 2; orchestra score completed the following year.
- 1929: *Legende Provençale,* opera in three acts. Act I completed.
- 1930: *Ka-mi-a-kin,* symphonic poem. Completed in January. String Quartet in F Minor. Completed November–December.
- 1931: *Los Rubios,* three-act opera. Vocal score and orchestra score completed between May 5 and July 29.
- 1932–34: *Flutes of Jade Happiness,* three-act operetta.
- 1933–34: Piano Concerto in F Minor.
- 1935: *Legende Provençale.* Vocal score completed in June and July. (Orchestra score completed in 1938.)
- 1936: Trio in G Minor for violin, viola, and cello. Completed in April.
- 1926–36: Numerous songs, piano pieces, and instrumental pieces; various arrangements of the above compositions.

Her outpouring of creative energy is the more remarkable, given her enormous commitment of time and energy to teaching and promotional activity. She clearly aspired with each of these works to take her rightful place among the serious composers of art music of her time and generation.

Two operas, *David Rizzio* and *Legende Provençale,* are the most significant works from this period. Though they differ from *Narcissa* and from each other in conception, style, and character, they are as remarkable as the earlier opera. Few other composers of the First Los Angeles School attempted full-scale opera more than once or twice, very likely because getting productions was so hazardous, but Moore's commitment to opera was overwhelming. Her experiences in attempting to get a hearing for her operas certainly illustrate the problems faced by all American opera composers, and women in particular, even in the relatively friendly environment of southern California.

David Rizzio is Moore's excursion into the field of Italian opera. Her motivation for undertaking it was a far cry from the idealism that had led to *Narcissa* almost two decades earlier. Italian opera has always been far more popular in the United States than American opera. Since she could no longer underwrite her own productions, as she had for *Narcissa,* but was still determined to write opera, it seemed quite reasonable to try her hand at an Italian opera on a romantic, violent theme. *Rizzio* was intended to be a commercial success, perhaps as a partner to *Cavalleria Rusticana* or *I Pagliacci.*[1] She later put it to a student that *Rizzio* was "out of her idiom, but that she had determined to write a genuine Italian opera."[2] "I've gone astray, in my last opera 'Rizzio' . . . because I am forced, to find recognition abroad, before America will accept my American operas."[3] Other American composers of her generation had been successful abroad; she now hoped for a production in Italy, based on her librettist's connections there. Emanuel Browne, the librettist, claimed an Italian prima donna as his mother and, through her, a connection with the Italian opera composer Mascagni.[4] His libretto is unique in its subject matter, for it treats the short, violent reign of Mary, Queen of Scots, rather than her imprisonment.[5] Mary, beset by the plotting of her violently anti-Catholic Scottish nobles, turns for help to the papal nuncio David Rizzio. The climax of the opera is Rizzio's murder.

As it turned out, composing the music was far easier than getting a production. Things started out well enough. Successful private readings, both in Los Angeles and San Francisco, were noted in the press.[6]

LOS ANGELES REVERSES PRECEDENT
BY SENDING AN OPERA TO ITALY

Mary Carr Moore's "Rizzio" with an Italian libretto by Emanuel Browne is to be produced in Venice next year. A reading of the work last Saturday night provided much interest for a group at the home of Mrs. Cecil Frankel. . . .

The author of the libretto is the son of the renowned dramatic soprano, Celestina Boninsegna. Last summer he took the piano reduction of the score to Italy, and showed it to Pietro Mascagni, who predicted both artistic and popular success for the work.

Mrs. Moore has utilized a resourceful and varied harmonic idiom that consorts with a fluent melodic line. The vocal writing avoids the set tune, at the same time retaining fluency and grace of phrase. The composer's knowledge of the stage, acquired in the writing of several earlier operas, is admirably evidenced in her present score.[7]

Moore was optimistic as 1928 drew to a close: "Dec. 31, 1928. . . . Emanuel wished 'Luck to *Us*' for 1929. Well—I hope we both may have the success that now seems *a wee bit* probable." At least for a time, Browne tried to promote an Italian production. A production was announced for 1930 at the Teatro Malibran in Venice, with specific singers named for the principal roles. Soon the San Francisco Pen Women announced a tour to Old World literary shrines for the summer of 1930, to end in Venice in time for the performance of the new opera. At that point the production had been postponed from January to August. Presently there was another postponement, this time until sometime in 1931.

It was said that the prospective Mary, none other than Mme. Boninsegna herself, had not yet returned to Italy from a prolonged stay in South America. Ellen Beach Yaw, Moore's distant cousin, who was far past her prime as a soprano but who had also sung at the Met, was mentioned as an alternative Mary. In March, 1931, Moore applied for a passport about the time that the instrumental "Intermezzo" from *Rizzio* was first performed on radio.[8] Doubtless the Depression had something to do with the postponements; a scheme for a Los Angeles revival of *Narcissa* had fallen through a few months earlier. Another Mascagni promise is mentioned as late as 1936, but no Italian production ever took place.[9]

It was clear that the Italy bubble had burst when, by early 1932, plans were announced for a Los Angeles premiere for *Rizzio*. Forty music clubs became joint sponsors of an ad hoc professional production. Impresario L. E. Behymer was involved in the organization, the barnlike Shrine Auditorium was booked, and the proceeds were bravely earmarked for charity. But the necessary funds were hard to raise, and it was uncertain whether the curtain would ever go up, even for the single planned performance. Moore suggests that the backers, probably including Behymer, had reneged on their contract, leaving her liable for the deficit: "May 23, 1932. At 11 P.M. the opera was 'dumped on our shoulders' contrary to contract."[10] "May 24, 1932. Pd. Musicians' Union $287.50 (one half) Pd. publicity."

May 25, 1932. 1st orchestral rehearsal, Shrine Auditorium—$287.50. All day raising money! At 4:30 Mr. Ramsey notified me that Mrs. Rubens' check was not good, and I must raise an extra $100!! And in *cash*. Dear Alice [Alice Preston Carr, Moore's sister-in-law] sent me over the $100 in a check. When I reached the Shrine, I was still $100 short. Emanuel had some, but not enough! Raised balance through *friends* in the cast, who gave me their *last* possible dollar, until little by little we reached the quota.

May 26, 1932. World Premiere of *Rizzio*, Shrine Auditorium. [Today at] 7:30 A.M., "Rizzio" trouble again. When Mme. Demetrio [the set designer] came, I found the scenery wouldn't be released, without three signatures. I was obliged to sign. . . . Such difficulties! George McManus lent me $100 also; managed to get the curtain up. A really *lovely* performance. Col. Huntington made a long speech, representing Gov. Rolph. Very kind and complimentary. I was so tired I was afraid I'd faint. Had no dinner, and I guess no lunch. . . . Mr. Behymer and Mr. Spaulding *so* kind. *Rizzio* is full of lovely music; I am glad it was heard. At such a cost?

In addition to paying the bills for the production and rehearsing the singers, Moore had experienced other complications in the six weeks before the production. She traveled to Washington, D.C., to receive the first of her three composition prizes from the National League of American Pen Women.[11] An ulcer in her right eye threatened to impair her sight permanently. Her bank advised her that Arthur Duclos had forged her name to a check; she accepted the loss and did not bring charges against him. She was so shaken by the kidnapping and murder of the Lindbergh baby on March 1 (the body was found May 12, two weeks before the production) that she closeted herself for some hours following the news to sketch out what much later became the tone poem *Kidnap*.[12]

The *Rizzio* cast included Dorothy Francis as Mary, Rosalie Barker Fry as Lady Argyle, William Wheatley as Lord Darnley, Rodolfo Hoyos as Murray, and Luther Hoobyar as David Rizzio. Alberto Conti conducted. One must wonder, even given an excellent and well-prepared cast singing music that lies well for the voice, what the audience actually saw and heard at that one performance. The pickup orchestra had read through a brand new score only once; there was not enough rehearsal time to find all the errors in the parts, let alone develop a sense for the musical flow. The singers had never seen the sets before the performance. There was none of the basic cohesiveness that might have come from a production, even one as little rehearsed, given by an opera company that had worked together on other productions. Still, critical reception was generally friendly.

Los Angeles took a decisive step forward in musical renown, with the impressive presentation of Mary Carr Moore's two-act grand opera, "David Rizzio," at the Shrine Auditorium last night, when the unusual thrill of a genuine operatic premiere was experienced by a large and discriminating audience, which did not begin to applaud freely, until the very beautiful score of the ingenious musician began to take a firm grip on the heart-strings. . . . The opera is solidly musical, with no attempt at ultra-modernism, but with an abundance of motive, richly suggestive in orchestration, and decidedly unlike any other work, so far as memory goes back, so that Mrs. Moore can be doubly accredited with a free muse that does not stoop to borrow. The whole sweep covers every phase, from shadowy softness to the most dramatic intensity, and the opera will undoubtedly be accepted in the great centers of musical appreciation as a work of genius.[13]

The cast of the opera, chosen from local ranks, was, with one or two exceptions, weak dramatically. . . .
When the opera is produced professionally, as it surely will be, we feel confident that it will gain unlimited popularity. This performance is a bold attempt to produce an opera without the sponsorship of an established opera company, and has proven itself a successful idea.
The orchestra selected by Mr. Conti provided a gratifying setting for the chorus and soloists. The second act particularly was impressive from the orchestral standpoint.[14]

One is left with the sense that the critics liked the music, but that they were uncertain whether to blame the lack of dramatic impact on the production or the score itself. Only one critic was negative and condescending in his review. His commentary may reflect an attitude that helped *Rizzio* to its present obscurity.

A world opera premiere has recently been heard in Los Angeles! That sounds big and important. It probably was just that for the composer, Mary Carr Moore, and the principals taking part. . . . When one considers that the entire score was the work of a tiny, unassuming lady, then no matter what may be said or thought, the fact remains that it was quite an achievement. There are not so many women in America who can write an opera—even a feeble one.[15]

Excerpts were performed by the Chicago Women's Symphony under Ebba Sundstrom in July, 1933, for a Pen Women convention, the only known performance of any of *Rizzio*'s music outside California. A Chicago critic reported, "The music is exceptionally attractive, well written, brilliant and melodic. It shows undeniable gift for musical form."[16] Moore was particularly pleased by the response of the Chicago audience, which was not influenced by her "hometown" status: "July 14, 1933. Ebba Sundstrom conducting. Fine musician. . . . Rec'd a wonderful ovation for *Rizzio*. . . . Very happy over reception. Almost *no* acquaintances in audience, yet was recalled again and again."

There were later productions, though never another one with orchestra. When the Opera and Fine Arts Club staged a reading with piano in 1937, Moore had to borrow some hundreds of dollars in order to discharge the five-year-old lien Demetrio had put on the sets in 1932. There were two concert performances of parts of Act I by Federal Music Project orchestras in 1936 and 1938, and numerous performances of the "Intermezzo." "Sola, abbandonata," Mary's aria, was performed many times, and the duet that follows it quite often as well. The Euterpe Opera Reading Club staged revivals in 1940 and 1948, again with piano. The 1948 performance took place at the Biltmore Hotel; Moore noted that all seventeen hundred seats in the house were filled for the morning performance. This production, though technically private, drew another favorable critical notice.

Dr. Moore is an American contemporary who is not afraid to use melody rather than confused harmonic cacophony and the result is that her opera is imbued with an expressiveness and a beauty sorely lacking in many new works of other composers. The opera has dramatic intensity and the story is worked out with a musical logic which many composers might do well to emulate.[17]

A revival of *Rizzio*, in which the opera was staged and two pianos replaced the orchestra, was heard in 1982.[18] Notice of the revival drew at least one recollection of the original 1932 production:

you must remember that this event took place fifty years ago and I was only thirteen years old at that time. . . .
    The part of the action that I recall most was the scene when the courtiers rushed in and murdered Rizzio. This was done very effectively, and the opera

ended in tragedy, with Mary and Rizzio the victims of cruel plotting. I was very sorry for them both. . . .

My overall memory of attending the premiere of *Rizzio* is that the music and the opera were better than the performance. For years I kept hoping that the opera would be revived in Los Angeles with a big production and a really good cast of singers. But this was the era of the Great Depression, and *David Rizzio* never got another chance.[19]

In 1982, once again various constraints on the production made a fair evaluation impossible. The authors were left with the sense that, given reasonable funding and rehearsal time, the opera would be stageworthy for modern audiences. One of Moore's former students who attended the 1982 revival pointed out, "The whole opera has a dramatic impact that somebody someday is going to rediscover."[20] A modern reprint of the vocal score (New York: Da Capo Press, 1981) makes *Rizzio* the only one of Moore's operas easily obtainable.

In the flush of her anticipated success with her Italian opera, Moore looked around for another opera subject. She considered Lola Montez (1818–61), a dancer who lived for a time in California's Mother Lode country, as a possible subject. Edna Buckbee is mentioned as the librettist for this project, but the sketch she produced is far from a libretto.[21] Instead Moore settled on *Macabre,* a play written by a young Los Angeles dancer-writer-composer, Eleanore Flaig. At the time Moore selected *Macabre* (variously named *Drascovie, The Promise, Love and the Sorcerer,* and simply "the French opera" before it was done) Flaig was in her late twenties; she had danced with the Pavley-Oukrainsky Ballet and with the Chicago and San Francisco operas. One of her poems had been selected by *Literary Digest* as a "best poem" of 1928. In 1930, she was called the "Dancer Divine" in the pages of the *American Dancer,* to which she contributed a series of articles on the history of the dance. Through the Depression years she eked out a living for herself and her mother with occasional film assignments and as a dance teacher. The Flaigs, mother and daughter, lived with Moore at one point. Flaig thought highly enough of Moore to write an "Homage to Mary Carr Moore," which includes these lines:

> Sweet Schubert's lyricism sings again
> In you—Puccini's melancholy haunts the score
> Where retrospect gives place to exultation;
> Again your passion verges upon the sublimity
> Of Wagner, the Viking.[22]

The history of Moore's work on this opera is both tantalizing and elusive. All the other large works she ever produced were written over a relatively short period of time, in one or several intense periods of composing. The pattern for this opera, which is surely one of her very finest achievements, if not the finest of all, is rather different. The first act was completed in 1929; she played extracts for her friends as early as 1930.[23] Though she may have worked on the project from time to time thereafter, her main energy went to *Los Rubios* and the piano concerto, along with a string quartet and the operetta *Flutes of Jade Happiness,* which all demanded prior attention for one reason or another. In addition, there were flurries of activity involving planned or actual productions of *Narcissa, David Rizzio,* and *Los Rubios.*

A summer respite to complete the work, such as the MacDowell Colony in New Hampshire offered some of her Los Angeles colleagues, was beyond her financial reach. Finally, in the spring of 1935, Lucy Sherman Robertson, a cousin, came to the rescue, giving Moore the funds to free her summer from teaching.[24] She rented a cabin high in nearby Topanga Canyon, leaving her family obligations behind, and set to work. The respite lasted two months. As fast as she could write, she put the remaining two acts of *Legende Provençale* down in piano-vocal score form. Only on the Fourth of July did she turn aside long enough to write out her own setting of "My Country 'Tis of Thee" in memory of her father's long-ago patriotic orations on Decoration Days in St. Helena. By early August she had finished; she turned without pause to Harry Noyes Pratt's libretto, *Atlantis,* which she envisioned as a pageant with film potential. *Atlantis* was abandoned after a few numbers, but when she returned to her family and her teaching duties in the fall, *Legende* was apparently complete. The full score took three more years. She did not press for a production, however. Perhaps her other commitments made it impossible. Certainly she recognized that the music was too difficult for many of her usual local performers to handle. Then too, she had been criticized in the past for her "weak" orchestration. This time, she did not want a repeat of that old saw. She could wait for a decent production with a proper orchestra.

In 1941 she took the score to Eugene Zador, a film composer who was particularly well known for his skill as an orchestrator.[25] In September of 1942 she spent an afternoon with Stiles Johnson, once her student and by then a Catholic priest, going over the treatment of the plainchant that underlies the final scene. Again, in 1943, she saw

Zador; then she sent the score to the conductor James Sample in New York. At one point, in September, 1941, she had begun to extract the orchestral parts from the full score, a long and tedious job she soon abandoned. In all this time, she had heard only one aria from the opera, "L'étoile du soir" ("The Star of Eve"), sung in public.[26] She may have taken the score to other conductors, although she made no note of it in her datebooks. As late as November, 1947, she took the vocal score and librettos in English and French to Vladimir Rosing, director of the American Opera Company in Los Angeles.[27]

Suddenly, in March 1949, as she moved from the Leeward Avenue house, she could not find the orchestra score. How it disappeared she did not know, though she looked for it diligently before giving it up. The individual parts she had copied also vanished, then or later. She set to work at once to reconstruct the opera, probably from sketches and drafts, or from the earlier piano-vocal score. A new piano-vocal score, with some different indications about orchestration, was completed on January 20, 1950. Twenty-one years from start to finish! By that time, she did not even attempt a new full score, for her hand had grown shaky and the time was past for such a large project.

The play on which *Legende Provençale* is based was written in English. Flaig then translated it into French, providing the text that Moore actually set.[28] Flaig's source is said to have been a legend in very old French. The presence of Agnes Sorel, "Queen of Beauty" and mistress to Charles VII, places the action in the fifteenth century, between 1429 and 1450. The simple faith and patriotism of the young lovers, Amiel and Rozanne, are no match for the sorcerer Drascovie's evil manipulations. Nevertheless, the disaster he causes is made to have a happy ending, for *Legende Provençale* is a celebration of the triumph of romantic love over both religious obstacles and death. The final scene portrays Rozanne's funeral procession on the night of All Souls' Day. As the monks in the chapel sing the requiem, spirits of the dead drift around the courtyard. The restless ghost of Amiel, a suicide, appears on a knoll and calls his dead love three times. The funeral procession emerges into the churchyard. Rozanne, in her shroud, slips from her coffin and joins Amiel. Their love duet rises over the chanting of the monks, which has continued throughout the scene. "Redeeming Love and vanquished Death . . . Beloved of my soul, Echo of my desire" rises over the monks' "Dona eis requiem, miserere nobis."

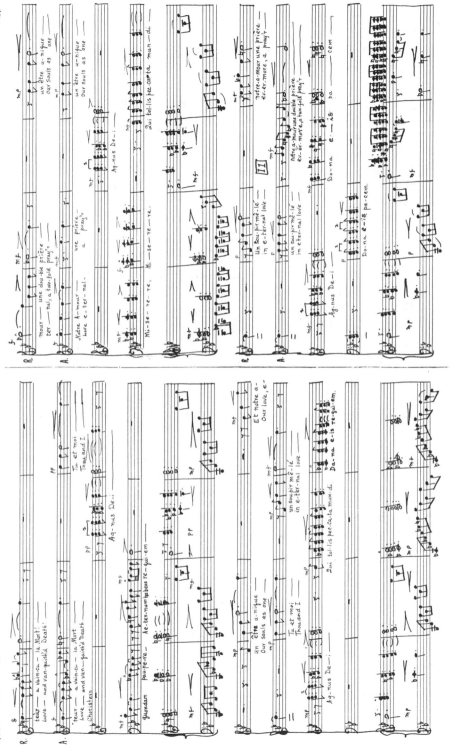

Pages from *Legende Provençale*, Act III, scene 2. (Reprinted, by permission, from the composer's 1950 copy of the piano-vocal score [composed 1935], Mary Carr Moore Archive, Music Library, UCLA.)

Moore set this story with great skill, employing a subtlety and rich variety of expressive means unique in her catalog. Most striking is her treatment of French diction. The rhythmic inflection of the musical setting is surprisingly well adapted to the needs of this language, which she had never before attempted to set and which she probably had never studied except with tutors as a student, no more recently than 1894. On the basis of treatment of text alone, there is not a page of the vocal score that is quite like any of her settings of English or Italian. In addition to this, she put her widened harmonic vocabulary to work with unprecedented resourcefulness, expanding and altering it to fit the needs of the drama.

Legende Provençale, alone among Moore's operas, has never had a production. The only published critical comment deals with a performance of Rozanne's Act III aria, "L'étoile du soir," performed with orchestra in April, 1941. It is unusually enthusiastic: "richly emotional in character, of lovely melodic line and opulent orchestration."[29] "This, incidentally, proved to be the best piece of music I have heard by this talented, lovable, and industrious American composer."[30]

James Sample, the conductor at that 1941 performance, later studied the now-missing full score and wrote Moore a long letter discussing it.[31] His friendly but quite professional commentary is more enlightening than most of the published criticism about Moore's work.

I believe the *Legende* is the best work of yours that I have had the privilege to see. The story, and both librettos (Fr. & Eng.) are excellent. . . . You have caught the atmosphere of the story, and of Provence. . . .

I don't agree with Zador and his ideas AT ALL. He is Slav—has no possibility of understanding the subtleties of the French. . . . He (Zador) speaks of too much French influence; Europeans will never understand the American, who is a *composite* European, with all the possibilities of French, German, Slav, etc.

I have only one adverse criticism of the work as a whole, and that is, I would like to see more dramatic sections, as a contrast to the many delicate sections. I believe, that only you can accomplish this—but it can be done, by lengthening some of the dramatic passages, and making them, possibly, stronger. The lyricism of the opera is delightful; but occasionally I feel the need of contrast. Now I may be wrong; it will be hard to say, before we are able to see and hear the whole production, in a continuous performance. I like the Latin at the end, and under no circumstances would change it. It makes a wonderful atmosphere, which sets itself apart from the realities of this world. . . . The vocal lines of the work are really fine, and I mean that. I don't know of one

American opera that even approaches it in this respect. . . . Yours are genuine and natural, and really inspired.

I would attempt to make no change in the character of the work, as Zador suggests. His orchestration is really superb, and you can pay attention to his comments there, but not in any other way. . . .

There are a few spots I would someday like to discuss with you, as it is difficult to write in detail, but I feel they are comparatively unimportant. I believe you have accomplished what *is* important. That is, atmosphere, style, story, vocal line etc. With a bit more dramatic punch here and there (which must come from the libretto) it is by far the best of the American operas I have come across. I see the influence of many composers, not in style, but in atmosphere. That is not wrong, but right. I believe the public will take the work to its heart when it gets a chance to be heard. *Manon* of Massenet, is so popular, but this is a better work in all ways—and if *Manon* is popular, how can this fail? . . . If the music is good, I am convinced that it can't be lost or buried long.[32]

Because the orchestral score is lost, there is no way of knowing how Moore actually dealt with Zador's suggestions, or Sample's. Quite apart from its content, Moore's transcription of Sample's letter reveals one of the most remarkable circumstances of all about Moore's work as an opera composer: So far as is known, it is the only written criticism of a score she ever received from anyone who was willing, genuinely interested in her work, and professionally competent to offer advice.

The indigenous musical culture in which she worked provided her with encouragement, with a way to earn at least a modest living through her teaching, and with a certain amount of opportunity. But in *Legende Provençale*, Moore transcended its resources. From her background of home dramatics, community theatricals, and personal studies, and virtually without the cosmopolitan intellectual and artistic exposure that the very concept of opera implies, Moore succeeded in writing viable opera. *Legende Provençale* represents the highest point in Moore's aspirations as a serious creative artist and, as she herself knew, the peak of her achievement. That this ghost story, which could so effectively be staged with modern lighting and projections, should almost have become a ghost itself, is perhaps the saddest irony of Moore's career.

CHAPTER 16

Los Rubios and Other Los Angeles Music

The invitation to compose another opera on an American subject came in the spring of 1931, about the time that the hope of an Italian production of *Rizzio* was fading. At first Moore was merely asked to supply music for a pageant to be staged the following September as part of La Fiesta, the city's 150th birthday celebration. Somehow the pageant grew into a full-length opera, to be based on a recently completed novel by local writer and English teacher Neeta Marquis.[1] The time was desperately short for such a large project, but Moore agreed to do it anyway. She never found it easy to say no, and there were several compelling reasons for trying it. She wholeheartedly agreed with her fellow members of the newly formed Society for the Advancement of American Music (SAAM) that a native school of opera should be encouraged. The idea of opera as a popular art with wide public participation for a public celebration is not so different from the pageant put on by the village folk in Sarah's "Water of Eden" of two decades earlier.[2]

In *Narcissa* and *The Flaming Arrow*, Moore had already demonstrated her commitment to American opera, but neither one was appropriate for this specific occasion. A production outdoors, in the city's new Greek Theatre in Griffith Park, by largely amateur forces, open to the public without charge, was guaranteed if she could meet the deadline. She would not be paid, but she would be performing both a civic and an artistic service that might set a precedent for other civic and artistic services, for herself or for other composers. Besides, she would own the music, and there might be other productions. The compatibility of the project with her aesthetic ideas about American music made it easy to take on what was, when it came down to it, an intriguing challenge to her professional skill.

The unpaid commission had come about through her association

148

with Lulu Sanford Tefft, the organizer of the Society for the Advancement of American Music. The project was SAAM's first major undertaking. Among SAAM's other charter members were Neeta Marquis, the novelist-turned-librettist; Laura Sweeney Moore (no relation), a member of the board of directors of the playground and recreation department; and Glenn M. Tindall, music supervisor of the playground and recreation department. A formal agreement was signed in Los Angeles City Hall on April 28, for an opera to be performed on September 10. There was to be an amateur chorus of several hundred, plus dancers and an orchestra. The orchestra would be the Playground and Recreation Department Symphony, which represented the apex of the department's huge participatory music program. Moore's friend and Laura Sweeney Moore's close relative, Mildred House, would train the chorus. The city budgeted a skimpy four thousand dollars for the project.

A week after the agreement was signed, Moore received the first part of the libretto. Her confidence of the previous week that she could set Marquis' text was quickly shaken: "she had a musician's difficulties with the unfit libretto. It was mostly in narrative form, even the conversations being largely of intrigues in business. The book itself is a long novel being more historical than romantic in plot and theme. It was almost entirely devoid of poetical or rhythmic language—full of hard, unsingable words."[3] Apologetically, she prodded Marquis to make changes that would make a text practical to set and produce: "Your letter received with the altered plot, which I deeply appreciate. It is a pity to put you to so much trouble, but I believe the ultimate result will save so many stage difficulties, that it will be worth the trouble."[4] Though several weeks remained in the school term at California Christian College and the Steeb School, she set to work at once, for the performers had to have their music well ahead of the performance. Sarah described the regimen her daughter followed once school was over.

She lived alone in her house, doing her own cooking and housework, because she could not have any one around her. She rarely left the house, seeing no one but her mother who came at times to stay ten or fifteen minutes between sunset and dark.

She hardly averaged five hours of sleep at night. When sleep conquered, she would set the alarm clock fifteen minutes ahead, throw herself on the bed and sleep as if dead; wake and go on again. Toward the end she must every hour or so, lave her eyes in cold water to keep her vision clear enough to continue.[5]

The piano-vocal score, something over 100 pages, occupied her through June. July was taken up with the orchestra score, some 286 pages worth; and August was spent frantically copying parts, attending daily rehearsals, and attempting to soothe the continually ruffled feelings of the singers and everyone else involved. Some excerpts from her datebook give an idea of the chaos. For starters, there was not even an agreement about who was in charge of rehearsals.

August 17, 1931. Copied parts until 4:30 A.M., got up at 9, worked until rehearsal. Went to Hollywood High to help conduct . . . and was taken aside by Mr. Tindall and told very kindly that it would go better if I would keep off the stage!! Also I find that I am not to conduct the opera. That, at least, is a relief—if they will not distort the tempi.

At orch. rehearsal tonight, Mr. Tindall said to his *very* amateur orchestra— with horns—(and *everything* off pitch) that "some of the orchestration would doubtless have to be re-arranged!" But when Mr. Adam labored with them, it sounded as intended. I feel like getting a little temperamental myself!

August 19, 1931. . . . I got ready to go to the rehearsal, expecting Mrs. House to call for me. No one came, no message. . . . Found, by inadvertent remarks, conflicting explanations, etc., that I had been "forgotten" purposely. Mildred is doing a double deal. Sorry, I didn't quite expect it from her. . . . But what is the cause? Have I worked myself to death all summer, to be thrown aside like a worn garment, now that the opera is ready? I am not unduly sensitive, but I do not understand. . . .

August 20, 1931. . . . I think best to ignore Mildred's part in it. . . . Possibly she expected to conduct it herself? But if so, she lacks judgment, for she is not experienced in such matters.

Tindall settled that dispute by conducting himself. Then the librettist, who anticipated eventual financial success, demanded a larger cut.

Aug. 25, 1931. . . . Miss Marquis signed one [contract] with me in which I granted her 35% of possible profits (are there *ever* profits?)

She now considers that inadequate, and wants me to sign a contract which eliminates me entirely from any Moving Picture rights. I think that is exceedingly grasping! 15% is usual for Grand Opera libretti—more is generous. This is her first attempt and was very difficult for me to set.

August 28, 1931. . . . Neeta's last letter. Doesn't she realize I *want* to be fair with her? *More* than fair? But I cannot let my entire work go for nothing at all. I have absolutely nothing to *leave* my dear children, except my music. If there should be any money in it ever, they must not be deprived. If I were thoroughly dead, or perhaps, when I am, there may be some value to it.

Sept. 1, 1931.... Met Neeta Marquis ... amicable meeting. I agreed to give her 50%. I think that is out of all proportion! Rehearsal at night ....

Moore could not defend her own interests in a forthright manner, but she tried to look after the interests of her singers, especially publicity for them.

Aug. 26, 1931.... Still puzzled—getting no publicity for any of the singers. At the City Hall they lay it all to Miss Marquis. She went to the papers and complained! That is fatal!

August 29, 1931.... Official news, lists all "Major Events" for the Fiesta, including street parades, Rodeo, etc.; *no* mention of the opera!!

Sept. 3, 1931.... Mr. Tindall told me he considered me "ungrateful!" Said many unkind things! I told him I felt the Department was very "ungrateful" to me, after all my hard work for their Department, with neither remuneration nor publicity for my singers.

Sept. 6, 1931. Mrs. Herzinger threatens to remove Harold Hodge from the cast, as he has had insufficient publicity. I urged that it was too late to leave honorably. She is determined! Lots of worry! I hardly feel he will do it—but, who knows?

Sept. 7, 1931. Spent most of the day phoning, about Harold Hodge; terribly worried.... But in the end, Harold came around and took me out to rehearsal, and agreed to stand by! ... I am glad these worries don't affect me as they used to!

She dealt with the cumulative fatigue and pressure as best she could.

August 1, 1931.... Like all young people, [the potential singers] think they are professional when they have sung one role and "gotten by!" They *should work as I had to!*

August 16, 1931. Opera is a funny game—sometimes I wonder *why* I keep on writing them!

August 18, 1931. The "way of the composer" is a hard one! But it is my way of expressing my faith. It is the truest expression of myself. I believe God gave me the gift—to use.

Somehow she managed to get through the preparation, buy a new dress for the occasion (pink instead of her usual discreet black), and welcome Marian and Wesley, who came for the performance. Sarah, who had fled during the final week of rehearsals, returned as well.

The day of the performance brought a fleeting but satisfactory climax to her summer of superhuman labor.

Sept. 10, 1931. Spent the day copying the 1st act parts for trombone. The telephone rang incessantly. Night. Premiere of *Los Rubios*, Greek Theatre. It was packed *full*—people sitting on the walls, standing up, etc; nearly 13,000 turned away. Performance was smooth. Everything went well except the orchestra could hardly be heard. Bass trombone missing. Only 3 horns, half the time, missing cues, or coming in too soon. How one suffers! But on the other hand, the stage pictures were lovely, the singers did well, and it went "moving along."

Los Rubios was very well received by both press and public, though the free outdoor performance created problems for the audience. One critic wrote to Moore of his difficulties.

I had a row trying to get into the theater, then scraping for a seat, bothered by later comers climbing over me and talking, so that combined with the imperative need of leaving early in order to meet presstime, likely enough I could not view quite the right perspective of either score or libretto. The facts you give in your letter make it plain that hardly anyone could fairly judge the opera by that production. I more emphatically even than at first, am of the opinion that the work should be repeated in proper raiment of orchestra, singers, and direction; it is quite possible that you have in it the living lasting California opera.[6]

Published critical comment was favorable. It complimented the city for underwriting the enterprise, and Moore for her work. Bruno Ussher, who was still friendly toward Moore's music, wrote a review that is typical.

Taking all things into account, this present manifestation of community effort merits cordial approval and should encourage authorities to cultivate creative and executant talent of the community for like undertakings in the future. If opera is to become a native art in this country then it must be part and parcel of the language life and living of this country. Last night's music, text and enunciation, proved indeed that English is a singable idiom. . . . Mrs. Moore's score is facile, has melodic and emotional appeal and indicated a practiced hand. A second and lively performance might reveal dramatic elements missing now.[7]

One critic called attention to Moore's newly demonstrated potential for light opera: "This is not this talented musician's first attempt at opera. . . . But this production looks as if it might be the birth of a new flare for light opera upon a scale that will become permanent."[8]

Los Rubios is indeed light in character. Its story revolves around land-office chicanery and scarcely rises above the level of barroom melodrama. The libretto's claim to authenticity appears to rest on its progression from an Indian prologue to a Spanish-dominated first act to an Anglo-dominated conclusion rather than on the characters or details of the plot.

Moore handled the special demands of the libretto and the projected performing forces with seemingly effortless skill (to judge from the score, not the datebooks). Her recent Indianist tone poem, *Ka-mi-a-kin,* became the overture, supporting the opera's prologue. The song "Querida mi vida" of two decades earlier became the central feature of the Act I choral-dance sequence. The traditional dance tune "Sir Roger de Coverly" appears as part of the American square dance sequence of Act III. There are her own tangos and waltzes and songs of suitably folklike character, with straightforward diatonic harmonies. These are embedded in relatively long and complex recitative- and arioso-like passages, which use her current and, by then, finely honed post-romantic harmonic language. The handling of the English text is sufficiently sure to disguise the problems it presented to her. She was even able to set Marquis's panegyric to the prospective fortunes to be made in Los Angeles real estate, "Some day . . . these noble acres of Los Rubios will be a treasure," as if it were a classical aria text. For some of the more crass business details, she fell back on the technical device of melodrama: spoken dialog against the opening waltz, distorted to symbolize the evil nature of the discussion. The performing forces may have been amateur, but her work was thoroughly professional.

Despite the huge audience and the good press, further performances did not materialize. A planned repeat had been scratched before the performance; the production had already strained the playground and recreation department's human resources even without reference to the state of its budget. There was talk of another production, and even a hint in the *Times* of a nibble from Hollywood: "The two women have already had an offer from a publisher for their work; they have been flirted with by motion-picture scouts, and they are retaining all rights to it. While only one performance is scheduled for La Fiesta, it is quite possible that it will be given for a season if it

Pages from *Los Rubios*, Act I. (Reprinted, by permission, from the composer's 1931 manuscript copy of the full score, Mary Carr Moore Archive, Music Library, UCLA.)

friend, These no-ble acres of Los Rubios, Will be a trea-sure, Wide-ly sought

measures up to expectations."⁹ But *Los Rubios* seems not to have interested the film colony. The opera's only revival was for an opera reading club in 1936.

The speed and assurance with which Moore produced the music for this opera suggest that she could have worked on film scores successfully, as many male composers did from time to time. A few film assignments would have relieved the relentless pressures of her heavy teaching obligations and her financial burdens. There were no women among the film colony's composers and arrangers, however, and Moore did not become an exception.

Two months after the performance, Neeta Marquis was still trying to obtain a copy of the score. For her part, Moore wrote "Copyright Mary Carr Moore" on every page of the piano-vocal score and then filed it with the Copyright Office. It is the only opera score she treated in that manner. Moore did not attempt to work with this librettist again. But she did patch over her differences with the Sanger-Moore-House clan. Two years after *Los Rubios*, Laura Sweeney Moore approached her with another libretto, this one for an operetta that Laura Sweeney Moore wished to direct and conduct herself. Again the production was sponsored by the playground and recreation department; again amateur forces were used. *Flutes of Jade Happiness* was done at Los Angeles High School and, later on, in the Greek Theatre, where Laura Sweeney Moore also directed *The Flaming Arrow*. A review gives an idea of what the work was like.

> Reflecting the strange fatalistic creeds of the East, the story and music naturally bore the flavor of oriental moods. There was the plaintive and wistful elusiveness of Chinese poetry in the midst of the fluid lyricism of its musical score. The choruses with their reiteration of theme brought strength and dramatic splendor to the operatic content. The music though rich in color and filled at times with a certain mysterious sensuosity, somehow failed quite to reach the grand gesture. However, oriental music as we conceive it perhaps is unable to encompass the high emotion of real operatic tragedy.¹⁰

A few years later, Laura Sweeney Moore attempted a performance of *Beyond These Hills* with her amateur forces. Moore, who was remarkably tolerant of bad performances, finally threw up her hands: "June 5, 1942. Recreation Dept. Chorus and Orch. . . . Mildred is a dear; so is Laura Moore, and Mrs. Sanger, but not professional enough for such difficult work. Mildred conducted from the piano score, instead of conductor's score. So with only two rehearsals (orch.) and some there for the first time, it was very hard on *me*."[11] *Los Rubios* and *Flutes of Jade Happiness* thus joined *The Flaming Arrow* as works appropriate for amateurs to perform. But the quartet cycle *Beyond These Hills* belonged to a different category. Like *David Rizzio, Narcissa,* and *Legende Provençale,* it required professional treatment in performance.

In the space of eight years, between September 1927 and August 1935, Moore had written three operas and an operetta, each with a totally different locale, in three different languages. Though none won more than local recognition and certainly none brought her fortune, three of the four are successful in achieving the artistic goals she had set for herself.

A series of pieces for various instruments with piano indicates that Moore had more instrumental performers available for club concerts and musicales in Los Angeles than she had earlier. Such pieces as "Message to One Absent" for violin and piano, "Chant d'amour" for flute and piano, and "Nostalgia" for clarinet and piano are written in a latter-day salon style intended to show each solo instrument's traditional character and give their performers some sympathetic passages. A suite called "Forest Sketches," published by Carl Fischer in 1938, began as occasional piano pieces of the same type: "Murmur of Pines" (1928), "Before the Dawn" (1931), "Twilight in the Forest," and "Dance of the Wood Sprites" (both 1932).

The extended works for concert performance, such as the two string quartets, the string trio, and the piano concerto, are quite different from the shorter instrumental pieces or the songs. They are more tightly controlled in structure, more formal, and much more Germanic in their initial influences than the operas, though a steady loosening of the Germanic qualities of Moore's early training is evident as she gained confidence in handling the texture of the string ensembles. Moore probably had very little experience of the string quartet literature when she undertook the G Minor Quartet in 1926, as a thank-you to her Oakland friend, Orley See. Its effect is old-fashioned but competent. It does not sound at all like the music of *The Flaming Arrow* or *David Rizzio,* the two operas closest to it in time. Of its four movements, only the Scherzo was definitely performed, at one concert by the Bartlett-Frankel Quartet.

The second quartet dates from 1930, inspired by Bessie Bartlett

Frankel's generosity in founding the Bartlett-Frankel Quartet, to whom it was dedicated. Eventually, in 1934, this F Minor Quartet won a prize from the National League of American Pen Women. Though Bartlett-Frankel never took it up, it was played by two later quartets, in Los Angeles and Riverside. Of the three chamber works for strings from this period, only the trio for violin, viola, and cello of 1936 bears any resemblance at all to her more spontaneous operatic style. Its arrangement of the four movements in slow-fast, slow-fast order suggests a neoclassical shape, but its originality makes it difficult to categorize. In particular, the extended, serene lyricism of the third movement contrasts with a short final fugue that begins conventionally and winds itself into an Ivesian harmonic and rhythmic knot before unwinding again. Probably the trio was never performed in its original form. Several years after composing it, Moore arranged it for string orchestra. In that version, she heard a performance of it by a Chapman student orchestra at a Native American Composers concert, where it was well received.

Moore was influenced by the string quartet's reputation as the most intellectual and formal genre of art music.[12] These three chamber works for strings are conservative. Two later quartet movements, one incomplete, are far more experimental. The string chamber music does not reveal a single harmonic colloquialism of the sort that appears routinely in the songs and short instrumental pieces, but it does display a substantial evolution in Moore's style over the period in which it was written. The quality of her workmanship leaves one wondering why it did not gain more currency and wider performance.

The attitude of string quartet performers may have been a factor. The F Minor Quartet was performed by the Boris Morros Quartet in 1937 at the festival of the California Society of Composers. Phil Kahgan was the violist at that performance, which he remembered well forty-six years later. He was very complimentary about the music, which he said the members of the quartet had enjoyed playing. When asked why Moore's quartet had not been programmed again, he referred to the group's obligation to give weekly network radio broadcasts and shrugged, "she was a society lady. She wasn't a member of the profession."[13] In spite of this devastating statement of prejudice, the Boris Morros Quartet probably produced as polished a performance as any extended work of hers received in her lifetime.

Page from Trio in G Minor, op. 98, no. 3, first movement. (Reprinted, by permission, from the composer's 1936 manuscript score, Mary Carr Moore Archive, Music Library, UCLA.)

If the quartets and the trio never achieved the currency that the earlier *Saul,* in both trio and quintet versions, did, the piano concerto fared distinctly better. It was performed by the Federal Music Project symphony orchestra in Los Angeles by two different soloists and conductors; there were several two-piano performances as well. It had even more performances in a third version for piano and an instrumental quartet of violin, viola, clarinet, and cello. Five different pianists learned the solo part and performed it in one or another of these versions.[14] After hearing it in the quintet version in 1940, Bruno Ussher criticized its conservative style by wisecracking that Dame Ethel Smyth's memoirs, *Impressions that Remained,* were "an autobiography not a piano concerto." Ussher credited the concerto with "some pleasant and some pathos laden, again playful ideas to various moods, from the decidedly romantic and continental of convention to the pseudo oriental."[15] The concerto is not in the vanguard of ultramodernism, nor was it intended to be. If anything, it has a kinship with the work of Moore's exact contemporary, Rachmaninoff. Runs and flourishes, sonorous statements of lyrical melodies, and occasional whole-tone twists characterize each of the three movements, which are contrasted with one another in traditional fashion. It is a well-constructed work to which a recent evaluation of Rachmaninoff's work might as easily apply: "a highly individual, lyrical idiom which, if it has not had any lasting effect on the development of [American] music, nevertheless is characterized by sincere expression and skillful technique."[16]

A continuing stream of songs in the years 1927–36 reflects the flexible and experimental character of Moore's style during her early years in Los Angeles. "Highwayman's Hollow," "Japanese Night-Song," and "Blue Herons" are full of chromaticisms but are still very different from one another. "Lo, We Shall See the Veil Withdrawn" has the straightforward directness of expression of her best early songs but greater harmonic richness. Its text reflects the popularity of Christian Science among Moore's friends and contemporaries in Los Angeles. "Message," from 1936, is the last important song from Moore's burst of creative activity in Los Angeles. Its tightly controlled form and slightly more astringent chromaticisms are still balanced by the parlor touch, which had by then entirely disappeared from Moore's operas and chamber music. "Wings of Flight," which was sung quite frequently, is a tribute to her older son, who was making a career as a pilot.

A different approach and purpose is found in her dignified setting of "My Country, 'Tis of Thee," done in the summer of 1935. Except for the certainty with which it moves, this setting might have been composed in early Seattle days. It is a personal expression, which she dedicated to "My Father, Col. B. O. Carr: patriot, soldier, and citizen." Starting out as a four-part setting, it appeared in print as a song and eventually was given an orchestral accompaniment. It provides a musical link between Moore's early idealistic patriotism and her budding activism in behalf of musical Americanism. It also marks the end of Moore's decade of exuberant creativity, although a few interesting choral settings are scattered among her later works.

CHAPTER 17

The Federal Music Project

As the Depression wore on, a few larger performances began to come Moore's way in addition to the steady round of club hearings that her music was receiving. Most of them were connected with the Federal Music Project of the WPA. Begun in 1935, the Works Progress Administration (from 1939 the Work Projects Administration) was the product of federal legislation aimed at reducing the continuing and catastrophic unemployment that went with the bad times.

Early on, the WPA was committed to the support of public projects in the arts. By 1936 a Federal Theatre Project, a Federal Writers Project, and a Federal Music Project were under way. None of these ever represented more than a small fraction of the total WPA effort, but they sparked controversy out of proportion to their relatively small size.[1] The well-publicized Composers Forum Laboratory was pioneered by Ashley Pettis, earlier a performer of Moore's music.[2] It offered chamber-sized performances of music by composers who afterward answered questions from the audience about their work. This but small part of the FMP was apparently most successful in New York City and seems to have had little impact on Moore or other Los Angeles composers.[3]

Overall, the Federal Music Project included symphony orchestras, somewhat smaller concert orchestras, concert bands, dance bands, chamber music, and choral groups. There were teaching projects, folk music collecting projects, music copying projects, and innumerable radio broadcasts. The Southern California Music Project's thirty units gave 4,324 performances to a total audience of 2,415,497 during the year of the project that ended September 1, 1940.[4] A breakdown of attendance, nationwide, over the project's first four years, hints at the project's areas of concentration and/or the tastes of audiences in the late 1930s: concert and symphony orchestras, 37 percent; concert bands, 30 percent; dance bands, 16 percent; student recitals, 6 percent; chamber music, 4 percent; and opera and choral music, 5 percent.[5]

The bureaucratic clumsiness that might be expected in such a large undertaking did not prevent occasional excellence from developing among the various performing units. Gastone Usigli's work with the FMP Symphony of Los Angeles between 1936 and 1939 was particularly admired, as was his very frequent programming of music by American composers, including Moore.

The occasion was particularly a triumph for Gastone Usigli as conductor, not merely in the visual aspect of his adept handling of his orchestral and choral forces as seen by the audience, but in the more potent inculcated understanding between the performers and himself which permitted him to obtain from his singers and players a spontaneous response to his every expressive intent, seemingly of almost hypnotic power. Unless we are mistaken, this highly gifted musician eventually will be "discovered" with acquisitive intent by the powers-that-be of some of our major orchestras. He has accomplished remarkable results with the Los Angeles Federal Symphony Orchestra.

The combined chorus and orchestra obtained both beautiful and stirring effects in the scene from Mary Carr Moore's opera, "Rizzio," . . . The Moore work . . . gave more than a hint of . . . dramatic effectiveness and lyrical beauty.[6]

Performances of unfamiliar music by any orchestra rarely draw such unstinting critical praise.

The Los Angeles FMP had its share of political battles, occasionally touching Moore. The "ten percent" rule, which allowed Usigli to hire a few players who didn't qualify for relief for key positions in the orchestra, came under fire. There was criticism that the foreign-born were favored over native-born musicians in hiring. Moore was involved in a conflict between Usigli and Harlé Jervis, state director of the FMP, perhaps over Usigli's hiring practices. She agonized over her decision to take sides against Jervis, a woman, even though Jervis was viewed as a political hack without musical understanding.[7] "Jan. 17, 1938. Federal Music Board . . . . In no condition, physically or mentally to go thro' the ordeal of having to take sides against Harle Jervis; but felt compelled to do what I felt was right. On return home, went thro' a distressing telephone conversation with her. I regret the whole thing, but principle compels." Usigli left the project some eighteen months later. His departure came on the eve of a concert at the Greek Theatre of music by American composers given as part of a Society of Native American Composers festival. Moore's music was not on the program, but she was very active in the Native American Composers. She attempted to salvage Usigli's role in the concert without success.

June 21, 1939. Return to L.A. . . . a lot of trouble brewing in Fed. Music Project. Samoussoud had been suspended; also McKinley—Miss Bentley discharged—Usigli resigned—also Rubanoff [sic]. . . . Composers' Concert now in hands of *Altschuler!!* I wired Pres. Roosevelt and wrote Eleanor Roosevelt, hoping to get Permission for Usigli to be "guest conductor"!! He has been told he *may not* enter the Project Bldg! This, by a Ditch Digger.[8]

The *Pacific Coast Musician* tells the rest of the story.

That an interval of more than three weeks could elapse between the sending of an emergency telegram from Los Angeles to WPA headquarters in Washington and the receipt of an answer to that telegram, appears to be eloquent evidence of how "exceedingly slow" in grinding and uselessly late in starting, the Governmental mills can be. . . .
The WPA reply was received last Wednesday—more than two weeks after the final concert had taken place! It announced that the matter would be referred to the local WPA-FMP authorities, whom, incidentally, officials of the Native Composers had tried in vain to reach before appealing to Washington.[9]

Moore's personal aversion to Roosevelt and his New Deal was wholly predictable, given her family's longtime Republican loyalties. Probably the aversion was shared by many other American composers. Yet, in common with others, she could see the potential for American music, including her own, in the FMP, and she did her best to exploit the opportunity. She served repeatedly on the audition boards that screened and assigned applicants for FMP work to appropriate performing groups. She was often a member of committees involved with local FMP policy decisions. Her datebooks show her attending innumerable meetings as well as many concerts sponsored by the FMP throughout the period of its activity in Los Angeles, between Janaury, 1936, and early 1942. She became close friends with young James Sample, the conductor who was brought in to pick up the pieces after Usigli's departure. Though Moore's own notes are very sketchy and other information is incomplete, it appears that she was the only one among the many women composers working in Los Angeles in the 1930s to take so active a role in the administrative activities of the Southern California Music Project.

Whether her committee work helped or not, Moore's music received a respectable number of performances by FMP orchestras in Los Angeles. The orchestral performances were:

- May 8 and 23, 1936. Piano Concerto. Emil Danenberg, piano; Modest Altschuler, conductor.
- September 9, 1936. *Ka-mi-a-kin*, tone poem, reading. Alois Reiser, conductor.
- September 9, 1936. Scena, Act I, *David Rizzio*, concert version. Adolf Tandler, conductor.
- May 12, 1937. *Ka-mi-a-kin*. Mary Carr Moore, conductor.
- February 22, 1938. Scena, Act I, *David Rizzio*. Gastone Usigli, conductor.
- July 15, 1940. *Kidnap*, tone poem, reading. James Sample, conductor.
- October 23, 1940. Piano Concerto. Constance Shirley, piano; James Sample, conductor.
- April 2, 1941. "My Dream," orchestrated song. Ruth Miller Chamlee, soprano; James Sample, conductor.
- April 8, 1941. Rozanne's aria, "L'étoile du soir," from *Legende Provençale*. James Sample, conductor.

In addition, the F Minor Quartet was played twice in Riverside, in July, 1937, and February, 1940.

Moore's public conducting had previously been limited mainly to the performances of *Narcissa* in 1912 and 1925 and of *Memories* in 1914, and club performances of such works as *The Flaming Arrow*. Now she found herself conducting more of her own music in orchestral performances. The first of these was a performance of the "Intermezzo" from *David Rizzio* at the Ford Bowl in San Diego in August, 1936. The following year she conducted her own *Ka-mi-a-kin* in Los Angeles. Alfred Hertz, who conducted at the Hollywood Bowl for many years in addition to his San Francisco Symphony assignment, repaid an old debt and invited Moore to conduct the Bay Cities FMP Symphony in her own music. She conducted the "Intermezzo" and

Ka-mi-a-kin in two performances, one in Oakland, the other in San Francisco, in 1938. Some of the men in the orchestra had played under her direction in 1915 at the Art Palace Preservation Concert. Two years later, she was back in the Bay Area to conduct *Ka-mi-a-kin* at the World's Fair on Treasure Island, a performance that was broadcast on network radio. There may have been other performances of her orchestral music in these years, but they have not been traced.[10] When she began the lengthy task of copying out the orchestral parts to *Legende Provençale* just before school opened in the fall of 1941, she may have had in mind a concert performance by Sample's FMP orchestra. If Sample had contemplated such a performance, the opportunity soon slipped away; World War II and the effective end of the FMP would come within weeks.

The opportunity provided by the FMP orchestras could not give Moore much exposure, for she had written relatively little orchestral music. Further, the orchestral music does not represent her finest work. The FMP's schizophrenic treatment of opera, which was first assigned to the Theatre Project and only belatedly to the Music Project, meant that the federal programs could not help her get productions of her best works, the operas. It appears that, in addition to Moore, only Elinor Remick Warren, Frances Marion Ralston, and Fannie Charles Dillon among the Los Angeles women composers had orchestral works ready for performance when the FMP suddenly gave them an opening. But Moore was the most successful of them in getting performances of her own music, probably because of her diligent committee work.[11]

Other opportunities outside the Federal Music Project came and went. Mrs. Irish, manager of the Hollywood Bowl Association, phoned Moore one day, asking her to submit some scores for possible performance in the Hollywood Bowl. Moore duly carried the scores to the piano concerto, *Ka-mi-a-kin,* and the *Rizzio* "Intermezzo" to the Bowl office on July 26, 1940. It is not clear why she did not choose to submit, say, Act I of *Narcissa* or the complete *Rizzio.* The importance of the FMP to Moore becomes even more evident since she did not succeed in breaking into the Bowl.[12]

By 1942, as the FMP was shut down by the onset of war, the music scene in Los Angeles presented a far different picture from that of a decade earlier. The emergence of many local composers, and the creative ferment Moore had helped to foster, were overshadowed by events far beyond her, or anyone else's, control. The indigenous culture of the First Los Angeles School suddenly found itself situated next door to a huge film and radio industry, in a city well on its way to becoming one of the art music centers of the world. The number of composers, arrangers, orchestrators, and performers brought to Hollywood or attracted there by the film industry had soared by 1940. Along with the homegrown talent, which included students of Moore from Chapman College, there were many established European musicians. Often they had been sought out by the builders of the various movie companies, themselves frequently of European birth. Overlapping with this group of new arrivals was another group of composers and performers, some of them internationally famous. These were the exiles from Hitler's Germany, who came to Los Angeles in a steady stream in the late 1930s. The more innovative their music or the more left-wing their politics, the more likely they were to emigrate, for Hitler's government had no more use for radicalism, either in music or in politics, than it did for Jews.

By the time the United States entered World War II, some of the most famous composers of the twentieth century were living in Los Angeles, where they set about bringing their notions of "culture," "taste," and "modernism" to the provincial Americans among whom they found themselves. Among the émigrés were Arnold Schoenberg, Igor Stravinsky, Ernst Toch, Joseph Achron, Ernst Krenek, Hanns Eisler, Erich Korngold, and even Sergei Rachmaninoff. The established local composers had hoped that in the FMP they would finally find a way to break the longstanding domination of American art music by the foreign-born, but they were no match for this new wave of émigrés. Reflecting this change, the staid *Pacific Coast Musician*, which had always reported local music events as its main function, now became more cosmopolitan. Several pages of each issue were devoted to "Screen and Radio Music and Musicians." Music events from around the country were regularly reported more fully on the front pages, while recent Los Angeles musical events and the activities of prominent local teachers were given less space in the rear. The added pages and increased advertising space are indicative of the growing size and prosperity of the area's musical community, though it was a community in which the importance of the indigenous music culture was clearly diminished.

CHAPTER 18

The Ultra-Moderns

Moore's compositional style had evolved a long way from the "Lullabye" of 1889 by the time the émigrés began arriving in earnest around 1936. The Pre-Raphaelite influences of "The Quest of Sigurd" and the deliberate archaisms of *Narcissa*, the tonal ambiguity of "Mysterious Power" and the modal experiments of *Beyond These Hills*, and the whole-tone usages of *The Flaming Arrow* and "Highwayman's Hollow" had led to the distinctive post-romantic synthesis she had achieved in *Legende Provençale*. In the 1920s she had been thought of as a modernist. "Immortal Birth" at its publication in 1922 was said to contain "the new note"; *Beyond These Hills* was greeted with the remark that it was "modern in feeling."[1] In her early years in Los Angeles the "modern" elements of her teaching were stressed.

In spite of the continuing evolution of her style, in the 1930s the perception of Moore's music changed from modern to old-fashioned. Local critics had been shocked when Henry Cowell came from San Francisco in 1925 and again in 1926 to initiate the reluctant Los Angeles public into the works of the so-called ultra-moderns. But a few years later, in 1933, Bruno David Ussher, a local critic, was apologetic about liking Moore's violin sonata of 1918: "Some may call Mrs. Moore's melodic [style] old-fashioned in the manner of the romantic school. Very well, then, be it called thus, but at least it is sincerely expressive and not epileptic or asthmatic as so much, fabricated by our 'moderns.'"[2] Moore's younger friend Hugo Davise succinctly explains the shift in her perceived position from modern to old-fashioned by saying, "Around [1930], Debussy was the latest thing we knew around L.A. We never knew anything about modern music until the émigrés came."[3]

The musical style of American composers of Moore's generation was initially shaped by German Romanticism. Most had actually studied in Germany; Moore herself had been taught by two Leipzig-trained Americans. After 1900 they had gradually turned away from their old, exclusively German models. The French influences apparent in Moore's use of whole-tone techniques and her selection of English, Italian, and French texts for her operas are both consistent with the interests of her American contemporaries.

The search for a new aesthetic approach to replace the decaying Romantic ideal in music took a variety of forms after the First World War, attracting many composers a generation younger than Moore. The younger Americans, of whom the best known is Aaron Copland, also found their inspiration in European sources, but their interests lay in the variety of new approaches that were lumped together under the label "ultra-modernism." "The Six" in France had rebelled against the lushness of Debussy's Impressionism. After exploring atonality for some years, Schoenberg had formulated his twelve-tone theory, which he saw as a logical extension of the functional tonality of the eighteenth and nineteenth centuries. Bartók, Stravinsky, Varèse, and others also challenged traditional Romantic concepts of melody, harmony, rhythm, tone color, and form, leaving expanded technical resources and aesthetic confusion in their wake. Despite similar experiments by older Americans such as Charles Ives, the ultra-modern approach was effectively introduced in the United States in the 1920s from Europe through the efforts of the International Composers Guild (ICG) and the League of Composers. It spread only slowly from New York, making little impact elsewhere in the country even after the émigrés themselves began to arrive with the new aesthetic and the new techniques in their baggage. As late as 1941 the League of Composers' journal, *Modern Music*, reported that southern California "probably has the smallest audience for new music to be found anywhere," in spite of the presence of so many of the ultra-moderns there.[4]

The ultra-moderns may have formed a very small part of Los Angeles' musical life in statistical terms, but Moore as a creative artist had no choice but to address the issues they raised. In 1913 she had managed to ignore the aesthetic implications of the Armory Show during her single extended visit to New York. Now her negative response was more than a practical decision not to flout the audience that she had so carefully nurtured over the years, as the modernists were doing. It was profoundly visceral. Sometimes upon hearing a particularly outrageous work, she would have to leave during the performance to throw up. Other times she would have to stop her car on the way home as she grew ill.[5] Her aversion to the music of the new generation of modernists is expressed in this comment on a performance of the "Andante for Strings and Clarinet" by American composer Roy Harris (1898–1979): "Mar. 22, 1931. Either I am hopelessly out of date—or else he has not the divine spark. We work for American Music—and then listen to music (?) which puckers one's mind like a bite of green persimmon. Why are they *so* afraid something will sound pure and clean and sweet. So *much* of the *young* modern stuff sounds like a dose of typhoid fever."

Moore was by no means totally opposed to all aspects of the ultra-moderns' offerings, however. Like the composers a generation younger, she was dissatisfied with the older expressive means available to her. Two undated string quartet movements, one with chords built in fifths and another, later one with dissonant counterpoint, indicate that she was quietly experimenting with the new techniques herself. Datebook entries reflect her attitude. "Apr. 4, 1933. [Bartlett-Frankel Quartet] Program. Mozart Quartet, D Minor; "Indiscretions" by Gruenberg; Piano Quintet, Bloch. . . . Was not at all happy with any of the program. Tired of the Mozart harmonies; disgusted with Gruenberg; and horrified at the Bloch, though sometimes I like him. Guess I'm ready for an 'Old Ladies' Home."[6] Another hint of the stylistic conundrum she faced appears several years later: "May 26, 1937. Program was very excellent tonight thro'out. Willy Stahl's work modern but interesting and forceful, not *merely* one dissonance piled on another." Elsewhere, she admired the "splendid work" of Florent Schmitt in "The Tragedy of Salome" and found Alexander Borisoff's music "very well written and interesting" at another performance.[7] Other modernists didn't fare so well, though she continued to listen to their work: "May 24, 1941. . . . I went to Congregational Church at 8:15 for Festival of 'Modern Music'?! A *little* I liked, most of it was tiresome. 'Onward Christian Soldiers' in 'Swing' offended me, and many others! A very tiresome concert. But unless I had *heard* it myself, I wouldn't have known."

Moore's comments on a musicale in the summer of 1935 place the issue in focus and allow Moore to speak for herself. A newspaper announcement of the event sets the stage.

A salon to bring about mutual understanding and mutual appreciation among progressive composers will be given tonight by Verna Arvey in the

Norma Gould studio at 831 S. La Brea Ave. Among the participating composers are Arnold Schoenberg, Joseph Achron, Dr. George Liebling, Mary Carr Moore, Richard Drake Saunders, Henry Cowell, William Grant Still, George Tremblay, Sidney Cutner, Hugo Davise, Gilberto Isais and Charles Pemberton. . . . The evening is invitational.[8]

Moore came for the evening from her summer cabin in Topanga Canyon, where she was just finishing the vocal score to *Legende Provençale*. The datebook gives this laconic report of the proceedings: "Aug. 3, 1935. Composers' Symposium. Ida Gunnell sang 'Sunset' and 'My Dream.' Very ultra-modern program, my work was very 'passé.'" "Sunset," a whole-tone song which was one of the few to be published soon after it was written (1925), need not have embarrassed her. But the twenty-year-old "My Dream," with its slightly inflated parlorisms, must have seemed thoroughly out of place at this gathering. Clearly Moore felt that the selections she had offered were not appropriate, for a few days later she wrote to Arvey: "I am sorry to have 'let you down' but didn't realize you were having only the ultra-moderns. (altho' Dr. Pemberton and Dr. Liebling do not belong to that group, except in certain instances)." She took the occasion to express her ideas about ultra-modernism in more detail.

As for the voice, I am not willing to subject a "fluid instrument" without keys to set a pitch, to such distortion. I am a great admirer of Schoenberg's works—some of them! All of them are of interest; but human nerves are not built to stand a strain of that sort, except for short intervals.

Some critics felt that if Miss Rogers' voice had been of better quality, the songs would have been more interesting; but I maintain the opposite; I feel that her voice would have appeared to better advantage, had the intervals been less exacting, & her voice more free to express the exquisite poems. . . .

I shall not live to see whether I am right or wrong, but out of all this groping, some will find nobility & sincerity, the rest, who are merely trying to be different, will be forgotten! When you are my age, think about it, & see which works survive in the hearts of music lovers!

I do not mean things of the sort, necessarily, of the two songs I presented, the other night. They are already passé to many of the newer group, & exceedingly modern to the large majority!! But I mean, in general—the dissonant motives should be utilized to express tragedy, inharmony, mockery, etc. etc. but not for nobility, beauty or exaltation; tho again, I do not mean the old I, IV, V etc.!![9]

This session may have been a turning point for Moore, who very rarely associated with Schoenberg and his circle thereafter. After the string trio of the following year, which uses the harmonic language of *Legende Provençale,* Moore did not again attempt to compose a large work in a serious style that carried forward her harmonic vocabulary.

There was probably a personal element in Moore's alienation from the ultra-moderns, especially her hostility toward Schoenberg. He had arrived in Los Angeles late in 1934 as a fugitive, first from Hitler and then from the harsh climates of New York and Boston. A few months after Arvey's salon, Schoenberg wrote to Bessie Bartlett Frankel, Moore's student and patron. His letter cannot have failed to offend both Frankel and Moore with its patronizing attitude.

I would very much like to have you sometimes or at least once among the audience of this class, because I know what I am doing here is of the greatest importance for everybody who is interested in music. I know from my experience of nearly forty years that a real understanding for music has to be based on a sound capacity to distinguish between value and non-value. And I know, too, how new my attempt is, to bring not only the amateur, but also the musician, to a real knowledge of basic elements for appreciation. . . .

Frankly: I am very disappointed not to find the interest of the society in my doing, not to find appreciated what I am doing in favour of the future state of musical culture in this city, not to find the support which is owed to such a doing. . . .

Yes, I want you and many other of the society people among my audience and making propaganda for my work in favour of the musical culture of Los Angeles.[10]

Schoenberg's implied attack on Frankel's taste in music helped widen the gulf between the émigré faction that formed around him in Los Angeles in the late 1930s and the "resident" composers, including Moore and her circle. Some time later Schoenberg confirmed the split with a direct attack on Frankel and impresario L. E. Behymer for allegedly suppressing publicity for a concert of his music.[11]

Only one other incident involving both Moore and the leading ultra-moderns of the day is known. A few years after Arvey's fateful musicale, Aaron Copland visited Los Angeles and attempted to organize a chapter of his American Composers Alliance; Moore attended the organizational meeting: "Dec. 21, 1939. Am. Composers' Alliance, 8 P.M. Arnold Schoenberg, Ernst Toch, Jos. Achron, Aaron Copland, Davise, Stahl, Leftwich, Strang, Ruegger [*sic*], George Tremblay. (15 including myself—the only woman.)" Next to her clipping from the *Pacific Coast Musician,* which reported the meeting, Moore noted in the margin of her scrapbook that they had invited her to become secretary of the new chapter and that she had refused, claiming "other commitments." The appearance of the notation makes it clear that she relished the chance to turn them down.

It is tempting to ascribe the hostility of Moore and other older composers toward the younger ultra-moderns to a generation gap. Moore was in her early sixties at the time of Arvey's salon, after all, while Henry Cowell and Aaron Copland were more than two decades younger. But that hardly explains the depth of her aversion. There must have been other reasons.

First, the American ultra-moderns, like their European counterparts, presented themselves as rebels against the established order. As a young woman Moore had been too much inculcated with the notion of a lady's place and function to present herself or her art as expressions of rebellion. She could hardly be expected at this point to applaud such a posture on the part of other, younger composers. Second, there were often leftist political overtones associated with the newer music that were bound to offend her. Third, and perhaps far more important, is the resentment suggested in an interview she gave at about the same time as the Arvey salon.

But of all the difficulties I encountered, perhaps the greatest has been in the fact that I am an American and a woman. That combination, I assure you, has been the most discouraging obstacle of all! So long as a woman contents herself with writing graceful little songs about springtime and the birdies, no one resents it or thinks her presumptuous; but woe be unto her if she dares attempt the larger forms! The prejudice may die eventually, but it will be a hard and slow death.[12]

Moore grew up, as did her Eastern contemporaries, in a society in which music was studied mainly by women and pursued by them as an accomplishment, not a profession. By contrast, professional musicians were typically foreign-born males. Serious music and music study were often considered a sign of effeminacy in American men. If they would gain a place in the art music establishment for themselves, the younger American men apparently believed they had to make the public distance between this older notion of the place of art music and their own aesthetic posture as wide as possible.

While the influence of the ultra-moderns was increasing in the period between the two world wars, women composers overall were receiving less recognition. Very few new female faces appeared in the course of the 1930s to balance the increasing numbers of male composers active in Los Angeles.[13] A 1942 survey of music as a vocation in the Los Angeles area notes the increasing sex prejudice in the profession: "[There is a] preference of men by the motion picture industry and by radio, both of which are of recent growth. On the basis of these figures, we may assume that the 1940 census will also reveal an increase in both the total occupational figure and the number of men."[14] Even though many women had been active as composers in Los Angeles when Moore arrived on the scene in 1926, she was the only one invited to present her music at Arvey's salon in 1935; the only one present at the American Composers Alliance's organizational meeting in 1939; and the only one to have her music performed on the FMP concerts of 1940–41. Of the women active in Los Angeles in 1930, many had retreated by 1940 to silence or to club performances, an artistic outlet that was doomed to steadily decreasing importance in the decades following World War II.

The relationship between the rise of the ultra-moderns and the decline in activity of woman composers is probably not so direct as stated here, since other, extramusical factors were also at work, but the correlation is sufficiently striking to deserve more attention. It suggests that Moore's visceral reaction to the ultra-moderns of the 1930s was an intuitive response, made in self-defense. By her vigorous FMP participation, as well as her work with the Manuscript Club and the American music movement, Moore did all she could to encourage the "resident" composers of the First Los Angeles School, including the other women, and to keep avenues open for her own music beyond her frequent club performances. She would not let go of her opportunities, however imperfect they might be, without a struggle.

CHAPTER 19

Musical Americanism

Organizing in behalf of her music seemed entirely natural to Moore, since she had done it all her life. As a student of seventeen, the young Mary Louise had followed her mother's example and organized her own students in the community of Felton for homegrown performances. It would be difficult to count the number of performances, productions, classes, and musicales she had organized since then. Almost from the moment she arrived in Los Angeles, she turned her gregarious nature and her enthusiasm for organizing toward American music, often following the model of the American Music Center she had started twenty years earlier in Seattle. The Manuscript Club, an outgrowth of her work as a teacher, was her most lasting success as an organizer, but her work in behalf of the music of more established American composers sometimes drew more attention. Much of her activity was in cooperation with one or two noncomposer associates and with her composer friends Homer Grunn and Charles Wakefield Cadman.

All three composers shared a distinctly populist view of art music. They favored a larger share of the art music establishment, which was heavily dominated by performances of European composers, for American music. In addition, they favored more recognition for regional American composers, in opposition to the cultural hegemony over American music held by New York City. They wished to write serious music that would appeal to a wide audience. A statement by Arthur Farwell, who had been a source of inspiration for all three, reflects the underlying principle for their concerted activities: "To create an American musical life means to liberate and educate popular and social opinion until every community is as ready to give support to an American as to a European product or enterprise of equal or similar worth."[1]

Grunn taught piano in his own studio and, after 1935, at Chapman College, where Moore probably saw him frequently.[2] Like Cadman, he had become very interested in the music of American Indians. He frequently used Indian themes in his music, as both Cadman and Moore had done at one time. Cadman remains the best known of the three, as he was then. His song "At Dawning" had been a big commercial success as early as 1905; from that time he supported himself through the sales of his music and lecture-recital tours rather than teaching. His Indianist opera, *Shanewis, or The Robin Woman,* was produced at the Met in 1918 and revived the following year. Cadman had lived in southern California for at least a decade before Moore arrived there. He enjoyed enormous popularity in Los Angeles from the first. Though he lived in San Diego some of the time and was often away on tour, his popularity and prestige were very useful, as were his frequent writings in behalf of American music.[3]

A Cadman Creative Club with national aspirations was organized in Los Angeles just before Moore's arrival in 1926, with Cadman as honorary national president and Grunn among its charter members. It offered several national competitions; in 1929 Moore won a first prize for her 1915 song "My Dream" and a second for her more recent piano work "Murmur of Pines." By 1931 the club had dropped its national goals and reorganized as the Creative Arts Club, with organist Dudley Warner Fitch as president and Grunn as program chairman. Its new purpose was to support any opera or other original work by a local composer.

Mr. Grunn believes that such composers as Charles Wakefield Cadman and Mary Carr Moore, now of international reputation, and other artists should be given proper recognition and support, through an organized body, in presenting their works. He calls attention to the fact, obvious to most of us, that the composer coming here from the East almost always received far greater recognition than the artist who is local and perhaps in reality a more important one.[4]

The Cadman Creative Club offered a program of Moore's music in 1929, including *Saul* and excerpts from *David Rizzio.* In 1930, there was a program of *Narcissa* extracts. By 1935 Grunn was still program chairman, emphasizing both the American and the nonmodernist character of the club's offerings: "According to Homer Grunn

. . . there is still a wide difference between compositions by old and modern composers so far as public interest is concerned. Therefore, on Wed. . . . members and guests will have an opportunity to hear a program having an air of responsible musicianship."[5] Moore was the "responsible" composer in this case.

Mrs. Lulu Sanford Tefft, a friend of Moore's and an admirer of her music, was "Chairman of Musical Americanization" in the Cadman Creative Club. It was she who traveled to Chicago and New York in behalf of their cause in 1930 and who called the attention of Eleanor Everest Freer's American Opera Society to *Narcissa,* thus garnering a belated David Bispham Medal for Moore and presenting it to her at a dinner in Los Angeles.[6] It was she who had taken on the Met in the *New York Times* over the old but still lively issue of opera in English.[7] And it was she who joined the public criticism of Toscanini when he took the New York Philharmonic on a tour of Europe without performing a single work by an American composer. Several of her articles published at about that time express an "American point of view" whose strong political and nativist overtones reflect Moore's views and those of her associates.

Tefft championed American opera not only because it could teach proper American values ("In the advent of historical American opera—New England, Spanish, Indian motifs, etc.—national educational interests would become dominant and constructive . . . a just pride in the Homeland. . . ."), but also because it could insulate us from insidious foreign ones ("lest insidious influences creep in and gnaw at the foundations of all the institutions we have so laboriously built up"). She preached a patriotic distrust of the foreign musicians who dominated American art music, particularly opera: "There are works available that could and should be used. . . . They need careful handling, however, by directors that unquestionably grasp the American point of view. . . . Such a task takes deep loyalty and cannot be intrusted to an alien."[8] There was still hope for American music, for: "thank God, they have not as yet wholly robbed us of our birthright of individual national expression." Mrs. Tefft's "vast storehouse of native material" available for American composers included an indirect reference to *Narcissa:* "the intriguing trek of Marcus Whitman, the missionary to the Indians, who withal proved himself a loyal statesman in quest of Empire."[9] It almost goes without saying that Tefft's value system for music included avoiding "the bad characteristics of the so-called modern school," as Cadman and the other resident composers were thought to do.[10]

Nothing written by Moore herself attaches such heavy political freight to the cause of American music. But she and many other composers in Los Angeles, and in other parts of the country, seem to have gone along with Tefft's ideas. These values were scarcely new to Moore, for Sarah had fretted over the evils of "foreignization" many decades earlier, expressing similar ideas and even advocating, in *Billy To-Morrow in Camp*, a dramatization of *Narcissa* as a way to teach American values. It should be pointed out with respect to what follows that the term "native" in connection with American music was and is used in a neutral way by musicians having diverse political points of view. In this context, it implies neither the music of American Indians nor the literal exclusion of foreign-born musicians from the country.

Tefft's Society for the Advancement of American Music (SAAM), organized in 1930, included local composers Louis Woodson Curtis and Guy Bevier Williams on its board of directors, along with Moore's friend and supporter Mildred Sanger House. A bulletin, "American Music Notes," dated November, 1934, announces that dues were abandoned because of the Depression. It asks members to sign and return: "THE PLEDGE. I, a native born American, desire the Advancement of American Music, and shall lend my support to furthering its best interests." It announces Eleanor Everest Freer as an honorary member, carries an appeal for orders from Daniel Gregory Mason's New York–based Society for the Publication of American Music, and lists recent doings of Los Angeles composers Frances Marion Ralston, Fannie Dillon, Ann Priscilla Risher, Mrs. M. Hennion Robinson, Moore, Cadman, Curtis, and Williams.[11] A two-piano performance of Moore's piano concerto and *Beyond These Hills* made up one of its concerts in 1935; there were other concerts at least as late as January, 1937. At least nineteen composers had works performed on SAAM concerts.[12] Nine of these nineteen composers were female, a feature that might not have been explicit in Mrs. Tefft's rhetoric but which reflects a certain sexual egalitarianism in her organization, as well as its identity as a music club rather than a professional society.[13]

With the organization of the Federal Music Project in early 1936, a new opportunity presented itself for the resident composers in Los Angeles, especially those who had written orchestral music. The new

FMP orchestras would very likely be more receptive to American music and new music than the Philharmonic was. But there was no guarantee that they would play the residents' music. Los Angeles composers would have to compete with both the European-dominated art music establishment and the New York establishment. It was time for the older, more conservative resident composers who had supplied programs and support for groups like the Creative Arts Club and SAAM to move away from the old club orientation if they were to secure performances for their orchestral music. A composers' organization able to make professional and independent musical judgments was needed. Moore, Cadman, and Grunn talked about the need to organize as they sat with local critic-composer Richard Drake Saunders at the annual Los Angeles Music Teachers' Association dinner in late June, 1936. Saunders quickly publicized the project, advising those interested to contact its new secretary-treasurer, none other than Mary Carr Moore. Moore herself provided a succinct account of the new California Society of Composers' genesis in her monthly column for *Music and Musicians.*

A new group is being formed, composed of American composers of Southern California, who have written works in the more serious forms; orchestral scores, operas, chamber music, etc. It is hoped that the combined efforts of this group will eventually succeed in gaining the attention of Symphony and Opera conductors, most of whom are foreigners and cannot know of the material available, unless it is brought to their attention. That the general attitude on the part of the thoughtless to the effect that America has achieved nothing of moment in the larger forms is undoubtedly due to lack of information, and possibly of interest on the part of European conductors. Until the country as a whole is willing to accord the same interest to its own composers to the extent of insisting on well-rehearsed performances and enough repetitions to familiarize the hearers with the musical content, the American composer is in danger of smotheration. How many listeners were sympathetic to the works of many, now considered great, at first hearing? History tells the story.[14]

Saunders expanded in his article on Moore's reference to the possible self-interest of European conductors.

The real fact is that European trained artists have long held a virtual monopoly, which they are desperately afraid of losing. If the American public takes to American works, it will obviously soon progress to taking up American performers, and the third-rate Europeans who have long flooded this country will find their jobs non-existent.

But in the last year a new factor has been injected into the equation, the WPA music projects. There are now symphonic orchestras available, and moreover symphony orchestras which have no prejudice against American music, but which are willing to lend a helpful hand.[15]

By October, the group had refined its leadership. Moore eased herself out of the onerous duties of secretary-treasurer and joined several others on an advisory board. Very soon the organization claimed a membership of twenty-five, though no list of names survives.

In addition to encouraging more FMP performances of their orchestral music, the membership settled on the format of an annual festival of American music. Two such festivals were held, in the spring of 1937 and 1938, each consisting of three or four concerts. At least one FMP orchestra concert was a part of each festival. Mrs. Frankel made the Friday Morning Club's building available for the chamber music concerts, and even rounded up the Boris Morros Quartet, bringing Moore her much-prized performance of the F Minor Quartet, and later of the quintet version of the piano concerto. The critics were receptive, giving the concerts plenty of friendly coverage. In all, music by some twenty-seven composers, nearly all of them Los Angeles residents, was performed at the two festivals.[16] Their success seems to have prompted a spate of other festivals and chamber music series in Los Angeles, of which Peter Yates's "Evenings on the Roof" is the most famous.[17]

At least three of the composers who had become members were foreign-born, including Vernon Leftwich, George Liebling, and Adolf Tandler. All three were naturalized citizens who had been longtime fixtures on the Los Angeles musical scene; none was a member of the new group of émigrés who were fugitives from Hitler.[18] Leftwich was a write-in candidate for president of the organization when elections were held after the 1938 festival. His election precipitated an ugly dispute over the organization's membership requirements. The issue was apparently simple, but it had no easy answer: Who is an American composer? The initial organizers were native-born and not ultra-moderns. They wished to break the domination of the art music establishment by the foreign-born; they also wished to get performances of music by American composers who were not ultra-moderns. They seemed to feel that if they allowed more foreign-born composers to become members, something that the English-born Leftwich's election seemed to presage, their own interests would be swamped in a sea of international-oriented ultra-modernism.

Their solution was to dissolve the successful California Society of Composers, then reorganize with a specific membership requirement similar to SAAM's earlier pledge of "native born composer." Frank Colby described their dilemma in the *Pacific Coast Musician.*

The Society was organized with the tacit understanding that its purpose was to advance the interests of American-born composers; consequently, it was assumed that foreign-born musicians were not eligible to membership. However, a number of naturalized citizens were early accepted into the Society without protest. Subsequent members, though native Americans, joined the organization unaware of any membership restrictions based on place of birth.[19]

Seventeen of the original twenty-seven, something over 60 percent, elected to remain with the newly organized Society of Native American Composers (SNAC), Moore among them. To replace the members lost in the battle, they recruited both locally and nationally. In addition, they loosened their requirement that members have composed in the larger forms. One result was that a larger proportion, nearly a quarter, of the new group's membership was female. A membership list compiled in 1943 or 1944 includes the names of sixty-three composers. Almost a third were national figures, including Amy Beach, Howard Hanson, Charles Ives, and Carl Ruggles.

Though there was a net gain in membership after their reorganization, the conflict precipitated a public controversy that cost the new SNAC goodwill among local critics. Saunders, one of the California Society of Composers' original four, defended the new group. He drew an analogy with the Russian Five, who had championed a national music in nineteenth-century czarist Russia.

Such an organization, definitely nationalistic in its formation and intention, will necessarily be the topic of much discussion and probably much dissension in musical circles. Some will hold such a group to be narrow, because of its expressed limitations. Others will declare it a necessary stimulant to musical progress in this country. As a matter of fact, it is both, and the two are not incongruous. . . .

The musical rise of every country is directly traceable to the efforts of a nationalistic group. As long as music is purely an imported article, the public as a whole will take comparatively little interest in it. The germination, the motivation, and to a certain extent the treatment of a musical subject must reflect a distinctively nationalistic psychology if it is to be more than a mere elongation of some other national school.[20]

The native American criterion for membership was, however, challenged by another critic.

I take it that emphasis is laid by the sponsoring society on the fact that composers are native to these shores. I am wondering whether the spirit of true Americanism as distilled in the ink of official signatures necessarily differs when used in the bureau of vital statistics from that of the immigration office.

Sometimes I wonder, too, whether the real nationality of music does not come with the emotional perception and expressional objective of the composer, rather than with the mere facts of locality of birth.

. . . Had the music performed particular flavor which one could easily recognize as American? . . . I have not been able to discover the "American" quality.[21]

As was her way, Moore was more tactful than some SNAC supporters, but there is no doubt where she stood. She attended all of SNAC's organizational meetings, holding some in her own home. She probably helped write the new bylaws, and she continued to defend them amid the continuing controversy: "July 9, 1941. Annual meeting NAC. Same discussion re admitting foreign-born members. A pity that Dr. Leach and Dr. Olds (first attendance) had to hear so much arguing! Clifford Vaughan quite determined to open membership; Arthur Lange too, of course. *Why,* another Society? There are quite enough of those. If we preserve the American tradition, we *must* go forward on the *Native* basis." As late as 1944, she gave her position in a radio interview.

Moore: We felt that we had fulfilled our purpose as a State Society and that it was time to branch out and assist other composers of other sections in our country. . . .

Our goal is still a timely American creative expression, different totally in its essence to anything the old world has yet offered. Personally I am a great believer in the wisdom and the responsibility of every national group, not only in preserving the folk songs of its country, but also, in recognizing its national characteristics. America is composed of such a wide heritage, from so many national backgrounds, that it is difficult to segregate that which is ourselves, and that which has been implanted. . . .

Reynolds: Then it is a difficult matter to develop a strictly American idiom?

Moore: Indeed it is. But I believe that we shall.[22]

Controversy or not, SNAC was a going concern for several years, until the onset of the war curtailed music-making in Los Angeles. A festival was staged in June, 1939, even though bureaucratic battles within the WPA almost disrupted the FMP orchestra's contributions to it. In two seasons between fall 1939 and spring 1941, SNAC sponsored nineteen concerts and workshops in which it presented music by some forty composers. In addition, James Sample proved to be a friend when he took over the FMP orchestra. Moore and two or three other SNAC members regularly served on the advisory committee that helped Sample screen new scores as they were submitted for performance.

SNAC's biggest success was in becoming the formal sponsor of the FMP orchestra's entire 1940–41 season. The program cover for each of its sixteen Embassy Auditorium concerts bore the rubric, "The Society of Native American Composers presents the Southern California Symphony." In that season, works by forty-six Americans, including several Latin Americans and many émigrés, were performed. Only nine of the forty-six were members of SNAC; the rest ran the gamut from Lionel Barrymore and Samuel Barber through Erich Korngold and Vernon Leftwich to Eugene Zador.[23] The New York–based journal *Modern Music* took negative notice: "The WPA Symphony runs a series in connection with an organization called 'The Society of Native American Composers.' Until now the output has been very depressing, the usual program featuring items like the *Symphony* by Charles Wakefield Cadman about which the less said the better."[24]

Arthur Lange succeeded Frank Colby as president of SNAC in 1940. Lange had recently left the film colony to start a small recording company featuring music by American composers (including émigrés and modernists). His monthly newsletter, *Co-Art Turntable*, became an advocate for SNAC and for American music in general.[25] Though Lange had wanted to admit the foreign-born to SNAC, his newsletter reflects many of the same conservative political views that Lulu Sanford Tefft had expressed a decade earlier. For instance, his editor "Henri Lloyd Clement" (the pen name used by Ethel Dofflemyer), a close friend of Moore's, fretted over the many performances of Shostakovich's Seventh Symphony in the United States during 1941–42, seeing in them the bugbear of Communist propaganda: "it announced itself the 'Gettysburg Speech' of Russia, written in music, for it definitely conveyed the birth and development of Russian Communism. . . . Make no mistake—*this is a work written for a definite purpose.*"[26] Moore, however, responded to Shostakovich's Fifth Symphony on strictly musical grounds in a private comment: "Feb. 19, 1943. . . . went to Symphony—Shostakovich 5th. Now I begin to see why he is considered great; this, while thin at first, and faltering, rises to great heights!"

Moore was involved in SNAC's last burst of controversy, this one transcontinental. Adolph Weiss succeeded Lange as president in 1942.[27] He persuaded his friend Charles Ives to become honorary national president; Ives responded with a contribution in cash and a column for SNAC's new newsletter.[28] But presently he had second thoughts about his association with SNAC: "Recently a report of some serious criticism of the Society has reached me—it is, that this Society is against all Jews, and also pro-Fascist. I cannot believe that this is true— but, if it is, accept my resignation immediately."[29] Ives was probably more concerned with Weiss's personal views than with SNAC's actual history or policies, but his letter gave Moore one more chance to express herself on the subject.

Mr. Cadman, Mr. Grunn and myself agreed (in 1936) as to the desirability of perpetuating, as a distinct idea, the music of Americans, of at least one generation; but, in reality, the spirit of those, who, having lived a lifetime, in our own United States, and having inherited the feeling of our progenitors for this great "Land of Freedom" where one may expand, and breathe, and follow his own bent so far as his capabilities will allow; and who, as such, has an individual feeling for his Native Land, such as is expressed by all Patriots, of all Lands, in their own idiom.

This was in 1936; there was no thought of antagonism to the music of other countries; we have all been brought up on it, and are imbued with the spirit of the classics, and through the centuries, down to the modern expression.

At the present time, there is no possibility of any claim that we are opposed to the music of any other Nationalities; we all know it, perform it, and enjoy the discovery of works, heretofore unknown to us, by composers of any country. We are also friendly with the composers of foreign extraction who have come to us, having been forced to flee their own countries. We have, as a city, and as a Nation, extended toward them, hospitality, and welcome.

It is therefore, not reciprocal on their part, to complain if we desire, also, to preserve our own traditions, in our own land, in our own way. That is the privilege of any country, in regard to its own art and music.[30]

A final meeting in June, 1944, attempted to revive the organization and select a new slate of officers. Moore, who acted as secretary, typed up a page of notes recording a lot of discussion but no real inclination to give SNAC a fresh impetus. There were no further concerts and no more meetings, though Clement sent out a letter later that year on SNAC letterhead, aimed at promoting the upcoming revival of *Narcissa*. In the end, SNAC died not so much because of the continuing controversy around it as because of the aging of its champions. Homer Grunn was gravely ill; Cadman's health was no longer strong; Frank Colby and some others were already dead. Moore had recently lost a son to the war and was in her seventies. The passage of time had taken the fight out of those who cared enough about the music of those "Americans, of at least one generation" to take on an agenda such as that of the California Society of Composers or SNAC.

If they had not come close to achieving the goals they had set for themselves, at least both organizations helped Moore get more performances than she otherwise might have had.[31] They brought her as close as she ever came to major recognition as a composer. But her advocacy of SNAC's membership policy and goals probably led some of the then-young American modernists to characterize her as "not very tolerant."[32] Her actions are regrettable, for the accident of one's birthplace would seem to be an arbitrary criterion indeed for membership in a composers' organization. Yet Moore's position had some justification, for she saw her choices concerning the politics of music as polarized into two alternatives, neither of them entirely satisfactory.

On one hand, an international approach was associated with ultra-modernism, implying continued European domination of the art music establishment as well as leftist political overtones. Moore was uncomfortable with both of these implications. On the other hand, she had long championed the American music movement, and with the passage of time she had clearly become a traditionalist in music. Her politics were staunchly Republican. If the alternatives were reduced to two and formulated in an even more simplistic way as émigrés-modernism-communism vs. Americanism-traditionalism-fascism, she was clearly more comfortable with the second. Still, neither side dealt with the basic prejudice she faced—namely, sex discrimination. The fact that the internationalists demonstrated so little interest in or sympathy toward woman composers strengthened her commitment to the native American cause.

Many people saw a need for SNAC and supported it, regardless of the conflict. After all, American composers, especially those not based in New York City, did need help in getting their works heard. European composers and musicians did dominate the art music establishment to the virtual exclusion of others. As James Sample, who cooperated with SNAC, said, "What's the fuss? Of course we should have played more American music." The only way Moore could find to fight for her own music was to fight as unequivocally as she could for American music. Given the circumstances, it is hard to imagine that she could have acted otherwise.

CHAPTER 20

The Cost of Empire

Moore's life had changed, as Los Angeles' musical life had, in the decade of the Great Depression. In 1930 she had just finished the orchestral score to *David Rizzio* and was planning on a production in Venice. She already had begun working on her next opera, *Legende Provençale*, still tentatively called "Macabre." She was confident enough to turn away from this promising new work temporarily to write a short orchestra piece and a string quartet, as well as some new and interesting songs. She wrote of her plans to set a second Italian libretto from Emanuel Browne, of her interest in setting *Atlantis*, and of her expectation of returning to American subjects in further opera projects.[1] She believed for a while that a Los Angeles production of *Narcissa* was imminent; belatedly, she received the David Bispham Medal for this grand opera on an American subject. She was also working intensively at her two teaching positions, whose classes were steadily growing; preparing numerous club performances of her music; and nurturing her new manuscript club. Her horizons were widening almost on a daily basis. In her late fifties, she was at the height of her career and her creative powers.

A decade later, she seemed the same indefatigable worker. She had made the best of the situation when she could not afford to retire at sixty-five, two years earlier. Only a quotation copied into her datebook acknowledged the moment: "October 11, 1938. 'They all worked until they died; that, after all is the final test of the degree of interest in one's work.' Hertzler, in 'Horse and Buggy Doctor.' "[2] She met as many students as ever, and to them, she was still "full of pep" and "at her best when she was the life of the party." But the emphasis of her activity had changed. By 1940 she was composing much less, only three short new pieces in that year. She gave considerable time to arranging, copying, and orchestrating older works. She completed the orchestration of *Kidnap*, which had a reading in a rehearsal of the FMP orchestra, and started orchestrating *Beyond These Hills*, which dated back to 1923. She copied out a shortened version, now lost, of *Legende Provençale*, probably for a contest, and arranged her string trio of four years earlier for string orchestra. There were performances, large and small, including the piano concerto and a December reading of *Saul*, which brought forth from her the comment, "How *many* times it has been done, since Lillian! 1916."[3] There were three club performances of *Narcissa* extracts that year, but still no production in Los Angeles of the opera that was her prime contribution to American music.

Organizational activities took far more of her time. Both the Federal Music Project and the Society of Native American Composers were at the peak of their activities. Having finally been elected to membership in ASCAP in 1940, she found herself, too late in some cases, keeping track of the copyrights on her earlier published music. She traveled to New York City to talk with her various publishers and meet Edward Hipsher, who was compiling a new edition of his book on American opera.[4] She was amused to see herself regarded as a historical figure when, in November, she was invited to speak at a local high school: "November 8, 1940. Talk to Music History Classes, about me!!??" Later, she would spend some time on a memoir, "My Little Story," probably based on Sarah's old notes as well as her own recollections. Her major contributions as a composer were, by 1940, complete; it remained for her to garner the recognition on the local level that had by now irrevocably escaped her on a larger scale.

As the country was drawn into the Second World War, Moore's teaching activities slowed down. Olga Steeb died at the end of 1941, and enrollment at the Steeb School soon dropped sharply. Olga's death was a personal blow as well. Six months later, Chapman College, whose enrollment had also fallen, closed its doors for the duration, sending its few remaining students to Whittier College outside Los Angeles. Moore continued to teach some Chapman students in her home for a year or two, in addition to private students, but her load was sharply reduced during the war years. She saw off many students and friends, including Arthur Carr and Albert Harris, who had entered the military. The war affected some students in other ways: "June 22, 1942. Shizuko Koda should have also been here, poor child! At a Concentration Camp, at Santa Anita." There were changes in her family as well. Byron, too old for a commission, was ferrying bombers to Australia as a civilian pilot. Wesley left his practice and his family in rural Quincy, California, to become a flight surgeon and was sent to the South Pacific. Marian remarried; the new couple lived with Moore in the big Leeward Avenue house for some time before they could find a place of their own.

A sprinkling of datebook entries as the war approached gives an idea of her activities and enthusiasms. She still liked to be the life of the party, in this case when the Manuscript Club meeting fell on the eve of April Fool's Day.

March 31, 1941. Arthur Carr, Polly Pruter, Morris Browda and I gave a "surprise performance." Beginning with me, as Mme. Adelina Patti in an amazing rig ("*positively final* farewell performance") singing "Last Rose of Summer." Arthur and Morris, in scene from last act of "Love of Four Onions" (Browda); then Polly, in "Fraulein Schmorgasbord" singing two songs of Arthur's; and finale-ensemble: Polly, musical glasses; me, crybaby and egg beater; Morris, "Sweet Patootie;" Arthur, piano—"arms, nose & feet."

There were some memorable performances of her own music: "Jan. 9, 1941. I was almost afraid to hear this work [the string trio-suite for string orchestra] for the first time! But I really like it. Mr. Pollak [the conductor] says it is 'very beautiful, but very difficult.'" The trio had taken five years and a new arrangement to find a performance; a hearing for one short extract from *Legende Provençale* had taken even longer: "April 6, 1941. Laura Saunders sang the 'Air of Rozanne' just beautifully, and the orchestration just as I wanted it! Started in 1929, this is the first time I have heard *any* of my orchestral score; of course, I could not, since I haven't yet extracted the parts." *Saul* continued to be popular in club performances. For the fifteenth anniversary of the Manuscript Club, in 1943, it was performed in an orchestral version. The Glendale Symphony was conducted by William Ulrich.

April 5, 1943. My first hearing of my orch. score, "Saul," was intensely interesting (of course) to me. It seemed to hold the audience, although poem and music lasted 40 minutes. My heart beat so fast I almost suffocated! Laura [Sweeney Moore] *gave* a perfect reading of the poem, and every word was heard; beside which, she looked *lovely!* It was an evening to be remembered. I *like* my orchestration, which Dr. Ulrich pronouned "masterly;" it pleases me, and I am rewarded for many long hours of work.

Moore composed *Brief Furlough,* a quintet, in recognition of the wartime activities of her sons. In January, 1944, she wrote to Wesley about a performance of it.

Next week, I shall have the unique experience of conducting an orchestra, made up of some of the finest players in town, for the Hollywood canteen, in my first performance of "Brief Furlough" which I have improved, and scored for full orchestra; and instead of ending as I did before, on some long chords, I have added the main theme of "Home-Longing"—all "pepped up" into a brisk marchtime, and the bugle "Call to Arms" with the assumption in music, that they are going in, double-quick, to win! I am anxious to hear it in this form. It was so inadequately done, when you heard it, as the clarinetist, who was unable to come at the last moment, was replaced by an unrehearsed player, who really did well to keep his place at all; let alone to supply the "pep" and color, I had allotted to that part. I was grateful to the clarinetist, for even coming at all; and I am sure he would have been all right, with an adequate rehearsal.[5]

Three months later, Marian brought her the news of Wesley's death in New Guinea. Wesley, her younger son, left a family of his own in Quincy.[6] It was terribly difficult to accept his death.

April 13 and 14, 1944. Strange, this dream: all these days and nights I've been trying to "contact" Wesley, or *dream* about him. I cannot get in touch with him, or feel any reality about his going on, we were so close. Now this *vivid* dream of Byron, and his voice in my ears. . . . As I sat at my desk, thinking, I had a momentary glimpse of Wesley, thin and disheveled, face looked bruised and he was standing in tall growth of *something;* just for a moment!

A few months later, she rewrote a song from 1917, "My Wonderful Boy," and called it "My Son." She tried going to church regularly for the first time in many years.

Painfully, life went on. She sent scores off to competitions: *The Flaming Arrow* to the Met and *Kidnap* to an unnamed contest. Dolly and Mary Pasmore, who had been infants when she had studied voice with their father, visited her during the annual visit of the San Francisco Opera. Clarence Mader directed her new choral piece, "There is No Death," on an evening concert at his Immanuel Presbyterian Church. Whatever the Federal Music Project had done for her music and that of other Americans, she had never resigned herself to Franklin D. Roosevelt's presidency: "Nov. 7, 1944. Alas! Roosevelt, 4th term! Dewey is so fine, courageous, young, and *suitable*. How can it be? Too many 'teamsters'."

The flurry of readings from *Narcissa* in 1940 suggests that Moore was once again working for the elusive Los Angeles production of her first big opera.[7] The coming of the war forced a postponement of her aspirations for a time. Still, the opera's themes of duty, personal sacrifice, and patriotism were more timely than ever. A private reading in the summer of 1943 sparked her hopes: "July 19, 1943. Such a *fine* reading of *Narcissa*! . . . Rev. Evans seemed most impressed & interested. I think plans are going forward for something very nice." But it was not until March, 1944, that a *"Narcissa* Committee" was assembled from leaders of educational, civic, religious, musical, and social groups. Mrs. Irish was chairman, a very positive sign. She was joined by Bessie Bartlett Frankel and Louis Woodson Curtis, both longtime friends.[8] Only in October, seven months after they organized, did Mrs. Irish feel sure enough of her organizational success to telephone Moore with the advice, "go ahead and raise [your] chorus."

The budget agreed upon by Moore, Irish, Frankel, and the rest was minimal, even though it was in the neighborhood of seventy-eight hundred dollars. The production would be an ad hoc affair. The two performances would take place in Philharmonic Auditorium. There would be a chorus of church choir members, friends, and former students. Local singers, inexperienced in opera, would take the principal roles; an understaffed pickup orchestra of twenty-six would have only two rehearsals, meaning only one with the principals and chorus onstage. Moore would be the conductor, as she had been for the two earlier productions. She had already begun making masters for the chorus parts since Witmark, her publisher, could no longer supply printed copies of the vocal score.[9] An advantage of this was that she could return to the opera's original title, *The Cost of Empire*. Adrian Awan, the producer, announced that the staging would be kept simple: "with wartime limitations on what we may do in the matter of stage settings we shall try through natural means . . . live trees and rich lighting effects to do justice to the sheer inherent beauty and the richness of entertainment value."[10] The costumes from the San Francisco production, now twenty years old, were still available and were pressed into service.

At seventy-one, Moore now became the first woman to conduct an opera in a major Los Angeles concert hall, though she was leading her fifteenth and sixteenth performances of this opera. The production was well received, as her operas had always been. A former student, then in his twenties, now remembers Moore's performance as a conductor better than he does the music: "This dear old lady conducted it from the pit. She did such a very, very good job. It was a tremendous endeavor on her part. Afterwards the orchestra stood up and cheered."[11] A grandson was surprised at seeing his normally sweet-tempered grandmother "screaming at the tenor" when he ventured backstage during an intermission.[12]

More formal, contemporary critical reaction was kind, as it had been toward the two earlier productions. It took note of the production's shortcomings, however: "The performances were conducted by the composer . . . who indicated more concern for detail than for the overall picture. This, and the understandable inexperience of many in the cast made for a rather slowpaced production. Cost of Empire really is a fine work and deserves a place among serious American operas."[13] "With an earnest but inexperienced cast and limited rehearsal time Dr. Moore chose to keep the performance on an even keel rather than to indulge in musical histrionics."[14] "Lack of rhythmic strength and contrast last night may have been due to performance rather than to inherent deficiencies in the score."[15] Pleased as she must have been with the audience's response and the critical reception, she must have prized most of all a letter sent her by Clarence Gustlin, who was a prominent Los Angeles pianist, teacher, and music patron.

Your excellent opera, "The Cost of Empire" . . . I regret very much . . . was not in my repertoire some years ago when I was touring the States, under auspices of the National Federation of Music Clubs, in a special effort to acquaint the public with the subject of American Opera. I recall making repeated references to your work, however, under its former title, *Narcissa*.

I can say, without hesitancy, that your work deserves a very high place among American compositions in this form. In fact, I have neither examined nor heard any other which I would consider its superior. . . . I heartily share Mrs. Francis Payne's contention that this work deserves annual featuring, possibly in one of the city's open air theatres.[16]

The few hours of glory in the theater were followed inexorably by the reckoning of the deficit. A month after the performances, the "*Narcissa* Committee" met to deal with finances. According to Adrian Awan's accounting, there was a final deficit of $505.37. Moore tells of the meeting:

April 23, 1945. Worried all morning about this meeting! Met Mrs. Irish at 3, took check for $50.00 to help on her Awan's bill (just a drop in the bucket!)

I handed it to Mrs. Irish; she refused it. Then I gave it to Adrian; he refused it and Mrs. Irish tore it up. Neither of them would allow me to use my money. I was so touched that, like a silly idiot, I wept! Adrian is a rare person, and there is *no* one, just like Florence![17]

Mrs. Irish, Mrs. Frankel, and the others, who had among them worked so hard to establish the big-time art music institutions of Los Angeles, the Philharmonic and the Bowl, must have been thoroughly pleased to have achieved this production for their friend of many years, even though they had never succeeded in getting her the recognition of a Bowl performance. As for the composer, she was certainly ready to celebrate the happy outcome when the cast party began later that evening: "April 23, 1945. . . . Lovely party tonight . . . I took Mrs. Carter and slipped over home and attired myself a la 'Mme. Patti' and went back again. They all went into gales of laughter when I sang the 'Last Rose of Summer!' Lots of fun being a 'blooming idiot.' 'Oh, what a day!'"

Two years later Whitman College, in Walla Walla, Washington, approached Moore about the possibility of producing *Narcissa* on the centennial of the massacre in November, 1947. She liked the idea: "It has always been my deep desire to have this opera performed at Whitman College, or in the vicinity of the Whitman Mission, where I was taken to view the terrain and surrounding landscape, in order to obtain a true picture of the locale."[18] She spent the summer of 1947 recopying the final three acts of the conductor's score, which had by now become too faded to read easily. But the college's people did not seriously look at the score until October, making it far too late to prepare a production. She was disappointed but not entirely surprised by this turn of events: "until the work has been fully appraised, it is natural to assume that any opera composed by a woman would be of sufficiently simple calibre for amateur performance."[19] Moore's faith in her first and largest opera remained unshaken: "I am convinced, not only by the profound impression the opera has always made, not only upon audiences, but upon critics (who as a rule do not take kindly to female American composers), that the work being based upon such a noble theme, and with the approval of so many notable critics, will keep its place long after I am gone; and that is (or should be) reward enough."[20]

CHAPTER 21

The End

The war in Europe ended about a month after the *Narcissa* production, and Chapman College announced its plans to reopen in the fall. At seventy-two Moore returned to the faculty, the only member to return after the four-year closure except for the college's president, George Reeves. Her routine of club performances continued. Charlie Cadman, Radie Britain, Grace Shattuck Bail, and Charles Ferry were among the Schubert Club audience that heard her "Poème" for piano, violin, and cello in January. The Manuscript Club celebrated its eighteenth anniversary with a concert of her music in the Chapman Auditorium.

> Mar. 1, 1946. This concert was probably the most *entirely* satisfying to me, in many years. Every number was *beautifully* performed. There was no "last minute change," the audience was responsive, in all, I was completely, and satisfyingly in enjoyment of my own work!! Felt as tho' I hadn't composed it, and was hearing it for the first time! So *wonderful* to have such fine artists to interpret my work!
> Concerto in F minor, Ethel Leginska, Viana Bey.
> June Howard & "Co.," "Poème."
> "Beyond These Hills." Dorothy Robinson, Mary Pauloo, Inez Halloran, Lee Telle, Leonard Morganthaler.[1]

Her student and Cadman's protégé, Edward Earle, had his tone poem, "Misbehaving Clocks," performed by the Pasadena Civic Orchestra.[2]

In spring 1947 she retired from Chapman. Former students flocked to the commencement luncheon to honor her. Near the end of the exercises she was surprised to be summoned to the platform and presented with the college's Distinguished Service Award, "in sincere gratitude for the blessing and influence of a gracious Christian personality; in honest recognition of a great musician; in humble thanks for a true and loyal friend." "June 8, 1946. No one can know how deeply I prize it," she wrote.

The deaths of more friends are recorded. Carrie Jacobs Bond was one. Her cousin Ellen Beach Yaw, who had actually had the career as a coloratura that had once been planned for Moore herself, was another. Homer Grunn and Frank Colby had already died. Claude, whom she hadn't seen since the Christmas celebration arranged by the children in 1928, died. It had been a half-century since she had met him in tiny Lemoore. Her idealized view of marrige had never changed in spite of everything. The most upsetting of all was the loss of Charlie Cadman, her friend and ally through all her Los Angeles days, in December, 1946. Her datebook shows that almost ten months later she was still upset, apparently trying to sort out details of his personal relationships.[3]

She didn't always feel very well herself. Respiratory infections plagued her in the fall and winter. She was bothered by crowds at times: "Mar. 16, 1947. Went to church—almost fainted—guess I'd better not try it again." In September she tried to attend a family reunion but could not find it. She drove around for nearly three hours before giving up and going home. But still she met students and attended concerts and club meetings, often hearing her own music. She supplied an article, "Keep your Tools Sharp," for the new *Music and Dance* volume, edited this time by her old friend Richard Drake Saunders.[4] In April, 1948, a staged production of *David Rizzio*, using two pianos instead of orchestra, filled the Biltmore Theatre. In May, when Leonard Morganthaler sang "Mysterious Power" on radio station KFI with James Sample's orchestra, she was announced as "California's beloved composer." A week or two later, she took "about a 'ton' of music" to the UCLA Music Library as a gift.[5]

If she was slowing down, it was not obvious to everyone. USC's Pauline Alderman, who first saw Moore at the 1945 performance of *Narcissa* and got acquainted with her after the 1948 production of *Rizzio* at the Biltmore Theatre, marveled at both her appearance and her achicvement: "How in the world the woman ever had the stamina and the courage to do all those operas, I mean, just to compose them! . . . And she was so debonair and lively, as though she had nothing else to do. . . . Yes, I can see her in my mind's eye, just the way she looked—very, very attractive, very petite, very tiny, full of motion, of course, very, very vital."[6]

The big Leeward Avenue house was now too large for Moore, who lived there alone with two spaniels, Daisy and Whizzer. In 1949 she moved into an apartment in a new house in one of the large new subdivisions; Marian and Cy lived in the main part of the house. She discovered the loss of the full score to *Legende Provençale* in the course of the move and set about making a new piano vocal score even while she was still searching for the lost one. She had broken her right wrist the year before, and her heretofore steady hand and clear, legible music notation were now shaky. Still, she worked at this, her last major project, as fast as she could, just as she had done during that summer of 1935 in Topanga Canyon when she originally completed the piano-vocal score. After completing the *Legende* reconstruction, she occupied herself with making new master sheets for many of her older songs, though there were always a few new ones, such as "Welcome to Donald" on the birth of her first great-grandson and a setting of Psalm 25 for Luther Hoobyar, her first "David Rizzio." She continued to go out to concerts and meetings, though it became increasingly difficult. One evening she gave the cab driver the wrong address and had to call a second cab: "Sept. 30, 1951. I *must not* go out alone again!! I get so confused. Went to two homes—wrong addresses! Both, so kind and helpful. But it *might* have been otherwise."

The record of the datebooks ends in 1952, but her routine continued for two more years. She still had students, among them Jane Church Porter, who had some of her work performed by the San Francisco Symphony before abandoning music in favor of painting.[7] But a series of small strokes was progressively robbing Moore of her memory.

Her musical following had ceased to grow by the time of the last revival of *Narcissa* in 1945. As it now shrank, she must have pondered her continuing obscurity. Moore paid a heavy price for remaining on the West Coast and for failing to make and cultivate Eastern and European connections diligently over the years, as Fannie Dillon, for one, had done.[8] Her failure to study or visit abroad cost her the lasting professional connections with the foreign-born artists who traveled in the United States and set tastes for American audiences. Wesley Webster was a good friend and steady supporter, but a part-time San Francisco publisher with a relatively short regional list was simply not in a position to do for Moore what someone like Arthur P. Schmidt had done for the composers of the New England School a generation earlier.[9] John Tasker Howard had omitted her from his initial edition of the voluminous *Our American Music: Three Hundred Years of It* in 1931.[10] She had had to do without the steady financial support or patronage that underlies the career of every successful art music composer. Claude had been able and willing to help financially after the lean early years of their marriage, but his help came to an end in 1914 with their divorce, even as the Carrs' hopes and ambitions for her had foundered two decades earlier. Clarence Gustlin was right in his 1945 letter about *Narcissa*. He wrote that Moore had just plain been overlooked at a time when other composers of her generation, the first Americanist composers, were being recognized and published and performed, if not by symphony orchestras and opera companies, at least by the music clubs. Now she was swept into obscurity with the rest, having received only local recognition even at the height of her creative powers.

As she grew more housebound, she focused her waning energy on the task of organizing the voluminous collection of music and papers that was the evidence of her long career. By her eightieth birthday few of the friends and students who came to call could remember her as a young woman, before she had come to Los Angeles. None could go back to her days in Seattle, before 1915, or to the time before the turn of the century in Lemoore and pre-earthquake San Francisco and St. Helena. None suspected that she had taken refuge from the conflicts of her young adulthood in fainting spells or bouts of invalidism. None had a sense of her entire career; mostly they thought of her as their splendid teacher, mentor, and friend, as well as a composer. She talked to her callers of her achievements as a composer, for she was well aware of her worth as a creative artist, but there is no record of what she had to say about the dynamics of her life. If she speculated on the ironies and anomalies that now seem evident, we cannot know. We can only guess at how she saw her own career, for though she was a good talker, she left little written evidence that she had engaged in aesthetic reflection.

It had been no easy task to live as a Victorian lady and still remain true to her talent for large-scale, serious composition. At twenty she had felt shamed by the appearance of her picture "in the public prints," where ladies' faces did not belong. It did not take long to overcome this early diffidence; soon she became adept at announcing her performances and publications in local papers and music journals. That part had been relatively easy, but learning to live with the internal restraints that her early conditioning imposed had taken much longer. Her strong-willed mother, Sarah, had provided her with a role model for a lifetime of achievement, while at the same time weaving a net of feminine family and community obligation so tightly around her daughter that Moore had almost suffocated before coming to terms with it. Having learned to live constructively with these internal restraints at last, she had run straight into the external obstacle of sex discrimination. Her experience in New York taught her that the more European-dominated the music of a city, the higher were the barriers that kept woman composers out of the concert hall except as curiosities to be covered in the society pages. Had her voice fulfilled its early promise, she would have had a chance to be heard widely as a singer, but as a composer the obstacles were insuperable. The models for American art music were European, and European domination of American musical life had buried American creativity, even more for women than for men. Moore's interests were American, Western, feminine, Victorian—out of step with the accepted models for her generation. "I have written *most* of my work for Western poets and subjects; it has seemed right to sing of what is near and dear to me."[11]

How many ironies! She had taken advantage of such modern developments as commercial aviation quite early, yet she could not adopt a "modern" persona that might have eased her way, however slightly. She had sought out and explored some aspects of modernist expressiveness in her art in the 1920s, only to be dismissed out of hand by younger and more experimental composers who could not credit the artistic commitment of such a "lacy" Victorian lady. Her tentative early exploration of popular influences had been left behind in Lemoore, at the turn of the century. In abandoning them, she had separated herself from the elements of American music that have since attracted the most attention and proved the most vital. She had once found her inspiration and the liberation of her spirit in the American music movement, only to see her vision founder in a sea of cosmopolitan internationalism and sexual chauvinism. She could scarcely have known that the entire culture of the First Los Angeles School in which she had thrived would be so thoroughly forgotten. Both her marriages failed, yet she went out of her way to attack the common choose-one-not-both cliché about career and marriage, for she had managed, one way or another, to have both.[12] She spoke up for the joys of family and children in spite of the pain they had cost her and advocated the satisfaction of her professional life even as she threw herself into an endless succession of twenty-hour workdays. The *Pacific Coast Musician* had solemnized this final irony when it editorialized on her seventieth birthday, "Professional work, however, did not deter her from leading a normal life."[13]

What of her music? At the distant moment when the ultra-moderns of the 1930s and the modernists of the 1940s would themselves be swept aside by the relentless tide of progress and the music of her generation would be taken from the dusty attics and garages where it had languished, how would hers compare with that of her fellows? She knew that her work would stand up well, if anyone would ever look at it. Several decades after she went to live in a small nursing home in nearby Inglewood in 1954, where Marian could visit daily and she could receive her friends as graciously as she ever had, her faith in her own work seems justified. *Narcissa, Legende Provençale, Saul, David Rizzio,* and other works besides contain many moments of eloquent and forceful expressiveness, set in scenes or movements that are very well crafted indeed. A handful of the songs are small jewels. Like many of the longer works, they bear as a hallmark a certain dignified but straightfoward simplicity. They carry, all of them, her unique creative imprint. Many of her works warrant rehearing, in far better performances than they often received in her lifetime.

Moore's memory for matters musical outlasted her ability to identify her callers, often distressing them greatly. Probably she did not remember the interview she had given twenty years earlier, in which she spoke of three strikes against her as a composer: that she was alive, that she was American, and that she was a woman. Her life ebbed at a time when the feminist movement had sunk to its lowest point since its beginning, and when recognition for women as composers had virtually disappeared as their numbers dwindled. Moore's position was similar to that of the other woman composers of her generation, whose careers and aesthetic outlook had grown out of an earlier American, middle-class parlor tradition.[14] All of them had come to maturity as the number of woman musicians increased very rapidly in the decades before 1910. Their creative potential, like Moore's, was circumscribed by both conditioning and external prejudice; the emotional struggle to be both Victorian ladies and serious composers overwhelmed many of them. Very few among them reached the level of creative and emotional self-sufficiency Moore had achieved. As their opportunities shrank, most creative women were realistic enough to find other outlets for their creative energy than composing. Was she also impractical? Of course she was. A practical woman would have given up writing operas after *Narcissa* and stuck to teaching pieces for piano, with perhaps a theory textbook or two. But Moore continued to storm the barricades. "I have composed as much as I have had time for; squeezing it in late at night . . . mostly because I just couldn't help it."[15] "She had so much that might have made her a great composer under certain circumstances. . . . I think she probably had great capacities beyond what she was ever able to realize, because you don't have that amount of creative energy unless you have the possibility of creating something substantial."[16]

In terms of values, Moore bent with the times as little as possible. She clung stubbornly to the Victorian ideals of the primacy of romantic love and family obligations for a woman, to the sense of duty and the patriotism she had acquired in her early years. She had no choice but to cling to those old values; but as time went on, she found herself progressively more out of step with her younger contemporaries. The very device that made it possible for her to continue growing artistically for so long was also the one that helped assure that her music would fall into oblivion even as she passed her last days in Inglewood.

By the time of her death on January 9, 1957, it seems that there were few creative artists left who associated themselves closely with her value system. Her audience had nearly vanished. But those who survived her knew that Moore was, in her integrity and her commitment and her achievement, a pioneer in music as her grandfather had been a pioneer in railroading and her mother a pioneer of domestic feminism. She swam with all her power against the receding current of feminism in the middle decades of our century in her attempt to fulfill her creative potential and was rewarded by becoming, for a while, an aesthetic anachronism. Perhaps now that the tide has turned, her music will get the reevaluation and recognition it so richly deserves.

Catalog of Compositions
by Mary Carr Moore

The primary sources for information on Moore's compositions, apart from the music itself, are a handwritten catalog and several typed lists of works apparently also prepared by the composer. The handwritten catalog and the various typed lists do not agree in every detail, nor do they always contain information identical to that appearing on the extant MSS. Moore sometimes assigned or changed opus numbers well after the works were composed. Therefore, the order of some of her opus numbers, particularly the earlier ones, does not reflect a strictly chronological sequence. Where discrepancies exist, published opus numbers have generally been preferred over MS opus numbers, and MS opus numbers over Moore's catalog listings.

Many of the earlier songs and piano pieces are lost; several of the later works are unlocated. With only a few exceptions, all of the works not designated "lost" are in the Mary Carr Moore Archive, Music Library, University of California, Los Angeles. Where copies of works missing from the archive have been located elsewhere, this information has been noted.

Within each category, works are listed by opus number. For each work, the following information has been given, as appropriate: opus number, title, author of text, instrumentation, date of composition or arrangement, publisher, date of publication, and notes concerning arrangements, opus number conflicts, etc. The publishers identified by shortened names in the catalog are:

San Bruno, Calif.: Wesley Webster
New York: M. Witmark and Sons
New York: G. Schirmer
New York: Carl Fischer
New York: Da Capo Press
Boston: Oliver Ditson Company
Los Angeles: W. A. Quincke and Co.
Los Angeles: Saunders Publications
Hanford, Calif.: Charles W. Barrett
Seattle: Sterling Music Company
Spokane, Wash.: Harry L. Stone
San Francisco: Sherman, Clay and Co.
San Francisco: J. M. Byron (Composer's own imprint)

Stage

Opus	Title	Libretto
25	The Oracle, operetta, 2 acts	Composer
—	The Oracle, operetta, 3 acts	Composer
51	Music for Harry B. Smith libretto	Harry B. Smith
52	Music for Mr. Mead (children's operetta)	?
68/1	Incidental music for The Shepherd	Olive Dargan
71	Narcissa, or The Cost of Empire, opera, 4 acts	Sarah Pratt Carr
74	The Leper, tabloid grand opera, 1 act	E. Dudley Burrows
78/1	Memories, operatic idyll, 1 act	Charles Eugene Banks
78/2	Potato Salad à l'Opéra, vaudeville sketch	Mabel Crane
78/3	Three and a Pool, musical farce	Mabel Crane
78/4	Come to 'Frisco, vaudeville sketch?	Composer
—	The Firemen of the Wissahickon Inn, vaudeville sketch	H. F. Norton
79/10	Harmony, musical farce, 1 act	Composer and students?
82	Mother Goose Revue, musical revue for children	Traditional; added text by composer
83/1	The Flaming Arrow, Indian intermezzo, 1 act	Sarah Pratt Carr
83/2	The Shaft of Ku'pish-ta-ya, opera, 1 act	Sarah Pratt Carr
84/5	The Immortal Lovers, a Chinese Legend, pantomime	Flora Howell Bruner
84/6	Japanese Fantasie, pantomime plus 2 arias	Flora Howell Bruner; arias: Sydney Harris
88	Avalon, musical comedy	Maurice Salzmann
89	David Rizzio, opera, 2 acts	Emanuel M. Browne; Italian and English
90	Legende Provençale, opera, 3 acts	Eleanore Flaig; French and English
93	Los Rubios, opera, 3 acts	Neeta Marquis
95	Flutes of Jade Happiness, operetta, 3 acts	Laura Sweeney Moore
97	Atlantis, musical pageant	Harry Noyes Pratt

Composition	First Performance	Publication/Remarks
1893–94	San Francisco, March 28, 1894	
Rev. 1899, 1901	Seattle, January 10, 1902	Expanded version of op. 25
ca. 1902	Seattle, n.d.	Lost? Possibly same as untitled vocal score (6 numbers only) in Moore Archive
ca. 1902	Seattle, n.d.	Lost
1909	Seattle, n.d.	Lost; 2 numbers and instrumental passages?
1909–11	Seattle, April 22, 1912	Vocal score, Witmark, 1912
1912	Concert performance, n.d.	
1914	Seattle, November 1, 1914	Played 1 year on the Keith-Orpheum vaudeville circuit
1915	?	
1915	?	Sketches only
1915	?	Lost
1915	?	Music lost; libretto in Library of Congress
1917	San Francisco, May 25, 1917	Composed for Mission High School
ca. 1920	San Francisco, ca. 1920	Op. 82, nos. 13–24
1919–20	San Francisco, March 27, 1922	
Rev. 1926?	Los Angeles, November 25, 1927	Revision of op. 83, no. 1
1922	San Francisco, 1922	Also listed as op. 84, no. 4
1922	San Francisco, n.d.	Rev. of op. 84, no. 5; also listed as op. 84, no. 5
1927		2 numbers only; abandoned
1927–28	Los Angeles, May 26, 1932	Vocal score, Webster, 1937; reprint, Da Capo, 1981
1929–38		Original title: Macabre; full score lost
1931	Los Angeles, September 10, 1931	MS vocal score in Library of Congress
1932–34	Los Angeles, March 2, 1934	Additional numbers added 1938
1935		Act 1 (incomplete) only; abandoned

Orchestra

45/2 Spanish Dance, from The Oracle, 1901, lost

69/2 Brahma, baritone with orchestra, 1915; arr. of song (1909)

72/2 Mexican Serenade, baritone with orchestra?; arr. of song Querida mi vida, op. 72, no. 1 (1912)?; included in Los Rubios

79/3 My Dream, voice with orchestra; arr. of song (1915)

80/3 Saul, suite, 1930?; arr. of piano trio, op. 80, no. 1 (1916)

85/3B Rêvons, 1924; arr. of piano piece, op. 85, no. 3 (1923)

89 L'Intermezzo, from David Rizzio, 1927–28

91/10A Before the Dawn; arr. of piano piece, op. 100, no. 1 (1931); also arr. for flute, clarinet, violins I, II, viola, cello

91/10C Dance of the Wood Sprites; arr. of piano piece, op. 100, no. 2, unfinished (1 page only)

92 Ka-mi-a-kin, or Totem Vision, an Indian Idyl, 1930; also listed as op. 90

94/1 Concerto in F Minor, piano, orchestra, 1933–34; arr. for quintet: piano, violin, viola, cello, clarinet, op. 94, no. 2

98/3B Suite for String Ensemble, 1940; arr. of String Trio, op. 98, no. 3 (1936)

99 Kidnap (The Lost Child), 1937–39

102/3 Brief Furlough, 1943; arr. of quintet: clarinet, 2 violins, cello, piano, op. 102, no. 2 (1942)

Chamber

72/5 Pastorale, violin, piano, 1912 (Witmark, n.d.?; Webster, 1930 and 1940)

75/7 Romanza, violin, piano, 1913; originally op. 75, no. 4

79/1 Longing, cello, piano, 1915

80/1 Saul, suite, piano trio with narrator, 1916; arr. for orchestra, op. 80, no. 3

80/2 Saul, suite, piano quintet, 1916; arr. of piano trio, op. 80, no. 1

81/6 Sonata in C Minor, violin, piano, 1918

85/2 Wiegenlied (Berceuse), viola, piano?, 1923; also listed as op. 85, no. 3; fragment only

87/3 Reverie, violin or cello, piano, 1926 (Webster, 1935 [cello], 1940 [violin])

87/4 String Quartet in G Minor (Miniature), 1926

87/6 Message to One Absent, violin, piano, 1926 (Webster, 1941)

91/3 Chant d'amour, flute, piano, 1930

91/8 String Quartet in F Minor, 1930

91/10A Before the Dawn; arr. of piano piece, op. 100, no. 1 (1931) for flute, clarinet, violins I, II, viola, cello; also arr. for orchestra

— Twilight in the Forest; arr. of piano piece, op. 100, no. 3 (1932) for flute, clarinet, violins I, II, viola, cello

— Murmur of Pines; arr. of piano piece, op. 100, no. 4 (1928) for flute, clarinet, violins I, II, viola, cello

94/2 Quintet in F Minor, clarinet, violin, viola, cello, piano, 1936; arr. of piano concerto, op. 94, no. 1 (1933–34)

96/2 Nocturne, flute, piano, 1934

98/3 String Trio in G Minor, 1936; arr. for string ensemble, op. 98, no. 3B

98/7 Magyar Song, violin, piano, 1937 (Webster, 1942)

98/9 Nostalgia, clarinet, piano, 1938

98/10 Mountain Call, trumpet, piano, 1938

102/1 Poème, piano trio, 1941

102/2 Brief Furlough (Reminiscences of a G.I.), clarinet, 2 violins, cello, piano, 1942; arr. for orchestra, op. 102, no. 3

105/1 Improvisation, clarinet, piano, 1945

105/2 Love Song, cello, piano, 1945

106/2 Moods, oboe, bassoon, piano, 1946

106/3 Early Spring, violin, piano, 1947

107/3 Fairy Tale, violin, viola, 1948

— String Quartet in E Minor, unfinished? (1 movement only), n.d.

— Aftermath of Flu, string quartet, 1 movement (incomplete), n.d.

Lost: 19/2, Night, violin, piano, ca. 1892; 21/2, Simple Simon March, violin, piano, ca. 1892; 27/3, Song of Love, violin, piano, 1896; 33/2, The Dream, violin, piano, 1895; 35, Piano Trio, 1895; 40/2, Love Dreams, violin, piano, 1896; 40/3, Romance, violin, piano, 1896; 47/2, The Lake—Cold, Dark, Silent, cello, piano, ca. 1901; 65, Piano Trio (Vacation Trio), 1906

Piano

1/5 Invention, ca. 1888
2/3 Canon, ca. 1888
2/4 Minuetto Piccoletto, ca. 1888
8/4 Little Canon, ca. 1888
8/7 Three Little Cousins!, ca. 1888
43/2 Reverie, 1898
75/8 Barcarolle, 1913 (Byron, 1917?; Webster, 1935?)
85/3 Rêvons, 1923 (Schirmer, 1931); arr. for orchestra, op. 85, no. 3B
85/7 Fragment, 1925
85/8 Initiation Ceremony, Music Teachers' Association of San Francisco (Frank Carroll Giffen), speakers with piano, 1924
87/9 Etude in E-flat Major, 1927; also listed as Prelude in E-flat Major
91/15 Marche Humoresque, 1932 (Webster, 1955); original title: March of the Toy Soldiers
96/1 Mary Magdalene, choreographic sketch, 1933
96/5 Two-Part Invention, 1934
96/6 Prelude and Fugue in C Minor, 1943 and 1934, respectively
96/7 Desert Nocturne, 1934
100/1 Before the Dawn, 1931 (Fischer, 1939: Forest Sketches I); originally op. 91, no. 10A; renumbered at request of publisher; arr. for flute, clarinet, violins I, II, viola, cello, op. 91, no. 10A, and for orchestra, op. 91, no. 10A
100/2 Dance of the Wood Sprites, 1932 (Fischer, 1939: Forest Sketches II); originally op. 91, no. 10C; first published as op. 91, no. 10B; renumbered

at request of publisher; arr. for orchestra, op. 91, no. 10C (unfinished)
100/3 Twilight in the Forest, 1932 (Fischer, 1939: Forest Sketches III); originally op. 91, no. 10B; first published as op. 91, no. 10C; renumbered at request of publisher; arr. for flute, clarinet, violins I, II, viola, cello
100/4 Murmur of Pines, 1928 (Fischer, 1939: Forest Sketches IV); originally op. 87, no. 14, then op. 91, no. 10D; renumbered at request of publisher; arr. for flute, clarinet, violins I, II, viola, cello
101/1 Easter Morning, 1941 (Edward Earle's Suite I)
101/2 Summer Night, 1941 (Edward Earle's Suite II)
101/3 Autumn, 1939 (Edward Earle's Suite III); originally op. 98, no. 14
101/4 Winter Rain, 1940 (Edward Earle's Suite IV); originally op. 98, no. 15
103/5 Vacation Journey, 1944; also listed as Summer Journey
103/6 Tricycle Trip (On a Sunny Day), 1944
105/4 April Shower, 1945; original title: Blue
105/5 Prelude and Fugue in G Minor, 1945
107/2 Springtime Birds, 1948
108/1 Humming Bird, 1949
108/2 Rainy Day, 1949
108/3 Mountain Hike, 1949
108/4 Christmas Night, 1949
109/1 Spring Rhapsodie, 1950
Lost: 2/2, Andante, ca. 1888; 3/3, Waltz, 1889; 4/2, March, 1889; 4/3, Marjolaine, 1889; 4/4, Waltz, 1889; 6/2, Dance of Love, 1890; 6/3, Hymn to Music, 1890; 6/4, Improvisation, 1890; 9/3, Allegro Vivace, 1890; 9/4, Prelude, 1890; 9/5, Three Preludes, 1890; 11/3, Dance of the Elves, 1890; 11/4, Dance of the Sunbeams, 1890; 14/4, Prelude, 1891; 18/3, Concert Waltz in A Major, ca. 1892; 18/4, Concert Waltz in B-flat Major, ca. 1892; 19/1, From Arabia, ca. 1892; 20/1, Waltz, ca. 1892; 20/2, Two Step,

ca. 1892; 20/3, Marjolaine, ca. 1892;
27/1, Wedding March, 1896; 32/2,
Grand March, 1895; 43/1, Salon
Valse, 1898; 98/1, Evening Song,
duet, 1935

Organ

10/3 Prelude, 1890
10/4 Postlude, 1890, lost
72/3 Prelude in G Major, 1912, lost
72/4 Prelude in F Major, 1912; originally op. 72, no. 3
98/12 Prelude and Fugue in F Major,
1939
98/13 Prelude and Fugue in D Minor,
1939

Choral and Partsongs with Solos

39/1 As When the Weary Traveler (Unknown), SATB with soprano solo,
piano, ca. 1896
59 How Sigurd Met Brynhild in Lymdale, or The Quest of Sigurd (William
Morris), cantata, SSAA with soprano
and baritone solos, flute, 2 violins,
cello, piano, 1905
61 Oh, Wind From the Golden Gate
(Virginia Harrison), SSA with solos,
piano, violin obbligato, ca. 1906 (Witmark, 1910)
67/1 Idlesse (The Touch of a Summer
Day) (Clinton Scollard), SSA with contralto solo, piano, 1909 (Witmark,
1910? and 1922)
75/2 The Birthday of Christ, or Love,
the Saviour (Unknown), SATB with
soprano solo, organ, 1913
84/1 The Mountain Lake (Tahoe) (Flora
Howell Bruner), from California
Cycle, TTBB with soprano solo,
piano, 1922 (Webster, 1927 and
1932); optional parts for flute, clarinet, harp, strings, lost
84/2 Half Dome (Yosemite) (Fay Jackson Van Norden), from California
Cycle, TTBB with soprano solo,
piano, 1922 (Webster, 1932); optional
parts for flute, clarinet, harp, strings,
lost

84/3 The Pine of Portsmouth Square
(San Francisco) (Charles Caldwell
Dobie), from California Cycle, TTBB
with soprano solo, piano, 1922 (Webster, 1932); optional parts for flute,
clarinet, harp, strings, lost
86 Beyond These Hills (Gilbert Moyle),
SATB solos, piano, 1924; arr. for
SATB chorus, SATB solos, orchestra,
1942
96/12 From the Heights (Edward
Lewis), SSA or SAT with baritone
solo, piano; another version for SSA,
piano; arr. of song Dim Vistas (1935)
104/2 There Is No Death (Stanley F.
Murray), SSAATTBB with baritone
solo, piano or organ, 1944
106/1 Behold, God Is My Salvation (Isa-
iah), SSA with baritone solo, piano,
1946; original title: Hear, O Heavens;
Give Ear, O Earth
— Wedding Bells (Unknown), from A
Military Manoeuvre, SATB solos,
SATB chorus, piano, n.d.
— The Forest Shall Conquer, sketch,
n.d.

Choral and Partsongs for Mixed or Men's Voices
*(For SATB, unaccompanied,
unless otherwise stated)*

62 Life of Life (Alice Carey), anthem,
SATB, violin, organ, ca. 1906
73/1 When Christ as Babe to Judah
Came (Catherine A. Glen), anthem,
SATB, piano, 1912
96/11 My Country (Samuel Francis
Smith), 1935 (Webster, 1939?); arr.
for solo voice, piano (Webster, 1939);
also arr. for SATB or SSA, orchestra
97/2 Ave Maria, motet, 1935
104/1 There Is a Dream (John Steven
McGroarty), SSAATTBB, piano or
organ, 1943
105/6 Wake! Singing with the Dawn
(Gilbert Moyle), 1946
— Aspiration, Hymn to C.C.C. (Unknown), n.d.
— The Flag of Freedom (Composer?),
SATB, piano, n.d.

— March On with Freedom's Flag Un-
furled (Composer?), SATB, piano,
n.d.
— Oh, Land of Mine (Text by a survivor of Libby Prison), n.d.
— Prayer (Unknown), sketch, n.d.
— Response, 2 keys: E Major, G Major,
n.d.
— Untitled; text: "All hail to Thee,"
sketch, n.d.
— Untitled; text: "Draw near, draw
near and praise Him," sketch, n.d.
Lost: 1/3, Jesus, Lover of My Soul,
1889; 1/4, Heaven Is My Home,
1889; 12/2, Abide with Me, 1890;
12/3, Rock of Ages, 1890; 14/2, Boat-
ing Song (Anon.), TTBB, 1891; 29,
Arrangements with sacred words of 6
of Mendelssohn's Songs without
Words, SATB?, 1894; 36, 2(?) wom-
en's rights songs for San Joaquin Valley Campaign (Charles W. Barrett?),
TTBB?, 1896; 39/2, Father, Hear Us
(Unknown), anthem, ca. 1896; 46/1–
6, Six Responses, SATB, organ, 1901
or 1902; 70/3, Arrangement of
Schubert's Guide Post, 1909; 70/4, Arrangement of Schubert's Courage,
1909; 72/7, Madrigal (Unknown),
1912

Partsongs for Women's Voices
(For SSAA, unaccompanied,
unless otherwise stated)

13/2 Two Thrushes (Louise Chandler
Moulton), 1890 (Witmark, 1909: Bird
Songs I); originally op. 13, no. 1
22 My Lover Will Come Today (Phoebe
Carey), 1891 (Witmark, 1910); originally op. 14, no. 1
27/2 Bridal Song (Composer), 1896
63/2 Summer Passes (Arthur Powell),
SSA, piano, 1934 (Fischer, 1938); arr.
of song (1906)
— The P.E.O. Spirit (Unknown), 1907
or 1908
66/2 The First Singing Lesson (Claudia
Tharin), 1907 or 1908 (Witmark,
1909: Bird Songs II)
66/3 Farewell to the Birds (Good Bye)

(Composer), 1907 or 1908 (Witmark,
1909: Bird Songs IV)
68/3 Cedars of Lebanon (Alphonse de
Lamartine), 1909 (Witmark, 1910)
70/1 Barnyard Symphony (Anon.), 1909
(Witmark, 1909: Bird Songs III)
70/2 Welcome Song (William Cullen
Bryant), 1909 (Witmark, 1910? and
1922)
72/1 Songs for Waning Autumn (Clinton Scollard), SSA, piano, 1909 (Witmark, 1910); originally op. 67, no. 3
77/3 You (George Mellen), SSAA, piano
(Schirmer, 1931); arr. of song, op. 77,
no. 2 (1914)
87/11 Because It Is the May (S. H. M.
Byers), SSA, piano, 1927
96/11 My Country (Samuel Francis
Smith), SSA, orchestra; arr. of SATB
partsong (1935) (Webster, 1939?);
arr. for SATB, orchestra; also arr.
for solo voice, piano (Webster,
1939)
96/12 From the Heights (Edward
Lewis), SSA, piano; another version
for SAA or SAT with baritone solo,
piano; arr. of song Dim Vistas (1935)
—Arrangement of Thomas
Bradsky's(?) Thou Art Mine All, SSA,
piano, n.d.
Lost: 13/2, The Bridal Morning (Composer), 1890; 13/3, The Pale Moonlight (Composer), 1890; 13/4, Hedge
Roses (Composer?), 1890; 48/2, Sweet
Song-Bird Flown, or Valentine Song
(Jean Bryan), SSAA?, 1901 or 1902
(arr. of song, op. 48, no. 1); 48/3,
Sweet Song-Bird Flown, or Valentine
Song (Jean Bryan), SSA, piano?, 1901
or 1902 (another arr. of song, op. 48,
no. 1); 53, Arrangements (3?) of secu-
lar works, ca. 1902; 54, Arrangements
(21?) of sacred works, ca. 1902; 67/2,
May Time (Unknown), SSA, piano,
1909; 70/5, Arrangement of Dudley
Buck's In Thy Dreams, 1909; 81/9,
The Weeping Willow (Anna Young),
SSA, 1940; arr. of song (1920); 98/8,
A Yuletide Message (John Haraden
Pratt), SSAA?, 1939; arr. of song
(1937)

Solo Songs
(For 1 voice, piano, unless otherwise stated)

1/1 Lullabye (Composer), 1889 (Lincoln, 1909; Witmark, 1910?; Webster, 1932); also arr. for duet (Webster, 1932)

2/1 Forget-me-not (Henry Wadsworth Longfellow), 1890?

3/1 Lyric (Thomas Bailey Aldrich), 1891?

3/2 Love Song (Composer), 1891?

5/1 They Didn't Think! (Phoebe Carey), 1891?

5/2 Little Boy Blue (Traditional), ca. 1891

6/1 Where Art Thou Dreaming? (Thomas Moore), 1891?; original title: Thou Comest Not

7/1 Water Lillies (Elizabeth Akers), 1891?

8/1 Summer Love Song (Composer), 1892?

8/2 Let Me See (Anon.), ca. 1886

8/3 Dolly's Cradle Song (Composer), ca. 1886

9/1 The Russian Lover (Thomas Moore), 1892?

10/1 At the Making of the Hay (Samuel Minturn Peck), 1892?

11/1 The Brooklet = Mother's Song (Harriet McEwain Kimball), ca. 1893 (Webster, 1922)

11/2 Mother's Song (Harriet McEwain Kimball), ca. 1893; same text as op. 11, no. 1

12/1 There Is Nae One Like My Lassie (Susie M. Best), 1893

15/1 The Butterfly (Lucy C. Browne), 1894? (Lucy Croghan Browne, *California Carols* [Oakland, Calif.: The Author, 1897], pp. 42–45)

15/2 The Wild Flowers (Lucy C. Browne), 1894? (Browne, *California Carols*, pp. 59–61)

15/3 The Boy and the Moon (Lucy C. Browne), 1894? (Browne, *California Carols*, pp. 15–18)

16/1 I Promised My True Love (Unknown), ca. 1894

17/1 Goodnight, Sweetheart (Samuel Minturn Peck), ca. 1894

18/1 Could I Find a Word (Anon.), ca. 1894

19/3 A Princess Fair (Mildred Howells), ca. 1894

22/1 The Divine Lullabye (Eugene Field), voice, piano, violin obbligato, ca. 1894; originally op. 22, no. 4

26/2 Northern Love Song (Sarah Pratt Carr), voice, piano, violin obbligato, 1894 (Stone, 1906); original title: Eastern Love Song; in Library of Congress

28/1 May, or May with Life and Music (William Cullen Bryant), 1894 (Witmark, 1910 and 1912; Schirmer, 1929?; Webster, 1932?); originally op. 28, no. 2; in Library of Congress

30/1 The Rose (Phoebe Carey), 1895

32/1 My Love Hath Smiled on Me (Alfred Tennyson), 1895

33/1 Where the Reeds Dance (Olive Schreiner), 1895

37/1 We'll Never Let Old Glory Fall (Charles W. Barrett), ca. 1898 (Barrett, n.d.); also listed as We'll Never Let Old Glory Die

38/1 Sweet Belle of Mars (Charles W. Barrett), ca. 1896 (Barrett, 1897); private collection

38/2 The Mosquito (Charles W. Barrett), ca. 1896 (Barrett, 1897); private collection

— Untitled; text: "I'm in love with a laddie" (Charles W. Barrett?), ca. 1896

41 I'm Going to Vote, John! (Charles W. Barrett), 1896

42 Arrangements for Charles W. Barrett: Maginnis's Billy Goat (private collection), A Giddy Bright Star (private collection), Pretty Little Jane (Library of Congress), ca. 1896 (Barrett, 1897)

— Yankee Dewey Do (Charles W. Barrett), 1898 (Barrett, 1899), private collection

44/1 For Love of Her (Ethel E. Kelly), 1901 (Stone, n.d.)

47/1 The Tryst (Winston Churchill), 1901 or 1902 (Witmark, 1910; Webster, 1930)

48/1 Sweet Song-Bird Flown, or Valentine Song (Jean Bryan), 1901 or 1902; arr. for SSAA? and for SSA, piano?

49/1 What Thou Art to Me (R. M. Gilder), 1901 or 1902; in Library of Congress

50/1 Flower of My Heart (Unknown), 1901 or 1902; also listed as The White Flower of My Heart

55/1 Homeward (H. J. Lyle), 1902 or 1903

56 The Window, or The Song of the Wrens, cycle of 12 songs (Alfred Tennyson), 1902 or 1903: On the Hill; At the Window; Gone!; Winter; Spring; The Letter; No Letter; No Letter [different text]; The Answer; "Aye"; When?; Marriage Morning; originally op. 51

57/1 The Splinter Song (Sarah Pratt Carr), 1902 or 1903

57/2 The Robin (Composer), 1902 or 1903

58/2 I Love Thee (Thomas Hood), duet, 1902 or 1903 (Witmark, 1910; Webster, 1933)

58/4 Oh Sweet Thou Little Knowest (Thomas Hood), 1902 or 1903 (Witmark, 1910; Webster, 1933)

58/5 On the River (Phoebe Carey), 1902 or 1903; originally op. 53, no. 5

60/1 The Call of the Open Sea (Daisy Rinehart), 1905 (Witmark, 1910; Webster, 1933?); in Library of Congress

63/1 A Road Song (Mary Lowell), 1906? (Witmark, 1910); in Library of Congress

63/2 Summer Passes (Arthur Powell), 1906; arr. for SSA, piano (Fischer, 1938)

63/3 Midsummer (John Curtis Underwood), ca. 1906 (Sterling, 1907)

63/4 September (Helen Hunt Jackson), ca. 1906

64/1 Fate (Susan Marr Spaulding), voice, piano, cello obbligato, ca. 1906 (Witmark, 1910)

64/2 The Desert Road (Gilbert Parker), 1908?

66/1 The Rockabye Lady (Eugene Field), ca. 1908 (Witmark, 1910); in Library of Congress

69/1 Forever and a Day (Thomas Bailey Aldrich), 1909

69/2 Brahma (Unknown), 1909; accompaniment arr. for orchestra

70/6 Dream-Best (Carlin Eastwood), 1909 (Carlin Eastwood, *The Master Road* [New York, Seattle: Alice Harriman Co., 1910], p. 110); also listed as Castle of Dreams

— They Ain't No Swell Like Me (Carlin Eastwood), 1909 (Eastwood, *The Master Road*, p. 22, words and melody only)

— 'Tis Now a Well Told Tale, from Narcissa (Sarah Pratt Carr), 1909–11 (Witmark, 1912)

— When the Camas Blooms Again, from Narcissa (Sarah Pratt Carr), 1909–11 (Witmark, 1912)

72/1 Querida mi vida (Mexican Serenade), or Pancho's Serenade (Sarah Pratt Carr), 1912 (Webster, 1931 and 1940); accompaniment arr. for orchestra, op. 72, no. 2?

72/6 The Heart of the Water (Charlotte Perkins Gilman), 1912

73/2 To Mary, or Mary in Bethlehem (Catherine A. Glen), 1912

75/1 Compensation (Unknown), 1913

75/3 Autumn Lullabye (Susan M. Kane), 1913 (*Popular Educator* 32 [October, 1914]: 106)

75/4 Bright October (Susan M. Kane), 1913 (*Popular Educator* 34 [October, 1916]: 77)

75/5 November Song (Susan M. Kane), 1913 (*Popular Educator* 35 [October, 1917]: 99)

75/6 In Bethlehem Long Ago (Susan M. Kane), 1913

76/1 Mysterious Power (Composer), 1913 (Webster, 1922?)

76/2 Hark, the Herald Angels Sing (Charles Wesley), 1913

76/3 Finis (Rosamonde Mariott Watson), 1914

77/1 Dawn (Composer), 1914 (Byron, 1916); verse added, 1924 (Webster, 1928)

77/2 You! (George Mellen), 1914 (*Pacific Coast Musician* 4, no. 5 [May 1915]: 23–24; Byron, 1920?; Schirmer, 1921); arr. for SSAA, piano, op. 77, no. 3 (Schirmer, 1931)

79/2 My Sweetheart's Face (John Wyeth Allen), 1915

79/3 My Dream (Charles Phillips), 1915 (Webster, 1935); accompaniment arr. for orchestra

79/4 To Mother (Uintah Ruple Boyd), 1915 (Byron, 1916?; Webster, 1917 and 1941?)

79/6 Heart's Dawn (James M. Warnack), 1915

79/7 If the Stars Were Only Fishes! (Charles Caldwell Dobie), ca. 1916

79/8 The Cruise of the Pillowslip (Charles Caldwell Dobie), ca. 1916

79/9 O Wond'rous Soul (Composer), 1916

81/1 Consummation (Composer), 1917

81/2 The Bird of the Wilderness (Rabindranath Tagore), 1918

81/3 Peace, My Heart (Rabindranath Tagore), 1918

81/4 Love, My Heart Longs Day and Night (Rabindranath Tagore), 1918

81/5 Son (Composer), ca. 1918; original title: My Wonderful Boy; rewritten 1944

81/7 Your Hand on Mine, at Eventide (Composer), 1919

81/8 My Own Beloved (Elizabeth Barrett Browning), 1919?

81/9 The Weeping Willow (Anna Young), 1920; arr. for SSA, 1940

81/10 Dweller in My Dreams (Rabindranath Tagore), ca. 1919 (Webster, 1922)

81/11 Immortal Birth (Composer), ca. 1919 (*Music Lover's Magazine* 1, no. 2 [September, 1922]: 9–11); earlier titles: Ascension; Life; Why Call It Death?

81/12 Shadows (Fay Jackson Van Norden), ca. 1919 (Webster, 1922); in Library of Congress and Seattle Public Library

81/13 Song of a Faun (Fay Jackson Van Norden), voice, piano, flute obbligato, ca. 1919 (Webster, 1922); in Seattle Public Library

81/14 Winter (Fay Jackson Van Norden), ca. 1919 (Webster, 1922)

81/15 Hope (I Heard a Bird Sing) (Unknown), ca. 1919

82/1 The Bird and the Squirrel (Fred Emerson Brooks), 1918 (Schirmer, 1922)

82/2 Freedom (Fred Emerson Brooks), 1918

82/3 The Meadow Lark (Fred Emerson Brooks), ca. 1918

82/4 Why Pussy Washes His Face, *After Meals* (Fred Emerson Brooks), ca. 1918

82/5 The Hen, or It Pays to Advertise (Fred Emerson Brooks), ca. 1918

82/6 Starry Flag (Charlotte Canty), ca. 1918

82/7 Little Miss Study and Little Miss Play (Fred Emerson Brooks), ca. 1918

82/8 On That Lov'd Yesterday (Jesse G. M. Glick), ca. 1919

82/9 Come into the Moonlight (Composer), ca. 1919

82/10 Hallowe'en (Composer), ca. 1919

82/11 Hushabye Dolly (Composer), 1920 (Webster, 1922)

82/12 I Am the Boy Who Delivers the Smiles (Composer), ca. 1920

85/1 Cicina mia (Fay Jackson Van Norden), 1923 (Sherman, Clay, 1925)

85/5 Awake! and Greet the Dawn (Composer), 1924

85/6 My Heart Awaits (Bridal Song) (Composer), 1924

85/8 Initiation Ceremony for Music Teachers' Association of San Francisco (Frank Carroll Giffen), 1924

85/9 Sunset (John Wesley Moore), ca. 1925 (Schirmer, 1927); in Library of Congress

85/10 A June Requiem (Mrs. N. Lawrence Nelson), 1925 (Webster, 1926? and 1940); mistakenly published as op. 85, no. 9

87/2 Eventide (Composer), ca. 1926 (Webster, 1933)

87/3 Sun of Our Life (Oliver Wendell
Holmes), 1926 (Quincke, 1927); also
listed as op. 87, no. 5
87/7 A Glimpse of Him (Lula Sellars
England), 1926 (Quincke, 1927)
87/8 Clouds (Composer), 1926
87/10 Consummation (Song of Joy)
(Walt Whitman), 1927; original title:
Two Together; retitled, and accompaniment arr. for flute, violin, cello,
piano in cycle Four Love Songs, 1932
(Webster, 1933); in Special Collections, Research Library, UCLA
87/12 Highwayman's Hollow (G. V.
Yonge), 1927
87/13 Japanese Night Song (Ellen Jan-
son), 1928 (Schirmer, 1930)
87/15 Desolation (Song of Grief) (Composer), 1928; original title: A Song of
Sorrow; title changed to Mist; retitled,
and accompaniment arr. for flute, violin, cello, piano in cycle Four Love
Songs, 1932 (Webster, 1933); in Special Collections, Research Library,
UCLA
87/16 Wings of Flight (Composer), 1928
(Webster, 1936 and 1938)
87/17 The Prayer of a Tree (Helen
Lukens Gant), 1929; also listed as op.
88, no. 1
87/18 Renunciation (Parting) (Grace E.
Bush), 1929; original title: Blue Day;
also listed as op. 88, no. 3; retitled,
and accompaniment arr. for flute, violin, cello, piano in cycle Four Love
Songs, 1932 (Webster, 1933); in Special Collections, Research Library,
UCLA
87/19 Compensation (Secret Tryst) (Eleanore Flaig), 1929; original title:
Samarkand; also listed as op. 88, no.
4; retitled, and accompaniment arr.
for flute, violin, cello, piano in cycle
Four Love Songs, 1932 (Webster,
1933); in Special Collections, Research
Library, UCLA
87/20 My Lover (Mabel E. Palmer),
1929; originally op. 87, no. 18; also
listed as op. 88, no. 5
91/1 If This Be the Hour (Kahlil

Gibran), 1929; also listed as op. 88,
no. 6 and op. 89, no. 1
91/2 Blue Herons (Eleanor Allen), 1930
(Saunders, 1937)
91/4 Lo, We Shall See the Veil Withdrawn (In Purple Seas) (S. H. M.
Byers), 1930
91/5 Of Wounds and Sore Defeat
(William Vaughan Moody), 1930
91/6 I Had No Songs until Today (Edward Lynn), 1930 (Ditson, 1936)
91/7 April Moment (Edward Lynn),
1930
91/9 Eternal Home (Ellen Beach Yaw),
1930
91/11 Sea Call (E. Leslie Spaulding),
1931
— Ramoncita mia, from Los Rubios
(Neeta Marquis), 1931 (Webster,
1940)
91/12 The Little Winds of Home
(George E. Curran), 1932
91/13 Spires of Sunrise (George E. Curran), 1932
91/14 Home-Bound (George E. Curran), 1932 (Webster, 1948)
91/16 Home-Coming Time (Grace Boles
Hedge), 1933; also listed as op. 91,
no. 17
91/17 When for Me, Shall Be Your
Love (Marie Ruelas), 1933; also listed
as op. 91, no. 16
95/5 Cho Lin's Song, from Flutes of
Jade Happiness (Laura Sweeney
Moore), 1932–34 (Webster, 1934)
95/6 The Song of the World, from
Flutes of Jade Happiness (Laura
Sweeney Moore), 1932–34, voice,
piano, flute obbligato (Webster, 1939);
in Los Angeles Public Library
96/3 Voice of the Flame (James Warnack), 1934
96/4 Build Me an Altar, Love (James
Warnack), 1934
96/8 Sanctuary (Composer), 1935
96/10 Purple Lilacs (Composer), 1935;
original title: Solace?
96/11 My Country (Samuel Francis
Smith), 1935 (Webster, 1939); arr. of
SATB partsong (1935) (Webster,

1939?); also arr. for SATB or SSA, orchestra

96/12 Dim Vistas (Edward Lewis), 1935; arr. for SSA, piano, and SAA or SAT with baritone solo, piano under title: From the Heights

98/2 My Song (Rabindranath Tagore), 1935

98/4 One Day of Golden Sunlight (Un di' brillava il sole) (Emanuel Browne), 1936; also listed as op. 91, no. 4, and op. 91, no. 5

98/5 Dance (Betsy Davis), 1936 (Webster, 1946; published with Intuition, op. 103, no. 1)

98/6 Message (Composer), 1936 (Webster, 1947)

98/8 A Yuletide Message (John Haraden Pratt), 1937; arr. for SSAA?, 1939

98/11 Vision (William Preston Bentley), 1938 (Webster, 1948)

101/1 Song for Theta Sigma Gamma (Esther Dennison), 1940

103/1 Intuition (Betsy Davis), 1941 (Webster, 1946; published with Dance, op. 98, no. 5)

103/2 Ten Years Old (Composer), 1941

103/3 We Answer, as One, to America's Call (Composer), 1943

103/4 En avant, pour la victoire (On to Victory) (Patrick McAuliffe), 1943

105/3 God in All (Composer), 1945

107/1 Love's Bouquet (Lowell H. Coate), 1948 (Webster, 1950)

108/5 At the Beach (Composer), 1949

108/6 Christmas Morning (Composer), 1949

109/2 Your Loveliness (Mildred C. Tallant), 1950 (Webster, 1950)

109/3 Welcome to Donald (Composer), ca. 1950 (Webster, 1951)

— Said Johnnie Jones to Mollie Moore (Composer), 1950

110/1 Psalm XXV, 1951

110/2 Who Walks in Beauty (Paul M. Gray), 1952

— Come to My Hopi Land (Unknown), sketch for duet?, n.d.

— Sonnet (Elizabeth Barrett Browning), n.d.

— The Wren and the Hen (Anon.), n.d.

— The Trooper's Song (Unknown; Civil War song as sung by Byron O. Carr), arrangement, n.d.

— My Little Irish Colleen (Jack Chancellor), arrangement, n.d.

— My Mother's Gone to Heaven (Jack Chancellor), arrangement, n.d.

— We've Come a Long Ways Together (Hal Kemper), arrangement, n.d.

Lost: 1/2, Birthday Song (Composer), 1889; 4/1, Love Song (Composer), 1889; 5/3, Tom, Tom (Unknown), 1889; 7/2, Roses in Dew (Composer), 1890; 7/3, Sunshine (Composer), 1890; 9/2, Sweetheart (Composer), 1890; 10/2, Crossing the Bar (Henry Wadsworth Longfellow), 1890; 14/3, Song of a Triton (Unknown), 1891; 16/2, Mavourneen's Smile (Unknown), ca. 1892; 16/3, Far from Old Ireland's Shore (Unknown), ca. 1892

17/2, The Stars Breathe, Goodnight (Composer), ca. 1892; 17/3, Dew on the Clover (Composer), ca. 1892; 17/4, Thy Dark Eyes (Composer), ca. 1892; 18/2, One Word from Thee (Composer), ca. 1892; 21/1, Othello (Unknown), ca. 1892; 26/1, Love Song (Sarah Pratt Carr), 1894; 26/3, Winter Solitude (Composer), 1894; 28/1, April (Byron O. Carr?), 1894; 28/3, June (Composer), 1894; 30/2, Heather Bloom (Composer), 1895; 30/3, Song of Love (Alice Carey), 1895 31/1, Mother and Child (Eugene Field), 1895; 31/2, Serenade (Thomas Moore), 1895; 31/3, The Letter (Thomas Moore), 1895; 32/3, In Venice (Unknown), 1895; 34/1, When Thou Art Near Me (Lady John Scott), 1895; 34/2, When Thou Art Near Me (Lady John Scott), 1895 [another setting]; 34/3, When Thou Art Near Me (Lady John Scott), 1895 [another setting] (Sterling, 1907?); 36, Women's rights songs (2 solos, 2 duets?) for San Joaquin Valley Campaign (Charles W. Barrett?), 1896; 37/2, Parade, Rest (Charles W. Barrett), ca. 1896 (Barrett, n.d.); 37/3, Taps (Charles W.

Barrett), ca. 1896 (Barrett, n.d.); 38/3, My Moon Lady (Charles W. Barrett), ca. 1896 (Barrett, n.d.)

40/1, A Little Goodnight Song (Unknown), 1896; 41–42, Arrangements of campaign songs, war songs, etc., for Charles W. Barrett, ca. 1896; 44/2, Brown Eyes (Composer), 1901 (Stone, n.d.); 44/3, Hail Beloved Dawn (Composer), 1901 (Stone, n.d.); 45/1, Hebe (Composer), from The Oracle, 1901; 49/2, Heart of Mine (Composer), ca. 1902; 49/3, Bird Songs (Composer), ca. 1902; 50/2, Love's Greeting (Composer), ca. 1902; 50/3, Entreaty (Unknown), ca. 1902; 55/2, Jesus, My Refuge (Unknown), ca. 1903; 55/3, Father, Grant Thy Tender Mercy (Composer), ca. 1903

58/1, My Soul I'll Pour Unto Thee (Robert Herrick), ca. 1903 (Witmark, 1913); 58/3, An Impertinent Sparrow (George Horton), ca. 1903; 60/2, On, to the Mountains (Composer), 1905; 64/3, Absence (Composer), 1906; 69/3, Echoes (Louisa Merrill Pratt), 1909; 79/5, Just Why (Anon.), 1915; 85/4?, Oh Love, the Shadows Part (Ina Coolbrith?), 1924; 88/2?, Sea Gulls at Night (Harry Noyes Pratt), 1929; 89/2?, California (Unknown), 1929

Extant Songs
(Listed alphabetically by title)

The Answer, 56
April Moment, 91/7
Ascension, 81/11
At the Beach, 108/5
At the Making of the Hay, 10/1
At the Window, 56
Autumn Lullabye, 75/3
Awake! and Greet the Dawn, 85/5
"Aye," 56
The Bird and the Squirrel, 82/1
The Bird of the Wilderness, 81/2
Blue Day, 87/18
Blue Herons, 91/2
The Boy and the Moon, 15/3
Brahma, 69/2

Bright October, 75/4
The Brooklet, 11/1
Build Me an Altar, Love, 96/4
The Butterfly, 15/1
The Call of the Open Sea, 60/1
Castle of Dreams, 70/6
Cho Lin's Song, 95/5
Christmas Morning, 108/6
Cicina mia, 85/1
Clouds, 87/8
Come into the Moonlight, 82/9
Come to My Hopi Land, n.d.
Compensation, 75/1
Compensation (Secret Tryst), 87/19
Consummation, 81/1
Consummation (Song of Joy), 87/10
Could I Find a Word, 18/1
The Cruise of the Pillowslip, 79/8
Dance, 98/5
Dawn, 77/1
The Desert Road, 64/2
Desolation (Song of Grief), 87/15
Dim Vistas, 96/12
The Divine Lullabye, 22/1
Dolly's Cradle Song, 8/3
Dream-Best, 70/6
Dweller in My Dreams, 81/10
Eastern Love Song, 26/2
En avant, pour la victoire (On to Victory), 103/4
Eternal Home, 91/9
Eventide, 87/2
Fate, 64/1
Finis, 76/3
Flower of My Heart, 50/1
For Love of Her, 44/1
Forever and a Day, 69/1
Forget-me-not, 2/1
Four Love Songs, 87/10, 87/15, 87/18, 87/19
Freedom, 82/2
From the Heights, 96/12
A Giddy Bright Star, 42
A Glimpse of Him, 87/7
God in All, 105/3
Gone!, 56
Goodnight, Sweetheart, 17/1
Hallowe'en, 82/10
Hark, the Herald Angels Sing, 76/2
The Heart of the Water, 72/6
Heart's Dawn, 79/6

The Song of the Wrens, 56
Sonnet, n.d.
Spires of Sunrise, 91/13
The Splinter Song, 57/1
Spring, 56
Starry Flag, 82/6
Summer Love Song, 8/1
Summer Passes, 63/2
Sun of Our Life, 87/3
Sunset, 85/9
Sweet Belle of Mars, 38/1
Sweet Song-Bird Flown, 48/1
Ten Years Old, 103/2
There Is Nae One Like My Lassie,
  12/1
They Ain't No Swell Like Me, 1909
They Didn't Think!, 5/1
Thou Comest Not, 6/1
'Tis Now a Well Told Tale, 1909–11
To Mary, 73/2
To Mother, 79/4
The Trooper's Song, n.d.
The Tryst, 47/1
Two Together, 87/10
Valentine Song, 48/1
Vision, 98/11
Voice of the Flame, 96/3
Water Lillies, 7/1
We Answer, as One, to America's Call,
  103/3

The Weeping Willow, 81/9
Welcome to Donald, 109/3
We'll Never Let Old Glory Fall, 37/1
We've Come a Long Ways Together,
  n.d.
What Thou Art to Me, 49/1
When?, 56
When for Me, Shall Be Your Love,
  91/17
When the Camas Blooms Again, 1909–
  11
Where Art Thou Dreaming?, 6/1
Where the Reeds Dance, 33/1
The White Flower of My Heart, 50/1
Who Walks in Beauty, 110/2
Why Call It Death?, 81/11
Why Pussy Washes His Face, *After
  Meals*, 82/4
The Wild Flowers, 15/2
The Window, 56
Wings of Flight, 87/16
Winter, 56
Winter, 81/14
The Wren and the Hen, n.d.
Yankee Dewey Do, 1898
You!, 77/2
Your Hand on Mine, at Eventide,
  81/7
Your Loveliness, 109/2
A Yuletide Message, 98/8

Notes

Chapter 1

1. The information on B. O. Carr's early career and his ancestors is drawn from the brief "Memoirs of B. O. Carr," written in B. O.'s own hand in the same leatherbound notebook later used by Moore to keep a catalog of her compositions. A microfilm of the notebook is in the Mary Carr Moore Archive, Music Library, University of California, Los Angeles (hereafter cited as Moore Archive).

2. George Pitt Carr, *The River of Life* (Baltimore: Turnbull Brothers, 1871). "The Spirit of Battle," one poem in the collection, ends with these lines:

> For blood is more savory than wine is,
> And flesh is more tasteful than bread,
> And victory's song more divine is
> Than craven laments for the dead.

This youngest Carr brother also produced an epic poem on the Civil War, *The Contest* (Chicago: P. L. Hanscom, 1866), dedicated to Gen. E. A. Carr, the oldest brother.

3. Clark E. Carr's books include *History of Bringing the Atchison, Topeka & Santa Fe Railroad to Galesburg* (Galesburg, 1913); *History of the Galesburg Postoffice* (Galesburg, 1910); *The Illini: A Story of the Prairies* (Chicago: A. C. McClurg, 1904), a slightly fictionalized account of the Civil War; *Lincoln at Gettysburg* (Chicago: A. C. McClurg, 1906), a short account of the circumstances of the Gettysburg Address, along with Lincoln's text; *The Lincoln-Douglas Debates* (Galesburg, 1907); *My Day and Generation* (Chicago: A. C. McClurg, 1908); *The Railway Mail Service: Its Origin and Development* (Chicago: A. C. McClurg, 1909); and *Stephen A. Douglas: His Life, Public Services, Speeches, and Patriotism* (Chicago: A. C. McClurg, 1909). Extracts from his numerous political speeches are printed in *Portrait and Biographical Album of Knox County, Illinois* (Chicago: Chapman Bros., 1886). Clark Carr also wrote the introduction for Sarah Pratt Carr's *The Iron Way*.

4. General Carr is the subject of a modern biography, James T. King's *War Eagle: A Life of General Eugene A. Carr* (Lincoln: University of Nebraska Press, 1963). Carr was often at the second or third level of command, just

below the officers who are remembered in place names around the West. He fell one rank behind his contemporaries in 1866, when he turned down a chance to command a newly organized Negro regiment, and never was able to make up for his mistake. According to King, he was not so affable as his younger brothers obviously were, a fact that also helps explain his modern obscurity.

5. The reader is referred to King, *War Eagle,* for an account of this incident, which caused considerable controversy and probably held up General Carr's final promotion. General Carr's son, another Clark Carr, later served in Cuba in the Spanish-American War before becoming a rancher in New Mexico.

6. Mary Carr Moore, "My Little Story," Moore Archive, pp. 33–34 (hereafter cited as Moore).

7. Eugene A. Carr, speech to the Kansas Commandery of the Military Order of the Loyal Legion of the United States, 1886, quoted in King, *War Eagle,* pp. 232–33.

8. *Cleveland Plain Dealer,* July 25, 1898, quoted in King, *War Eagle,* p. 253.

9. *Galesburg Republican Register,* 1898, quoted in King, *War Eagle,* p. 253. This clipping also appears in the Carr family scrapbook, private collection, Marian Moore Quinn.

10. Lora Altine Woodbury Underhill, *Descendants of Edward Small of New England and the Allied Families with Tracings of English Ancestry,* rev. ed. (Boston and New York: Houghton Mifflin Co., 1934), vol. 2, p. 950. Information about Simeon Pratt's descendants comes from pp. 952–61.

11. Underhill, *Descendants,* reports that R. H. Pratt went to Europe for a couple of years around 1860. But there is no reference to the trip in Louisa Merrill Pratt's scrapbook or in any of the family's published writings.

12. George Kraus, *High Road to Promontory: Building the Central Pacific (Now the Southern Pacific) across the High Sierra* (Palo Alto: American West Publishing Co., 1969), p. 75. Other information about Pratt comes from the Biographical Card File, California State Library, Sacramento; from Tom Gregory, *History of Solano and Napa Counties, California* (Los Angeles, 1912), pp. 685–86; from Underhill, *Descendants;* and from Moore. The famous "Big Four" railroad builders had been Sacramento merchants who were not a part of San Francisco's power structure until the success of their audacious venture. They were Leland Stanford, Collis P. Huntington, Charles Crocker, and Mark Hopkins.

13. A volume of her poetry was published much later: Louisa Merrill Pratt, *Old-Fashioned Songs* (San Francisco: Sunset Publishing House, 1911). There are also several undated poems in her scrapbook.

14. "Good Morning," n.d., in Louisa Merrill Pratt's scrapbook, private collection, Marian Moore Quinn.

15. "The Story of the Old Woman Who Lived in a Shoe," n.d., in Louisa Merrill Pratt's scrapbook.

16. Biographical card filled out by Sarah Pratt Carr, Biographical Card File, California State Library.

Chapter 2

1. Catharine Beecher and Harriet Beecher Stowe, *The American Woman's Home* (New York: J. B. Ford and Co., 1869), pp. 13, 15–16.

2. Beecher and Stowe, *American Woman's Home*, includes a chapter, "Health of Mind," that contains the following subheadings, which may explain the ban on reading: "Uncommon precocity in children usually the result of a diseased brain—Idiocy often the result, or the precocious child sinks below the average of mankind . . . Some pupils always need restraint in regard to study."

3. William Mason (1829–1908) was a member of America's foremost musical family of the nineteenth century. Trained abroad as a pianist, he settled in New York City and became a teacher. He published a number of piano methods. As a student of William Mason and one of his assistants, Emma Dewhurst would have received excellent training as a musician and teacher.

4. Moore, p. 19. This is the first mention in Moore's autobiography of "Uncle John," her great-uncle John Haraden Pratt.

5. Sarah Pratt Carr, "Out of the Far West," ca. 1935, Moore Archive, p. 3 (hereafter cited as S. P. Carr).

6. S. P. Carr, p. 2. Moore adds that Hannah would sway to the music and sometimes sing along, "Go chain de lion down."

7. Thomas Moore (1779–1852), Irish poet, published several volumes of Irish melodies, which enjoyed lasting popularity. The best known is "Believe Me, If All Those Endearing Young Charms."

8. See Julian Mates, "The First Hundred Years of the American Lyric Theatre," *American Music* 1, no. 2 (Summer, 1983): 22–38. Mildred J. Hill reports a series of festivals of singing societies. The North American Saengerbund in 1877, for instance, was held in Louisville. It offered five days of concerts, a chorus of fifteen hundred, and an orchestra of seventy-five. ("History of Music in Louisville," chap. 8 in *Memorial History of Louisville from Its First Settlement to the Year 1898*, ed. J. Stoddard Johnston [Chicago: American Biographical Publishing Co., 1896], vol. 2.)

9. U. S. Grant was president when B. O. received his appointment. Carr's brother Gen. Eugene A. Carr had served with Grant at Vicksburg. General Sherman continued on active duty for some years following the Civil War. His brother, Senator John Sherman of Ohio, became B. O.'s supervisor during the Hayes administration. John A. Logan, a member of the Illinois bar, served in the U.S. Senate after the Civil War, in which he, too, had served as a general. President Garfield had time, after he took office in 1881, to renew B. O.'s appointment, but he was assassinated before the year was out. Colonel Watterson was a journalist who served briefly in the Confederate Army. He negotiated the merger of the *Louisville Courier* and the *Journal* upon his arrival in Louisville in 1868 and quickly made the merged paper a powerful political force. A Democrat, he used his influence to fight the Ku Klux Klan in Kentucky and to advocate reconciliation between North and South. He was almost surely responsible for the strong statements in the Louisville papers support-

ing B. O. at the time of B. O.'s resignation. Robert Ingersoll had been a cavalry officer; he became attorney general of Illinois.

10. *The National Cyclopaedia of American Biography* (New York: J. T. White and Co., 1907), vol. 9, pp. 255–56, reports of Ingersoll:

> His widest reputation, however, rests on his numerous witty attacks on certain popular forms of Christian teaching, as well as on the divine authority of the Bible. His lectures, which were published complete in 1883, contain such titles as "The Gods," "Ghosts," "Skulls," "Some Mistakes of Moses." . . . He has also lectured repeatedly on the life and work of Thomas Paine and on Shakespeare.

Ingersoll may be the person who first introduced Sarah Pratt Carr to Unitarian thought, or who helped prepare her for some later introduction.

11. At least two bills were introduced in Congress in 1882 concerning riverboat regulation, including such things as the passing signals to be used by riverboat pilots: H.R. 742 (47-1) 1882; and H.R. 651 (47-1)2066 1882. B. O. was involved in their development and was in conflict with at least one supervising inspector of steam vessels over them. Much of the dispute is detailed in the highly partisan newspaper articles preserved in the Carr family scrapbook in the possession of Marian Moore Quinn. B. O.'s personal popularity is evident throughout. The supervising inspector who was his principal opponent is referred to as "an ignorant, vain and vindictive person, who is wholly unfitted for the place he occupies." Carr's case was argued in the press by his friend Colonel Watterson of the *Louisville Courier-Express*. He was seen as an advocate of the interests of "the Western river men" against the unreasonable expectations of his Washington superiors.

12. B. O.'s appointment came through the Treasury Department. George S. Boutwell, who initially appointed him, had been a leader in the unsuccessful movement to impeach President Andrew Johnson. William A. Richardson, his successor, resigned under pressure from the House of Representatives in 1874 during an investigation of the Sanborn contracts scandal. Benjamin H. Bristow, the next treasury secretary, is credited with breaking up the Whiskey Ring, a widespread conspiracy of some years' standing by persons who pocketed federal liquor taxes. Senator John Sherman was Hayes's treasury secretary. That Sherman, who was considered an unusually able secretary, reappointed him speaks particularly well of B. O.'s record. After Garfield's death in 1881, President Arthur appointed Judge Charles J. Folger of New York to the Treasury Department, signaling a move away from the old radical Republicans of Reconstruction days with whom B. O. remained closely identified.

Chapter 3

1. Sarah's recovery seems to have been so complete that one wonders whether the diagnosis was correct. She had been "unwell" fairly often in Louisville, but no serious illness was attributed to her for the rest of her life— more than fifty years.

2. Moore, p. 30. The Grand Army of the Republic (GAR) was the Civil War veterans' organization that included veterans of the Union armies only. Decoration Day is now observed as Memorial Day.

3. *Napa Reporter*, October 15, 1886.

4. The *Napa Register*, October 22, 1886, carried Carr's reply to the latter charge. He personally had a standing offer to pay his white workers half as much again as Chinese workers; he preferred white labor over Chinese; he opposed the use of force against the Chinese. The proper solution was for employers not to hire Chinese labor, in his view.

Chinese laborers were brought into the United States to help build the western railroad system. There were many incidents of violence in the West involving attacks on them. Employers had the luxury of decrying the violence and defending the civil liberties of the Chinese workers, whose presence helped keep wages low, while mercilessly breaking up strikes brought by other workers in protest against poor working conditions.

5. Two of Sarah's articles for the *Woman's Magazine* (Brattleboro, Vermont) were "The Rights of Children," published in 1884, and "Old Maids," published in 1886. Moore's autobiography suggests that she had published other articles there, however.

6. *St. Helena Star*, December 23, 1887. In two performances, two hundred dollars were netted for the Woman's Relief Committee.

7. *Napa Register*, December 23, 1887.

8. William B. Bradbury, *Esther, the Beautiful Queen: A Cantata or Short Oratorio Designed for Musical Conventions, Festivals, and Musical Societies*, text by C. M. Cady (New York: Mason, 1856).

9. Carl Reinecke (1824–1910) was a late Romantic composer very popular in his own time. From 1897 he directed the conservatory at Leipzig.

10. Alice Edwards Pratt earned the Ph.B. in 1881 at the University of California, where she was elected class poet. Pratt's Ph.D. dissertation, "The Use of Color in the Verse of the English Romantic Poets" (University of Chicago, 1897), was reprinted (New York: Haskell House, 1971). She also published *The Sleeping Princess California* (San Francisco: W. Doxey, 1892), a long poem with a conservationist tone. There are several occasional poems from her undergraduate years in Louisa Merrill Pratt's scrapbook, private collection, Marian Moore Quinn.

11. San Diego Normal School is now the University of California, San Diego. Alice was the first English instructor hired when the school opened in 1898. She taught there until 1911 or 1912. From 1902 she had a joint appointment as registrar and member of the English faculty.

12. "Which is Best," poem dedicated to the Class of 1885, Santa Rosa Seminary, in Louisa Merrill Pratt's scrapbook, private collection, Marian Moore Quinn.

13. Dwight L. Moody (1837–99) and Ira D. Sankey (1840–1908) began their joint evangelical mission in 1870. Moody's sermons and Sankey's hymns became widely known in the late nineteenth century as they took their message throughout the United States and to England.

14. Mathilde Marchesi (1821–1913) had studied with Otto Nicolai and the fabled Manuel Garcia. She ran a school for singers in Paris for twenty-five years starting in 1881. She attracted many American students, including Emma Eames, Mary Garden, and composer-patron Eleanor Everest Freer. See Elizabeth Forbes, "Marchesi," in *The New Grove Dictionary of Music and Musicians*, ed. Stanley Sadie (London: Macmillan, 1980) vol. 11, p. 650.

15. As his problems multiplied in 1888, B. O. could not expect another federal appointment, since the president was a Democrat, Grover Cleveland. But in March, 1889, he traveled to Washington, D.C., to attend the inauguration of a Republican president, William Henry Harrison, and probably to seek another federal appointment. At about this time his brother Clark E. Carr became U.S. Minister to Denmark. If an appointment was the purpose of his trip, B. O. was unsuccessful.

16. The *Napa Register,* January 10, 1890, reports that the Carrs leased Valle Vista to one Vanaerd late in 1889. Vanaerd promised to invest sixty thousand dollars in a cognac factory on the property. He turned out to be a confidence man and left St. Helena with numerous unpaid bills. Although B. O. may not have lost any cash in this transaction, it may have delayed the sale of the property, which was not completed until 1892, when the Carrs had left San Francisco for Lemoore. Their investment in the extravagant house, with its wood paneling and specially made tiles, was never recovered. They suffered not only from depressed values in the Napa Valley because of the grape epidemic, but also from a nationwide depression.

Chapter 4

1. Carlin Pratt Eastwood's plays registered in the U.S. Copyright Office are "Brethren of the Summit," four-act play (Corte Madera, Calif., 1909); "Family Pattern," three-act play (Los Angeles, 1917); "King in a Blouse," three-act play (Corte Madera, Calif., 1912); and "The Master Road," four-act play (Corte Madera, Calif., 1910). *The Master Road* was published as a novel (New York and Seattle: Alice Harriman Co., 1910).

2. "Lullabye" is included in Mary Carr Moore, *Twenty-Eight Songs* (New York: Da Capo Press, 1987). The extant version of Moore's catalog was presumably copied from an earlier source in 1926 or 1927. It was periodically updated and annotated thereafter. The catalog is in a bound journal (microfilm, Moore Archive) that also contains a short memoir by B. O. Carr, poems by Moore, and a few clippings (hereafter cited as Moore, catalog).

3. The offer came through a family connection. Lucy Pratt Lillis, another of Grandfather Pratt's numerous younger siblings, was married to the owner of a Mexican land grant in the area, which is near Fresno. Sinon Lillis also owned several banks in that part of the state. He offered B. O. part ownership and the opportunity to manage one of them in Lemoore.

4. H. Rosenthal, ed., *The Mapleson Memoirs: The Career of an Operatic Impressario, 1858–1888* (New York: Appleton-Century, 1966), describes the companies' enormous popularity, which led to the printing and sale of coun-

terfeit tickets and other shenanigans in San Francisco. The American-born Nordica (1857–1914) was a prominent operatic soprano. Patti (1843–1919), one of an Italian family of singers, was among the greatest of bel canto singers. Her pure and flexible coloratura must have been an important model for Moore.

5. Steiner (1852–1927) is reported in Christine Ammer, *Unsung: A History of Women in American Music* (Westport, Conn.: Greenwood Press, 1980), pp. 167–68, as a composer of operas and a conductor. Ammer reports that Steiner produced "seven operas, a number of musical dramas, ballets, and many songs and dances."

6. Lawrence Estavan, ed. *The History of Opera in San Francisco*, vols. 7–8 of *San Francisco Theatre Research* (San Francisco: Works Progress Administration, 1938). Opera in English became a rallying cry for the American music movement later on.

7. "Gertrude Stein," in *Notable American Women, 1607–1950*, ed. Edward T. James (Cambridge, Mass.: Harvard University Press, Belknap Press, 1971), vol. 3. Stein grew up in an entirely different, and much less protected, family atmosphere, outside the Victorian conventions that shaped Moore's life so strongly.

8. Moore's daughter remembers Buffalo Bill riding up to shake hands with all the family during one of his shows some years later (Marian M. Quinn, letter to Smith and Richardson, February 15, 1984).

9. Alfred Frankenstein reports in *The New Grove*, vol. 16, p. 471, that Fritz Scheel conducted some concerts given by a "Symphony Society" in the 1890s. After Moore left San Francisco, H. B. Pasmore organized his Apollo Chorus, which sometimes performed with the Symphony Society. The San Francisco Symphony was not organized until 1911. Alfred Metzger, "Symphony Concerts in San Francisco from 1877 to 1919," *Pacific Coast Musical Review*, December 21, 1918, reported three orchestras of varying sizes that gave concert series at various times between 1880 and 1894. One gathers that their repertoires had little in common with those of symphony orchestras today.

10. Cornel Lengyel, ed., *Early Master Teachers*, vol. 6 of *History of Music in San Francisco Series* (San Francisco: Work Projects Administration, Northern California, 1940), p. 5.

11. Marriner-Campbell's career as a singer and teacher in San Francisco is discussed briefly in Lengyel, *Early Master Teachers*, pp. 127–29. She made several trips to Europe for study in the course of her career. Moore listed her among her teachers on a biography card filed in the California State Library, but does not mention her in the autobiography.

12. Beatrice L. Harms, "Biographical Sketch of Henry Bickford Pasmore," October 14, 1937, C-D 5132, Bancroft Library, University of California, Berkeley. Salomon Jadassohn (1831–1902), teacher, conductor, and composer, taught at the conservatory in Leipzig from 1871. His texts on harmony, counterpoint, and canon and fugue were translated into English, French, and Italian. Moore's own teaching in the 1930s and 1940s, like that of most American professors, still followed his method and that of Alfred

Richter. George Whitefield Chadwick (1854–1931) studied in Leipzig and became director of the New England Conservatory. He was a leading American composer of the New England School.

13. Rupert Hughes, *American Composers,* rev. ed. (Boston: Page Co., 1914; New York: AMS Press, 1973). "The work of H. B. Pasmore is highly commended by *cognoscenti* . . ." (p. 272). This part of the book is apparently unchanged from the earlier edition of 1900; later chapters by Arthur Elson in the 1914 edition also mention Pasmore.

14. Quoted in Lengyel, *Early Master Teachers,* p. 56.

15. Shakespeare, a disciple of Lamperti, was the author of *The Art of Singing* (1898–99) and other books on singing. His text says that he has tried to pull together "traditions and hints" left from the late eighteenth century, a high point for vocal technique. His text for bel canto singing is full of scale patterns and exercises designed to develop accuracy and agility rather than volume. Shakespeare's texts were widely used in the United States.

16. Pasmore took his whole family to Berlin for three years, starting in 1905. He supported them by teaching in several conservatories. Mary, Dorothy, and Suzanne formed the Pasmore Trio (violin, cello, and piano), which made its debut in Berlin in 1908. Their ability to play from memory long works such as the Tchaikovsky Trio, then a novelty for a chamber group, became their trademark. After tours of Europe and the United States, they worked with their father in San Francisco, teaching in the Pasmore Conservatory. They would have been active there when Moore returned to San Francisco in 1915. Mary and Dorothy became members of the San Francisco Symphony. A fourth daughter of Pasmore, Harriet, had a very successful career as a singer. Under the name Radiana Pazmor, she introduced some of Ives's songs in New York in the 1930s.

17. *Alameda Times Star,* April 28, 1938.

18. Quoted in Lengyel, *Early Master Teachers,* p. 67.

19. Alfred Richter (1846–1919) taught at Leipzig from 1872. One of his texts went through sixty-four editions before 1952, according to *Baker's Biographical Dictionary of Musicians,* 7th ed. (New York: Schirmer Books, 1984).

20. A complete fugal exposition with four voices, dated 1891, is copied out in a book of exercises and examples (now in the Moore Archive) that Moore assembled some forty years later for her own counterpoint classes.

21. Frank C. Walker, *Penelope: or, The Milkman's Bride,* a comic operetta in one act, with words and adaptations by Frank C. Walker (New York: W. A. Pond and Co., 1878). The music was adapted from the works of many composers.

22. Sarah Pratt Carr, "Old Maids," *Woman's Magazine* 9 (January, 1886): 142–44.

23. Moore, p. 59. In "Out of the Far West," Sarah gives a different account, reporting that Mary Louise talked about writing an opera and speculated on a comic plot with a house guest, probably Bertha Stringer, while on summer vacation at Lemoore, and that she was able to produce a completed score when Mrs. Farnham asked her about it.

24. Mary Carr Moore, *The Oracle*, piano-vocal score, 1893–94, Moore Archive.

25. *San Francisco Town Talk*, 1894, clipping in Scrapbook no. 2, Moore Archive. The attitude expressed here of contempt for popular music is not at all unique to Moore.

26. The much better-known Bohemian Club productions, which began in 1902, were entirely closed to women, who were even barred from the audience.

27. Unidentified clipping in Scrapbook no. 2, Moore Archive.

28. For a detailed account of the Woman's Building, see Jeanne Madeline Weimann, *The Fair Women* (Chicago: Academy Chicago, 1981). The Rumford Kitchen, part of the Massachusetts exhibit, was a model neighborhood kitchen designed to feed a model working-class neighborhood of kitchenless homes. All this was part of the contemporary reform movement now labeled "domestic feminism," and was designed to relieve women from the drudgery of nineteenth-century kitchens. See Dolores Hayden, *The Grand Domestic Revolution* (Cambridge, Mass.: MIT Press, 1981), pp. 151–62. Very likely Sarah went along on this trip, and the exposition probably stimulated her to further community activism in Lemoore.

29. W. S. B. Matthews, "Music at the Fair: The Present Outlook," *Music: A Monthly Magazine* 3, no. 4 (February, 1984): 428, lists these concerts: hour-long band concerts, two to four daily; popular orchestral concerts, eighty minutes long, every noon, given by a one hundred fourteen piece orchestra, Theodore Thomas, director; twice-weekly afternoon symphony concerts, often featuring the work of a single composer. The music of American composers such as Beach, Chadwick, Foote, MacDowell, and Loeffler was performed at some of these concerts.

30. Amy Marcy Cheney Beach (1867–1944) wrote "Festival Jubilate," op. 17 (1892), which was performed at the dedication of the Woman's Building of the World Columbian Exposition. Moore met Beach in San Francisco a quarter century after the exposition.

31. S. P. Carr, p. 11. The explanation for Moore's fainting spells that Moore herself gave in her autobiography, and which Marian Moore Quinn supported in a February 15, 1984, letter to the authors, is that the spells were related in some way to heart trouble.

Chapter 5

1. "Give the Country its Due," *Impress* 1, no. 12 (June, 1894). The article is signed "S. P. C., Lemoore," and there is no doubt that Sarah Pratt Carr was the author. One wonders how Sarah would have responded to life in Paris, had the Carrs been able to take Mary Louise there.

2. Karen J. Blair, in *The Clubwoman as Feminist: True Womanhood Redefined, 1868–1914* (New York: Holmes and Meier Publishers, 1980), defines the term *domestic feminism* as "the extension of woman's domestically nurtured traits into the public sphere" (p. 117). Domestic feminists of the late nine-

teenth century organized clubs first for literary study, then for activism in the area of "municipal housekeeping": "In their attempts to achieve moral and domestic perfection, women ventured into schools and benevolent organizations which extended new influence on the male-dominated public sphere" (p. 117). Sarah was clearly in the mainstream of domestic feminism. Music and the arts were not the primary area of interest for most domestic feminist reformers, though many wrote and published poetry, as Charlotte Perkins Gilman and Sarah herself did.

3. Charlotte Perkins Gilman, a prominent feminist reformer of the day, lived in California ca. 1890–95. She describes her experience there in *The Living of Charlotte Perkins Gilman, an Autobiography* (New York: D. Appleton-Century Co., 1935). Gilman took on the Southern Pacific Railroad, which was the principal source of the Pratt family's prosperity. "That great railroad and steamship owner held the state in absolute control by land and sea. It held merciless power in the legislature, in the press, in the courts, even in the churches through wealthy patronage. In the very women's clubs it could not be criticized because some prominent member was sure to be wife to an official of the road" (p. 145).

4. "Sonnet in Answer to a Complaint: 'So Many Prayers and Tears Must Go for Naught,'" in L. M. Pratt, *Old-Fashioned Songs*.

5. "The Minister's Teaching," in Pratt, *Old-Fashioned Songs*. The poem is dated Easter, 1890, and in a footnote Louisa Pratt relates it to Stebbins's preaching.

6. Rev. Charles W. Wendte was her mentor. He was minister of the Unitarian Church in Oakland and was in charge of the denomination's missionary activities on the West Coast. At that time, the denomination was expanding very rapidly and could scarcely supply congregations with ministers. Wendte had welcomed a woman as his associate minister in Oakland for a time, and he must have been glad to help train so promising a prospect as Sarah. In 1904, after some years of struggle, and after Sarah had ceased to be active as a minister, he succeeded in founding the Pacific School of Religion in order to train ministers on the West Coast.

7. *Lemoore Centennial Book, 1873–1973* (Lemoore, Calif., 1973).

8. Mary Louise brought her version of *Penelope* from San Francisco for one of these fund-raisers. B. O., as manager of the local bank, was instrumental in obtaining the land for the park.

9. "Lemoore Woman's Club—Serving Community 90 Years," *Lemoore Leader*, March 2, 1983. The article includes photos of Carr and cofounder Emma Fox.

10. Unidentified clipping, n.d., in Carr family scrapbook, private collection, Marian Moore Quinn.

11. S. P. Carr, p. 11. These sentences are lightly crossed out.

12. "Notes from the San Joaquin Valley," *Impress* 1, no. 10 (April, 1894): 4, article signed "S. P. C." (Sarah's initials). The Tulare teacher to whom she referred was probably Ada Reed Kruse.

13. The slogan "Boston of the San Joaquin Valley" is not found in any of

the Carr or Moore papers that survive. It was quoted in the *Lemoore Leader* article of March 2, 1983 (see n. 9 above). But it may safely be assumed that Sarah, with her Unitarian affiliation, was well aware of the writings of Ralph Waldo Emerson (1803–82). Emerson's 1837 address, "The American Scholar," advocates cultural independence from European models.

14. "First Meeting of Woman's Congress," *Impress* 2, no. 19 (February, 1895): 7 (the magazine's penultimate issue).

15. Charles W. Wendte, *The Wider Fellowship* (Boston: Beacon Press, 1927), vol. 2, p. 131.

16. Sarah Pratt Carr to the Boston headquarters of the Unitarian Association, January 15, 1904, Unitarian Universalist Association Archives, Boston.

17. *Christian Register*, March 14, 1895, 167, quoted in Catherine F. Hitchings, *Universalist and Unitarian Women Ministers* (Boston: Universalist Historical Society, 1975), p. 41.

18. "Health of Mind," in Beecher and Stowe, *American Woman's Home*, pp. 256–57.

Chapter 6

1. Charles de Bériot (1802–70), a Belgian, and Henryk Wieniawski (1835–80), a Pole, were both virtuoso violinists who also composed for their instrument.

2. A printed announcement in the Lemoore Public Library lists "Mrs. J. C. Moore, Mezzo-Soprano." Although described as "song recitals," the two surviving programs include works for violin and piano as well as readings. For the "Evening with German Composers," Moore sang a group by Mendelssohn, Grieg's "Outward Bound," a group consisting of Schumann's "A Forest Legend," Rubinstein's "Since First I Met Thee," Brahms's "Cradle Song," and Meyer-Helmund's "The Vow," as well as Mozart's "Dove sono." Her contribution to the French evening included: Chaminade's "Rosemonde," Delibes's "Bonjour Suzon," Lacome's "A Night in May," Massenet's "Air de Salome" from *Herodiade*, Saint-Saëns's "Moonlight in the Forest," Bizet's "In the Woods," and Gounod's "Jewell Song" from *Faust*.

3. Opp. 36, 37, 38, 41, and 42 are all assigned to the various songs written for Barrett's use. The two anthems in op. 39 were probably also for Barrett, who was a Presbyterian, rather than for Sarah's congregations. A few of these songs that were published have turned up in a private collection in Lemoore; a few more are in the Library of Congress. "I'm Going to Vote, John," the only unpublished one known to have survived, is written in Moore's hand and is in the Moore Archive. "We'll Never Let Old Glory Fall" lists Mary Louise Carr as arranger. Otherwise, the evidence for Moore's contribution is her own statement in her catalog. "I'm Going to Vote, John" and "Yankee Dewey Do" are recorded on Cambria C-1022; the first of these is in Moore, *Twenty-Eight Songs*.

4. For a modern account of the California state campaign of 1896, see Eleanor Flexner, *Century of Struggle: The Woman's Rights Movement in the United*

States, rev. ed. (Cambridge, Mass.: Harvard University Press, Belknap Press, 1975), pp. 230–31. San Francisco liquor interests rallied at the last minute to defeat the proposal by a narrow margin.

The temperance movement was closely associated with the women's rights movement, but the Pratts and Carrs, former wine growers, seem to have avoided this issue. In "Waters of Eden," some years later, Sarah stated her position on liquor: If taverns were closed and family-style wine gardens substituted for them, moderation would result and alcohol would no longer threaten the families of the working class.

5. Popular music was then considered disreputable by art music composers. But male composers who could wrote it anyway, apologizing but accepting the financial rewards. One well-known example is Victor Herbert, who always wanted to be accepted as a serious composer rather than as the composer of operettas. Whether Moore, if she had cultivated her gift for light music and musical comedy, would actually have had any commercial success, given the barriers against women in music, is open to question. There were women who published piano rags successfully, but most abandoned their careers within a few years and disappeared into the anonymity of marriage.

6. Moore, p. 79. Marian reports Byron's later comeback as "Yes, and I stood up to nurse."

7. Moore, p. 87. Clarkie was the son of B. O. Carr's brother Clarke E. Carr, of Galesburg, Illinois. Half a century later, Moore still marked Wray Torrey's birthday in her datebook every year.

Chapter 7

1. Eugene Carr had practiced law in Seattle, with time out for his trips to Alaska, since the early 1880s, when the town was very small. An officer in the state militia from the start, he had a prominent role in the anti-Chinese riots of 1885 and 1886. Nard Jones, in *Seattle* (Garden City, N.Y.: Doubleday, 1972), reports that E. M. Carr was one of five men arrested and charged with murder for their part in facing an angry white mob and protecting some hundred Chinese as they were being evacuated from the city. One person was killed and several more injured during the skirmish between the militia and the mob. Both sides were intent on removing the Chinese, who had been brought in to work on the railroad and, in 1885–86, were seen as unfair competition with unemployed white workers. The charges, brought by police officers in sympathy with the mob, were never pressed.

2. *Seattle Times*, January 11, 1902.

3. *Seattle Post-Intelligencer*, January 11, 1902. A repeat performance, this one to benefit the new Trinity Parish Church, was canceled when some of that church's members objected that *The Oracle* was unsuitable as a church fundraiser. One of the new numbers Moore had added dealt with the modern replacement of the nectar of the gods by Rainier beer. Moore was annoyed by this turn of events, for she had added that number at someone else's urging, and it was unnecessary to the plot.

4. Nellie Centennial Cornish (1876–1956) founded the Cornish School in

Seattle in 1914. The school rapidly acquired a national reputation, serving as a model for a private school built around a creatively integrated arts curriculum. Over the years well-known artists such as Mark Tobey, Martha Graham, and John Cage were associated with the school, which continues to play an important role in Seattle's cultural life.

5. Nellie C. Cornish, *Miss Aunt Nellie, the Autobiography of Nellie C. Cornish* (Seattle: University of Washington Press, 1964), pp. 59–60.

6. More than forty years later, however, Cornish's adopted daughter, Elena Miramova, would marry Byron Carr Moore, and Moore would speak of her contemporary as "my old friend Nellie Cornish" in her catalog.

7. Cornish, *Miss Aunt Nellie*, pp. 65–66.

8. Ibid., p. 64.

9. "Summer Passes" appeared in an arrangement for women's three-part chorus (SSA) some twenty years later under the imprint of Carl Fischer. "Brahma," op. 69, no. 2, was written in 1909. Moore scored the simple accompaniment for orchestra and conducted the orchestrated song at the Panama-Pacific International Exposition in San Francisco in 1915. Both appear in Moore, *Twenty-Eight Songs*.

10. Lionel Stevenson, *The Pre-Raphaelite Poets* (New York: Norton, 1972) describes the philosophy of Morris, who was close to several members of the original six young poets who banded together briefly in the 1840s to oppose the older, academic poets who then dominated English intellectual life. The present authors have relied on Morris's own statements in his Utopian sketch, *News from Nowhere* (1891), vol. 16 of *The Collected Works* (New York: Russell and Russell, 1966), for his view of the creative process and the role of the arts in everyday life.

11. The section set by Moore appears on pp. 162–68 of William Morris, *Sigurd the Volsung* (New York: Longmans, Green and Co., 1906). The poem first appeared in 1876. Though *Sigurd* tells a Norse saga, it is not so different from the medieval poems and tales of Sir Walter Scott, which Moore had heard from early childhood and read herself as soon as she was allowed to read.

12. Redfern Mason, review of Pacific Composers' Day at the San Francisco Musical Club, *San Francisco Examiner*, n.d., in Scrapbook no. 5, Moore Archive. Other composers represented were Albert Elkus, John Haraden Pratt, Arthur Fickenscher, Uda Waldrop, Oscar Weil, and Antonio de Grassi.

Chapter 8

1. B. O. Carr's military and pension records, as obtained from the National Archives and Records Service, Reference Services Branch, Washington, D.C., indicate that Colonel Carr filed three pension applications. He applied for an "Invalid Pension" on January 11, 1893, and on September 16, 1898. He filed for a pension on April 30, 1907, as well. Sarah applied for a widow's pension soon after his death in 1913. In 1936, Moore filed to recover Sarah's funeral expenses.

2. There are no known copies of many of the plays by Sarah Pratt Carr

registered in the U.S. Copyright Office. The Copyright Office did not require deposit copies for most of the time she was writing plays. The following are registered: "The Cost of Empire," four-act play (San Francisco, 1909) and libretto for the opera *Narcissa* (Seattle: Stuff Printing Concern, 1912); "Flash-Light" (with Lillian Volkman), sketch (San Francisco, 1912), Copyright Office; "Her Name," sketch (San Francisco, 1912), Copyright Office; "The Homesteaders," sketch (St. Helena, 1912), Copyright Office; "The Iron Way," four-act play, presumably a dramatization of her own novel (Seattle, 1907), unlocated; *The Jenkinses Go to the Circus, Rural Romp in One Act* (New York: Edgar S. Werner, 1912); "Kentucky Belle," four-act play (St. Helena, 1887), unlocated but described in chap. 3 above; "Lolita," five-act drama based on the career of Lola Montez (St. Helena, 1889), unlocated; "Love in Lucky Camp," three-act play (San Francisco, 1891), unlocated; "Madam, the Agent," four-act play (Lemoore, 1892), Rare Book Room, Library of Congress; "The Paper Table Mat," four-act comedy drama (Lemoore, 1898), unlocated; "Rock of the Sun," four-act play (Seattle, 1910), unlocated. "Reforming a Man, or Lemoore in 1919," play (Lemoore, ca. 1894), unlocated; "Ruins," one-act play, n.d., Moore Archive; and "Where Rolls the Oregon," screenplay scenario, n.d., Moore Archive, are other known dramatic works.

3. *The Iron Way* was published by McClurg of Chicago in 1907 and went through at least four printings. Clark E. Carr, Sarah's brother-in-law, had already published successfully with McClurg; he supplied a preface to Sarah's book. *Billy To-Morrow* followed two years later (1909). Its three sequels are *Billy To-Morrow in Camp* (1910), *Billy To-Morrow Stands the Test* (1911), and *Billy To-Morrow's Chums* (1913). "Waters of Eden" was serialized in the *Alaska-Yukon Magazine* (1909–10). The short story is "A Gordian Knot," in *Tillicum Tales* (Seattle: Lowman and Hanford, 1907).

4. Florence Martin Eastland, in "Does Writing Pay?" *Alaska-Yukon Magazine* 7, no. 5 (February, 1909): 425–27, describes the work of the Seattle Writers' Club, which Sarah had helped organize. In 1907, a volume of short stories (*Tillicum Tales*) including Sarah's "A Gordian Knot," was published by the Seattle Writers' Club. Sarah is described as "the banner seller of the clubs" and their "source of inspiration."

5. Sarah Pratt Carr, *The Iron Way: A Tale of the Builders of the West* (Chicago: A. C. McClurg, 1907), p. 69.

6. Sarah Pratt Carr, "Waters of Eden," serialized in *Alaska-Yukon Magazine* 9, no. 4 (March, 1910): 239.

7. Ibid., 239–40, 243.

8. S. P. Carr, "Waters of Eden," serialized in *Alaska-Yukon Magazine* 8, no. 6 (September–October, 1909): 455–56.

9. *Billy To-Morrow Stands the Test* (Chicago: A. C. McClurg, 1911), p. 232.

10. Sarah had attacked the unhealthy "foreignization" of San Francisco in an article for the *Impress* written from Lemoore in the 1890s. Census reports from this period break down the populations of cities by "native white, native parentage"; "native white, foreign/mixed parentage"; "foreign born, white";

and "negro and other." The percentages of the populations of San Francisco and Seattle falling into the "native white, native parentage" category were, respectively, 24.3 and 48.1 in 1900, and 27.6 and 44.6 in 1910. Both Seattle and Los Angeles, where Sarah passed her last years, had more homogeneous populations than San Francisco.

11. S. P. Carr, "Waters of Eden," serialized in *Alaska-Yukon Magazine* 9, no. 3 (February, 1910): 159.

12. Ibid., 150, 152; *Alaska-Yukon Magazine* 9, no. 1 (November, 1909): 50.

13. S. P. Carr, "Waters of Eden," serialized in *Alaska-Yukon Magazine* 9, no. 2 (December, 1909): 102–3.

14. S. P. Carr, "Waters of Eden," serialized in *Alaska-Yukon Magazine* 9, no. 4 (March, 1910): 243–44.

15. Sarah Pratt Carr to the *San Francisco Examiner*, September 19 (no year given; probably written during the suffrage campaign of 1896), in Carr family scrapbook.

16. *Billy To-Morrow in Camp* (Chicago: A. C. McClurg, 1910), p. 25.

17. Moore, p. 96. Two versions of the last three pages (96–98) of the autobiography, which describe her attempted suicide, exist in the Moore Archive. This and subsequent quotations from pp. 96–97 are taken from what appears to be the second version.

18. The strychnine episode was closely associated with "The Quest of Sigurd," but it is unclear which came first.

19. Mary Carr Moore datebook, August 18, 1931, microfilm, Moore Archive.

Chapter 9

1. Arthur Farwell, "Toward American Music," essay for December in *Musiclover's Calendar* (New York: Breitkopf and Härtel, 1906), vol. 2, pp. 21–24. Farwell produced many such homilies. Gilbert Chase, in *America's Music, from the Pilgrims to the Present,* 2d ed. (New York: McGraw-Hill, 1966), points out that Arthur Farwell was inspired by William Morris's work, as Moore and her mother had been. Morris's wide influence on the American music movement in the early part of the twentieth century bears further exploration.

2. Czech nationalist composer Antonín Dvořák suggested in "Music in America," *Harper's Magazine* 90 (February, 1895): 428–34, that Negro melodies might form a basis for a characteristically American art music. Edward MacDowell, who had made his reputation abroad, led the opposition to the concept, which nevertheless became popular.

A half-century earlier, however, William Henry Fry had completed the first grand opera composed in the United States, *Leonora,* and in 1852 had advocated "a Declaration of Independence in Art" in which "American composers shall discard their foreign liveries and found an American school." Writing in *Dwight's Journal* the following year, John S. Dwight of Boston had argued for the "universality" of music. Dwight's arguments, which as a practical matter asserted the primacy of German music, easily carried the day. See

Betty E. Chmaj, "Fry versus Dwight: American Music's Debate over Nationality," *American Music* 3, no. 1 (Spring, 1985): 63–84.

3. The Wa Wan Press published the works of thirty-seven American composers between 1901 and 1912. Some of the music used Indian themes. None of Moore's music was published by Wa Wan, since at that time Witmark seems to have published everything Moore chose to send them, including the piano-vocal score of *Narcissa*.

4. Among the others were Arthur Nevin (*Poia*, produced 1910), Frederick Shepherd Converse (*The Pipe of Desire*, 1910; *The Sacrifice*, 1911), Victor Herbert (*Natoma*, 1911), and Charles Wakefield Cadman (*Daoma*, 1912; *Shanewis*, 1918). These are discussed, along with Moore's *Narcissa* and *The Flaming Arrow*, in Harold E. Briggs, "The North American Indian as Depicted in Musical Compositions, Culminating with American 'Indianist' Operas of the Early Twentieth Century, 1900–1930" (Master's thesis, Indiana University, 1976). Of these composers, Cadman and Converse later became members of the Society of Native American Composers, which Moore helped organize; Farwell did not. The composers who attempted to write consciously American works, particularly those involving Indian themes or Indian-inspired music, are sometimes labeled American Romantic Nationalists.

5. Mary Carr Moore, "Writing and Producing an Opera," *Pacific Coast Musician*, July 7, 1915, 51. Dr. John McLoughlin's name was consistently misspelled "McLaughlin" by both Moore and Carr.

6. Henry Hadley (1871–1937) was another of the American nationalists. In the 1930s he founded the National Association of American Composers and Conductors (NAACC), an organization roughly parallel to Moore's American music groups of the 1930s, in New York.

7. Sarah acknowledged the following sources in her published libretto: Eva Emery Dye, *McLoughlin and Old Oregon: A Chronicle*, 5th ed. (Chicago: A. C. McClurg, 1903); Edmond S. Meany, *History of the State of Washington* (New York: Macmillan, 1909); [Stephen] Penrose, *Marcus Whitman* (probably published by Stephen Beasley Linnard Penrose, Walla Walla); Lee Moorhouse, *Indian Customs* (Moorhouse published souvenir albums of Indian photos in 1905 and 1906); and Edgar S. Fischer, *Indian Modes and Rhythm*.

8. Sarah Pratt Carr, foreword to *The Cost of Empire*, libretto.

9. Among other things, Sarah's play "Lolita," written in 1891, was based on the story of Lola Montez, a dancer who lived in the Mother Lode country of California for a time during the gold rush. More recently, she had written *The Iron Way*, a novel set in the Western locales of her own childhood.

10. "Club Hears Libretto," unidentified newspaper clipping, n.d., in Scrapbook no. 4, Moore Archive. This article includes a letter dated May 11, 1912, from Sarah Pratt Carr to the Walla Walla Symphony Club.

11. Mary Carr Moore to Robert L. Sincock, August 11, 1947, Northwest and Whitman College Archives, Penrose Memorial Library, Whitman College, Walla Walla, Washington.

12. Deciding that she needed additional study of orchestration for this very large task, Moore went for lessons to Edwin Fairbourn, who was associated with her American Music Center in Seattle.

13. Whitman did, in fact, make such an unprecedented winter journey to the East in 1842–43, and while there he urged the government to promote emigration to Old Oregon and provide much-needed protection to travelers over the Oregon Trail. However, there is no evidence that the United States was in any danger of losing Old Oregon to Britain at the time of Whitman's journey, and it is now recognized that Whitman's trip was also prompted by the American Board of Commissioners for Foreign Mission's order (later rescinded) to close his mission at Waiilatpu, and his concern about the growing influence of the Roman Catholic missionaries in the Northwest. Whitman's reasons for making this trip have been debated for over one hundred years, and the interpretation presented in the opera has come to be known as the "Whitman Saved Oregon" story. This version was widely accepted as fact when *Narcissa* was written, but is now regarded as myth. For further information on this historical debate, see Clifford M. Drury, *Marcus and Narcissa Whitman and the Opening of Old Oregon*, 2 vols. (Glendale, Calif.: Arthur H. Clark Co., 1973).

14. This use of "The Star Spangled Banner" may have been suggested by Puccini's use of the same tune in *Madama Butterfly*, which had its U.S. premiere at the Met in 1906. If Moore had not seen the opera, she had certainly read about it and must have been aware of this feature of Puccini's score. In *Butterfly*, "The Star Spangled Banner" symbolizes Pinkerton's despicable behavior; for Moore, it symbolized the winning of the American West, a noble cause.

15. Helen Ross, "Grand Opera of the West," *Town Crier* (Seattle), April 13, 1912, 11.

16. Mary Carr Moore to Robert L. Sincock, July 20, 1947, Northwest and Whitman College Archives.

17. Mary Carr Moore to Sarah Pratt Carr, n.d., Moore Archive.

18. Many of the costumes and props were loaned by Maj. Lee Moorhouse of Pendleton, Oregon, a noted collector of Indian artifacts. In some cases the singers wore the actual garments of the individuals whom they portrayed.

19. At the Wednesday matinee performance, the roles of Marcus and Narcissa were sung by locals Neal Begley and Maude Conley Hopper. Others who sang major roles in that first cast were: Alfred A. Owens (Elijah and Henry Spalding), Romeyn Jansen (Siskadee), Charles Derbyshire (Delaware Tom), Frederick Graham (Yellow Serpent), Henry T. Hanlin (Dr. John McLoughlin), Walter F. Paull (Reverend Hull), and Lottie Meeker Kessler (Eliza Spalding).

20. Ross, "Grand Opera of the West," 11.

21. Carl Presley, "Historical Opera of the Northwest," *Musical America*, May 11, 1912, 5.

22. Cyril A. Player, "'Narcissa' Sung; Well Received," *Seattle Post-Intelligencer*, April 23, 1912, 4.

23. "Music and the Musicians," *Town Crier*, April 27, 1912, 10.

24. Sydney Strong, "Whitman in Grand Opera," *Chicago Advance*, n.d., in Scrapbook no. 4, Moore Archive.

25. Player, "'Narcissa' Sung; Well Received," 4.

26. "Seattle's New Opera," *Musical America,* June 1, 1912, 20.
27. Ross, "Grand Opera of the West," 11.
28. Gem Harris, "Narcissa," *Overland Monthly and Out West Magazine* 83 (October, 1925): 380.
29. "Music and the Musicians," 10.
30. "New Grand Opera by Western Women," *Musical America,* March 9, 1912, 44.
31. Anna Cora Winchell, "San Francisco News," *Music and Musicians* 11 (October, 1925): 11.
32. Player, "'Narcissa' Sung; Well Received," 4.
33. Paul C. Hedrick, "Narcissa Approved by Large Local Audience," *Seattle Daily Times,* April 23, 1912, 7.
34. Sarah Pratt Carr, "Seattle Makes History in Music," *Nautilus* 14 (September, 1912): 67.

Chapter 10

1. Moore's autobiography ends about 1907; the datebooks begin in 1928. The authors have, therefore, depended more heavily for this section on the less-complete record of the catalog and the scrapbooks. In addition, conclusions about Moore's frame of mind at times during this period are drawn from the texts she chose to set. Information on New York's concert life is drawn mainly from the pages of *Musical America.*
2. Arthur Farwell, "Extremism in Paint and Tone," *Musical America,* April 12, 1913, 24. Farwell thought then that realism in music, in the form of the windmills, sheep, etc. in Richard Strauss's *Don Quixote,* had already been tried and rejected.
3. Royal Cortissot, "Ellis Island Art," quoted in Oliver Larkin, *Art and Life in America,* rev. ed. (New York: Holt, Rinehart and Winston, 1960), pp. 360–64. Larkin reports that Cortissot "concluded that Cézanne was a complacent ignoramus, Van Gogh a crazy incompetent, and Picasso a man whose unadulterated cheek resembled that of Barnum."
4. Conducted by Toscanini, on March 19, 1913. *Boris* was reviewed in great detail in *Musical America.*
5. *Musical America,* February 8, 1913, 13. Huneker ended by calling Schoenberg "a musical anarchist." Schoenberg and Stravinsky were highly critical of each other's music, and with the exception of Stravinsky's orchestration, Moore had little interest in either of them, then or later. It seemed totally unlikely in 1913 that the three of them would, all unwillingly, rub elbows with one another as residents of Los Angeles a quarter of a century hence.
6. *Musical America,* May 3, 1913. Peter S. Hansen, *An Introduction to Twentieth Century Music,* 4th ed. (Boston: Allyn and Bacon, 1981), pp. 80–81, gives a chart of the various noises to be considered as music as they appear in Russolo's manifesto, which was published in Milan.
7. *Musical America,* February 15, 1913, 37, quotes an unnamed English

writer in favor of ragtime as a source for American art music. European innovators such as Debussy had already borrowed ragtime rhythms.

8. John Kirkpatrick, "Charles Ives," in *The New Grove*, vol. 9, pp. 414–29. Ives was only a year younger than Moore, but his career was strikingly different from hers. Ives was well enough known by 1940 for Moore to have heard of his work, and for her associates to ask him to become involved in the Society of Native American Composers.

9. Claire R. Reis, *Composers, Conductors, and Critics* (New York: Oxford University Press, 1955). Reis had been trained as a pianist, and, like Moore, had to deal with a limited concept of how she should use her music: "My mother's ambition to make me a good pianist was primarily for 'home consumption' or at most to 'do good' by playing at charity affairs" (p. 26).

10. Emma Goldman, *Anarchism and Other Essays* (1910; reprint, Port Washington, N.Y.: Kennikat Press, 1969), p. 153.

11. See Lehman Engel, *The American Musical Theater*, rev. ed. (New York: Macmillan Co., 1975).

12. Oscar Sonneck was the head of the newly organized Music Division of the Library of Congress. Though German-born, he was already a strong champion of American music.

13. *Musical America*, March 15, 1913, reported the program, given for the MacDowell Club. The composers represented were Edward MacDowell, Mary Helen Brown, Max Liebling, Edmund Severn, Louis Campbell-Tipton, Emma Hanson Bartmess, Gertrude Sans Souci, A. Walter Kramer, Mary Turner Salter, J. Rosamund Johnson, John Alden Carpenter, Berthold Neuer, Alexander Macfadyen, Marion Bauer, Gena Branscombe, Ethelbert Nevin, Hallett Gilberte, Margaret Ruthven Lang, Ruth Helen Davis, Charles Wakefield Cadman, Louis Koemmenich, and Frank Bibb.

14. Both women seem to have invested their own resources to pay for their concerts, which were courteously reviewed in *Musical America*. The Hecksher review, which appeared on March 22, 1913, is accompanied by a reproduction of an oil portrait of the composer. A longer sketch on Ware, on March 15 (the concert was April 18), included photos of her "dainty workshop" located in an "exclusive" section of Long Island.

15. *Seattle Post-Intelligencer*, January 19, 1913.

16. *Musical America*, February 8, 1913, 22.

17. Richard Hageman (1882–1966) conducted at the Met for over twenty years. He wrote two operas. He was conductor of the Exposition Orchestra in San Francisco in 1915, where Moore certainly met him. Moore later included his songs among the models she offered her composition students.

18. Zoe H. Beckley, *New York Evening Mail*, 1913 (exact date unavailable), clipping in Scrapbook no. 4, Moore Archive.

19. There is no evidence that any of these promises were kept. One later report (by Dudley Burrows, unidentified clipping in Scrapbook no. 6, probably from September, 1925, Moore Archive) says that Moore conducted the orchestra of the Metropolitan Opera in a Sunday evening concert. There is no confirming evidence for this, however.

20. The "Barcarolle" was not published until 1935, when it was no longer a novelty. Pianist Ashley Pettis played it frequently during Moore's second San Francisco period, ca. 1920. He also played it at Steinway Hall in New York on November 9, 1925, as part of a group of pieces by California composers. He also recorded it on a mechanical piano roll (Duo-Art 66357).

21. Marian herself described the circumstances of her accident in interviews with the authors and in two letters to Smith dated February 15, 1984, and January 21, 1985. Claude did not marry the woman he was with on July 5, but he was married twice afterward; the third wife outlived him. In 1928 Moore noted in her datebook that a Christmas gathering of herself, Claude, and the three children was their first time all together at Christmas since 1911. This suggests the possibility of some earlier disruptions in their family life. In any case, Claude continued to take some responsibility for the children, who visited him periodically in later years and remained quite close to him. Claude later served a term as president of the King County Medical Society (Seattle), and traveled to update his surgical skills.

22. By that time the Pratts owned Valle Vista. Marian remembers getting a glass of wine for her mother, who fainted upon receiving the news of B. O.'s death. This may have been Moore's last recorded fainting spell. The cause of B. O. Carr's death is recorded as acute nephritis (Bright's disease).

23. The Scotsman Robert Burns (1759–96), the Irishman Thomas Moore (1779–1852), and the Persian poet-astronomer Omar Khayyám (ca. 1050–ca. 1123), whose poetry was adapted to English by Edward FitzGerald in 1859, were all widely read in late nineteenth- and early twentieth-century America.

24. Cyril Arthur Player reviewed this early production for the *Seattle Post-Intelligencer* (specific date unavailable): "too much brass. . . . The music, while pretty, is not compelling. . . . Somewhere 'Memories' will find its setting, but it was a pity that the crude and tepidly-appreciative local criticism was the first thing it faced." Things changed for the 1916 production, as the same paper later reported: "It is now in the big Orpheum time. . . . The Orpheum management has given 'Memories' a sumptuous setting." A program from the Minneapolis Orpheum lists *Memories* (Scrapbook no. 5, Moore Archive).

25. *The Firemen of the Wissahickon Inn* (Seattle: H. F. Norton, 1915). The libretto, by H. F. Norton, is in the Library of Congress. "Wissahickon Inn" is an ethnic reference to the Moravians who settled in the eastern United States.

26. *Potato Salad* is a rueful look back. In it, newlyweds make a shambles of their kitchen before the husband decides that maybe it is all right for the wife to hire a cook and return to her singing career.

Chapter 11

1. The Ada Clement Piano School, organized in 1917 with five teachers, four studios, forty pupils, and no capital, became the Ada Clement Music School three years later and took its present name, the San Francisco Conservatory, in 1923. When Ernest Bloch was recruited as its "name" director in

1925 and public fund-raising undertaken, it had grown to 43 faculty and 18 studios, with an enrollment of 560. Fund-raising was always necessary after that but became very difficult after 1930. (This information comes from the James D. Phelan Papers, Bancroft Library, University of California, Berkeley.) Nellie Cornish had started her Cornish School in Seattle in 1914 in much the same way, though she sought "name" teachers and remained the director herself. Moore joined the movement to organize private music teachers into conservatories with an attempt to start one at the same time Clement was beginning. Eventually Moore associated herself with the Olga Steeb Piano School in Los Angeles, which was probably the most profitable of the three West Coast conservatories that grew in parallel between the two world wars.

2. The text, by Charles Phillips, was selected in a competition sponsored for the occasion. "My Dream" seems to have had many performances before Moore recognized that it had become "passé" in 1935.

3. Ray Brown, review of the November 14, 1915, concert, *San Francisco Chronicle.* The song dates from 1909, but it was orchestrated for this occasion.

4. Redfern Mason, review of the November 14, 1915, concert, *San Francisco Examiner.*

5. Ellen Beach Yaw was related to Moore through the Carrs. Close to Moore in age, she was a coloratura soprano with a phenomenally high range. In an interview with *Musical America* ("Ellen Beach Yaw Travels 3,000 Miles to Sing for Thomas A. Edison," March 8, 1913), Yaw reports that she wrote two songs for herself that included c'''' and a sustained g'''. She sang them at one gathering attended by Moore in New York. Yaw studied aroad and sang at the Met before settling in Covina, California, outside Los Angeles. She was known as "Lark Ellen." A group of her recordings, made between 1899 and 1913, has been reissued on Pearl GEMM 239.

6. Moore, catalog. The first of these quotations is from "Longing," dated "San Francisco 1915, to J. C. M." The second comes from the previous year.

7. Stark apparently gave many poetry readings in the San Francisco area and elsewhere, concentrating on the very popular Robert Browning. She and Moore gave several joint programs, including one for the Saturday Morning Club in Santa Cruz, Calif.

8. Moore, *Twenty-Eight Songs.*

9. "Reading Browning," in L. M. Pratt, *Old-Fashioned Songs.* The existence of numerous Browning Societies confirms Browning's wide popularity in the United States.

10. Fred Emerson Brooks, quoted in an Ellensburg, Washington, paper, March, 1923, clipping in Scrapbook no. 5, Moore Archive.

11. Unidentified clipping, n.d., in Scrapbook no. 5, Moore Archive.

12. *Pacific Coast Musician,* quoted in *Pasadena Star News,* n.d., clipping in Scrapbook no. 5, Moore Archive.

13. Elsa Cross, *Pacific Commercial Advertiser* (Honolulu), March 6, 1920.

14. Adelyn Fleming, *Berkeley Daily Gazette.*

15. "Theoretical Music Subjects as Taught and Studied Today," a three-

page typed essay by Moore, prepared after 1945, Moore Archive. This essay has her teaching at Mission and Girls' high schools for two years, but Moore's catalog has only one year. Probably the catalog is correct.

16. *Pacific Coast Musical Review*, May, 1919, clipping in Scrapbook no. 5, Moore Archive.

17. Wesley Webster was a San Francisco engraver and part-time music publisher at one time associated with Harmon Langinger. He remained Moore's friend throughout her life, publishing many of her songs and those of her students, as well as the opera *David Rizzio*.

18. Undated clipping, probably from the *St. Helena Star* or the *Napa Register*, in Scrapbook no. 5, Moore Archive. The party was on April 19; Moore married Arthur on April 16.

19. Unidentified clipping from 1919, in Carr family scrapbook; also in Louisa Merrill Pratt's scrapbook, private collection, Marian Moore Quinn.

20. Moore's relationship with her mother is scarcely chronicled at all in this period. Sarah continued to work with the Whitman materials. She also offered her daughter several more librettos on different subjects. Moore set only one, "The Flaming Arrow."

21. All based on information in Scrapbook no. 5, Moore Archive.

22. A few years later, Beach was active in organizing the Society of American Woman Composers. (An undated invitation and a letter dated September 26, 1925, from Beach to Fannie Charles Dillon concerning the society are in Box 17, the Dillon Collection, Department of Special Collections, Research Library, University of California, Los Angeles.) Beach obviously knew about Moore, having met her; it is unclear why Moore did not join. Probably she was too occupied with the *Narcissa* revival. (A bio-bibliography of Beach by Jeannie G. Pool is forthcoming from Greenwood Press in its Bio-Bibliographies in Music series. A biography is in preparation by Adrienne Fried Block.)

23. Alfred Frankenstein, "San Francisco," in *The New Grove*, vol. 16, pp. 471–72, reports that the visit of the Boston Symphony Orchestra under Karl Muck to San Francisco for the Panama-Pacific International Exposition (PPIE) in 1915 resulted in the departure of Henry Hadley and the advent of Alfred Hertz, who promised something better than Hadley had been able to produce. Hertz remained until the symphony was forced to suspend operations in 1934. Hertz, a German emigrant, often conducted Wagner's operas at the Met; he conducted regularly at the Hollywood Bowl summer concerts after they were organized in 1922.

The switch from Hadley to Hertz tends to confirm the suspicion that Moore's earlier San Francisco training did not include the opportunity to hear a good orchestra on a regular basis.

24. Three letters in the Alfred Hertz Papers, Art and Music Department, San Francisco Public Library. The first letter from Moore is undated.

25. Such treatment is discussed in virtually every book on American music published after 1930. Frederick Search said of Hertz that "he is not interested in American music at all" (Frederick Preston Search to John Tasker Howard, December 2, 1937, Howard Collection, Newark Public Library). There were

no American-born conductors of major orchestras until 1943, when Alfred Wallenstein was appointed to the Los Angeles Philharmonic.

26. Review of a performance for the Philomath Club, March 27, 1922, *San Francisco Argonaut*. At this performance, three Hopi dances were interpolated.

27. *Daily Journal of Commerce* (San Francisco), April 9, 1922.

28. Anna Cora Winchell, review of a May, 1923, performance, clipping in Scrapbook no. 5, Moore Archive.

29. An interlude built on a dirgelike ostinato reference to the simple French round, "Are you Sleeping," is reminiscent of the slow movement of Mahler's Symphony no. 1. Hertz conducted the first performance of this symphony in San Francisco in October, 1921.

30. Mary Carr Moore to Sarah Pratt Carr, n.d., Moore Archive.

31. Gilbert Moyle also supplied the text for Charles Wakefield Cadman's "The Sunset Trail," a cantata for baritone solo and chorus composed in 1919–20. Cadman was the composer of several quartet cycles himself.

32. *Radiocast Weekly*, October 21, 1924.

33. Anna Cora Winchell, "San Francisco Notes," *Music and Musicians* 11 (March, 1925): 13.

34. The Casiglia Opera Company was a short-lived group that probably did not get beyond the low-budget productions of *La Traviata* and *La Bohème* mentioned in the *Pacific Coast Musical Review* at the time.

35. "Composer of Opera During Jubilee Sued," *San Francisco Chronicle*, September 6, 1925, 5. Davoust claimed that Moore had accepted less favorable terms from the Wilkes Theatre than he had offered: 75 percent of the gate as opposed to 50 percent of the gate. None of the newspaper reports about the suit are preserved in Moore's scrapbooks.

36. For the San Francisco production, stage direction was supplied by George Kegg; costumes, by Goldstein and Co. The local cast members were Florence McEachran, Flora Howell Bruner, and Stella Raymond Vought (Narcissa); Flora Howell Bruner and Martha Jalava (Waskema); Harold Spaulding (Elijah); Mary Hobson and Ruth Scott Laidlaw (Eliza Spalding and Siskadee); James Gerard and Glen Chamberlain (Marcus Whitman); Orrin Padel, Dixon Ervin, and Harry McKnight (Henry Spalding); Frederick Warford and Albert Tristram (Yellow Serpent); Albert Gillette and P. H. Ward (Delaware Tom); Frederick Levin and Andrew Robertson (Rev. Hull); and George Howker and Henry Perry (Dr. McLoughlin).

37. Curran D. Swint, "'Narcissa' Given Great Greeting," *San Francisco Daily News*, September 8, 1925, 8.

38. "Narcissa," *Argonaut*, September 19, 1925, 10.

39. John D. Barry, "Ways of the World," n.d., clipping in Scrapbook no. 6, Moore Archive, surrounded by other reviews from September, 1925.

40. Gem Harris, "Narcissa," *Overland Monthly and Out West Magazine* 83 (October, 1925): 380.

41. Ray C. B. Brown, "Alice Gentle, Guest Artist, in Title Role," *San Francisco Chronicle*, September 8, 1925, 11.

42. "Mary Carr Moore—American Composer," *Christian Science Monitor*, April 16, 1929, cites this production as an example of the fact that American artists must often sponsor their own works and "shoulder deficits that in many cases, as in Mrs. Moore's, more than swallow up all personal assets." A clipping in Scrapbook no. 6, Moore Archive, contains a report that Moore invested eight thousand dollars in the production.

43. "Charlotte Dunshee Interviews Mary Carr Moore," April 15, 1942, transcript, Moore Archive, p. 3. The interview was broadcast over KCFJ.

44. Even the records of the Sherman Clay Co., which mention some employees from the 1920s, omit Arthur, suggesting an unhappy ending to his career there. Arthur surfaced once more, when Moore was living in Los Angeles, but his eventual fate is uncertain. One clue is provided by the form Moore filled out in 1936 in order to recover funeral expenses for her mother from the Veterans' Administration; to a question about whether she was single or married, she wrote, "a widow."

Chapter 12

1. Seattle and San Francisco tended to level off in population growth after 1910, but Los Angeles kept on growing, more than doubling in size in the 1920s. In 1926, the *Pacific Coast Musician Year Book* estimated the population of the City of Los Angeles as 1.25 million, and of Los Angeles County as 2,147,788.

2. *Los Angeles County Culture and the Community* (Los Angeles: Civic Bureau of Music and Art of Los Angeles, 1927), p. 7.

3. Little evidence of these industrial orchestras survives outside the pamphlet. However, Barker Brothers had an auditorium in its store for many years and frequently sponsored afternoon concerts there, often using local musicians. The house orchestra at the Grauman Theatre gave a concert of music by American composers as early as June, 1920, and another of resident composers' music in July, 1921. Both concerts were reported in the *Pacific Coast Musical Review*.

The pamphlet's description of music deals only with the art music establishment. At that time, jazz was not respectable enough to discuss in a promotional brochure. The authors did devote one of their sixty-eight pages to the film industry in Hollywood, which was already making 85 percent of American films. Sound films would bring many musicians and composers to Los Angeles in the next two decades and help make Los Angeles the art music capital of the world for a time—a prospect entirely undreamed of in 1927, even by these community promoters.

4. John Sanders, "Los Angeles Grand Opera Association: The Formative Years 1924–1926," *Southern California Quarterly* 4, no. 3 (Fall, 1973): 261–302, describes the two competing week-long seasons staged by the San Francisco Opera and the Los Angeles Grand Opera Company in 1925, following a season in which the Los Angeles organization sponsored the San Francisco Opera for a week-long season. Merle Armitage as impresario and Richard Hageman as music director were pitted against L. E. Behymer and Gaetano

Merola in the 1925 competition. Moore was acquainted with all four of the combatants.

5. L. E. Behymer had been a prominent figure in both theater and music activities for several decades by 1926. Moore had numerous dealings with him in the ensuing years. A collection of his papers and memorabilia are at the Huntington Library in San Marino, Calif.

6. Joseph Zoellner and three of his children, Joseph Junior, Amandus, and Antoinette, were the members of this quartet. Their tours are reported in the *Pacific Coast Musician* and the *Pacific Coast Musical Review.*

7. Elizabeth Sprague Coolidge (1864–1953) was one of the best-known music patrons of her day. The Music Division of the Library of Congress is one of the principal beneficiaries of the Elizabeth Sprague Coolidge Foundation. Mrs. Coolidge was also a pianist and composer. Moore entertained Mrs. Coolidge, who was by then quite deaf, with a concert of her own music in 1938. The Coleman concert series of chamber music is still held in Pasadena. Early on, the Coleman sisters sometimes performed their own music.

8. The main campus remained in northern California, at Berkeley. The earliest version of UCLA had been as a branch of San Jose State College.

9. The Dominant Club continues as an organization of distinguished women in the field of music, its original hospitality function long forgotten. Moore became a member ca. 1940. The Gamut Club was involved in fundraising projects from time to time.

10. Moore soon became an honorary member of several of these clubs. A biographical card in the "Index of American composers" card file from the Federal Music Project, Music Division, Library of Congress, lists her as an honorary member of the following: Los Angeles Flute Club, Los Angeles Opera and Fine Arts Club, Cadman Creative Club, MacDowell Club, Euterpe Opera Reading Club, and Los Angeles Poetry-Music Club. In addition, she belonged to the California Federation of Women's Clubs, Ebell Club, Friday Morning Club, Browning Society, Los Angeles Athletic Club, Matinee Musical Club, Opera Reading Club of Hollywood, Southern California Women's Press Club, Surf and Sand Club, Women's Athletic Club, P.E.O. Sisterhood, Pen Women, Dames of the Loyal Legion, and her own manuscript club.

11. The figure for 1927 is taken from "The Music Program in Los Angeles," *Playground and Recreation* 24 (June, 1930): 177. This article reports an intermediate figure, for June, 1928, of 112,714 participants. The figure for 1929 comes from "Los Angeles Community Music," *Things Worth Knowing about Music and Art* 5, no. 6 (November–December, 1929). Neither article is signed. The first periodical was published in New York; the second in Los Angeles.

12. Photograph in Bessie Bartlett Frankel, *History of the California Federation of Music Clubs, 1918–1930*, 27 pp., pamphlet in Box no. 1, Bessie Bartlett Frankel Papers, Department of Special Collections, Research Library, University of California, Los Angeles.

13. Bruno David Ussher, ed., *Who's Who in Music and Dance in Southern California* (Hollywood: Bureau of Musical Research, 1933). Bond, Frankel, and Jamison were still active. Other women on the list are Madalyn Akers,

Alice Barnett (San Diego), Gladys E. Buell, Grace Bush, Roxane W. Byers, Mildred Couper (Santa Barbara), Joan Duff, Ella Duffield, Grace Adele Free-bey, Gloria Gage, Alice Maynard Griggs, Julia Howell, Moore, Frances Marion Ralston, Anna Priscilla Risher, Mrs. M. Hennion Robinson, Blanche Evert Seaver, Louise P. Stone, and Elinor Remick Warren. Fannie Charles Dillon and Elthea Turner are absent from Ussher's list.

14. Frank Colby (1865–1940) was editor and publisher. Vernon Steele took over after his death. Later on, the *Pacific Coast Musician* added regular space for the activities of musicians in the film colony. The *Pacific Coast Musical Review*, published in San Francisco, had a Los Angeles office and also reported extensively on Los Angeles' musical life until its demise in 1933.

15. For a recent example, see Paul Ditzel, "Classical Notes," *Westways* 76 (February, 1984): 71. "Los Angeles' Golden Age of Music started in 1934 when Schoenberg moved here from Europe." Howard Swan's standard *Music in the Southwest, 1925–1950* (San Marino: Huntington Library, 1952) covers Los Angeles' music history between the two world wars almost entirely in terms of L. E. Behymer's activity as an impresario.

16. Census figures supporting this claim are presented in Henry T. Harris, "The Occupation of Musician in the United States," *Musical Quarterly* 1 (April, 1915): 299–311. Harris is probably the source for L. E. Behymer, "L. E. Behymer Tells of California's Brilliant Music History," *Pacific Coast Musical Review*, July 21, 1917, 1, 3. According to both accounts, California had the most musicians, with 28.3 per 10,000 population. Western cities with populations over 50,000 dominated the list of the ten with the most musicians (including teachers) per unit population: Los Angeles, 45.8 per 10,000 population; Denver, 42.1; Boston, 38.9; San Francisco, 38.2; Seattle, 37.9; Oakland, 36.6; Kansas City, 35.6; Portland, Oregon, 35.5; Spokane, 33.4; Minneapolis, 32.7. Both articles are substantiated by the *Statistical Abstract of the United States* for 1910.

17. Bruno David Ussher claimed that in Los Angeles: "Our proportionate concert attendance is said to be eight times as large as that of New York City" (*Pacific Coast Musical Review*, October 18, 1919). For example, the Hollywood Bowl concerts inaugurated in 1922 drew a total audience of over 250,000 in their second season. For an early account of this very popular local enterprise, which was well covered in all the area's papers and periodicals, see Isabel Morse Jones, *Hollywood Bowl* (New York and Los Angeles: G. Schirmer, Inc., 1936).

18. The Oral History of the Arts Archive at California State University, Long Beach, and the longstanding collections of materials on California composers at UCLA are indications of renewed interest in this area, though resources of both are relatively limited. See C. Smith, "Resident Composers in Los Angeles Before 1935: The First Los Angeles School" (Paper read to Northern and Southern California Chapters, American Musicological Society, April, 1985). The May, 1985, meeting of the Northern and Southern California Chapters, Music Library Association, was devoted to sources for California music. A proceedings volume is in preparation.

19. "How Parents Can Influence the Life of a Child," talk prepared by Mrs. Leiland Atherton Irish, ca. 1946, typescript, Frankel Papers, UCLA. Most of the information about Mrs. Frankel comes from this source, but there are more of her papers and music at Scripps College. There are also entries for Frankel in various directories of outstanding women, particularly those from the West Coast.

20. In 1928 the quartet's members formed part of the faculty of the new Musart Conservatory, which Moore also joined for a time. At that point they called themselves the Musart Quartet. The Zoellner Quartet had been active for some time but lacked a secure financial base.

21. For a record of Moore's other income in those years, see chap. 13 below. Frankel's payments were clearly important.

22. Mrs. Cecil Frankel to Dr. Ernest C. Moore, March 21, 1932, Frankel Papers, UCLA. Theodore Stearns was hired instead of Moore. Stearns, like Moore, had been awarded a David Bispham medal for an American opera. Following Stearns's death in 1935, Arnold Schoenberg was appointed to the position.

23. Florence Irish (Mrs. Leiland Atherton Irish) was another prominent music patron in southern California. For some years she served as an unpaid full-time administrator of the Hollywood Bowl concerts.

24. Pro Musica was organized in New York by E. Robert Schmitz to bring prominent European composers to the United States for performances of their chamber music. Its concert tours were supported by chapters in the cities to which its artists traveled.

25. At first the school was at 4009 1/2 West Sixth Street, then at 453 South Wilton Place. The Steebs lived at the Wilton Place address themselves until their move to Mulholland Drive in early 1933. Moore occupied their apartment at Wilton Place for part of 1933. There is suprisingly little contemporary documentation of Steeb's career beyond the pages of the *Pacific Coast Musician* and a few mechanical piano rolls that record her playing. The authors depended on personal interviews with family and former students and on Jean Preston, "Olga Steeb: A Biography" (Senior paper, Music Resource Center, Department of Music, California State University, Long Beach, 1979).

26. Becker's other pupils included Lester Donahue, Fannie Charles Dillon, and Marguerite LeGrand. LeGrand became a colleague of Moore at California Christian College for a time. Dillon later denounced Becker's teaching.

27. *Continental Times*, November, 1909.

28. *Musical America*, December 18, 1909.

29. *Berlin Signale*, December 15, 1909. "A unique being, a piano-playing wonder."

30. On three separate concerts, Steeb played the following concertos: Beethoven, nos. 4 and 5, opp. 58 and 73; Brahms, no. 1, op. 15; Grieg, op. 16; Liszt, no. 1 in E-flat; Mozart, K. 537; Scharwenka, op. 82; Schumann, op. 54; and Tchaikovsky, op. 23 in B-flat Minor.

31. Alfred Price Quinn, *B'nai B'rith Messenger,* October 27, 1931. A series of scrapbooks assembled by the Atwood family in the 1920s, 1930s, and 1940s, now at the UCLA Music Library, which contains reports of piano playing as its main emphasis, includes numerous reports of Steeb's recitals.

32. During her student days in Europe, Steeb married an American, C. H. Keefer, who served as her manager for a time. A full-page advertisement, probably placed by Keefer, appeared in *Musical America,* June 3, 1911. It gives a photo of Steeb and quotes from seven different Berlin papers concerning her appearances with the Berlin Philharmonic. Keefer is listed as her manager; Hermann Wolff, Berlin, had charge of concert bookings. She was announced as available for concerts in America from July, 1911, to March, 1912.

In the early 1920s, Steeb married Charles Hubach, a singer who had been Dean of Fine Arts at Redlands University, where she taught briefly. He soon became an invalid, and seems not to have taken an active role in her lively musical circle.

33. Lillian Steeb French (Olga Steeb's sister), interview with Smith, November 7, 1980.

34. Margaret Ryan Sampson described these evenings in an interview with Smith, January 2, 1980. She was one of the privileged students. Sampson taught piano in Reno, Nevada, for many years.

35. Ted Gilbert, interview with Smith, June 12, 1980. Gilbert taught violin at the Steeb school.

36. The male students and teachers were drawn into World War II; some of the women probably also found jobs in the new war industries. Lillian Steuber, one of Steeb's more successful pupils, offered master classes for a time. Among the letters from Fannie Charles Dillon to Percy Grainger in the Grainger Museum, University of Melbourne, is an undated announcement, probably from fall, 1942, of classes at the Steeb School. Norma Steeb is listed as director and Fannie Charles Dillon as teacher of theory and composition. This effort to keep the school going appears to have failed. Norma Steeb presently took another teaching position.

37. For example, so strong was the anti-German feeling in Boston that Karl Muck, the great German conductor, was removed from his post as conductor of the Boston Symphony shortly after being appointed in 1917; he was actually interned as an enemy alien until the war ended. Because they typically contained many European-born musicians and played a heavily German-Austrian repertoire, orchestras seem to have been particularly vulnerable to that kind of hysteria.

38. Ted Gilbert, interview; Margaret Ryan Sampson, interview; Moore datebook, January 2, 1942, microfilm, Moore Archive.

Chapter 13

1. Unlabeled clipping among December entries, in Music Scrapbook for 1933, Los Angeles Public Library.

2. Scrapbook no. 7, Moore Archive. Moore taught in Berkeley for Marie Partridge Price in 1926, so this is probably from 1927. In Berkeley she had offered "Practical Instrumentation, Music History, and Harmony. Comparative system with attention to the principles of the standard authorities of Germany, France, England, and America," courses more similar to her later Chapman College offerings.

3. Among others, these briefly included actor Fred McMurray. Mrs. Frankel, J. Charles McNeil (who later became a benefactor of the Manuscript Club as well as Chapman College), and Dr. Lloyd Mills all figure prominently in the datebooks for several years. Dr. Mills, an ophthalmologist, treated her in the mid-1930s for an eye problem that threatened to prevent her from copying music on a daily basis. He was an amateur composer who sought her help with a piano concerto in 1932–33. Later, he hired her to orchestrate it.

4. Unidentified clipping, November 1, 1930, in Scrapbook no. 8, Moore Archive. The Los Angeles Music School Settlement, appropriately located on Mozart Street, was founded in 1916 by Mrs. Carrie Stone Freeman.

5. Parrish Williams, baritone, organized the school. Three members of the soon-to-be Bartlett-Frankel quartet were among its faculty: Emil Férir, Joseph Borisoff, and Nicolas Ochi-Albi, who later taught at Chapman College. Robert W. Major, advertised as the "Miracle Man of Acting," was the theater instructor.

6. Moore wrote that the invitation to teach at Chapman came over a dinner conversation with Otto Hirschler of the college at the annual meeting of the Music Teachers Association. The other two who began teaching at Chapman in 1928 were Marguerite LeGrand, piano, and John Clair Monteith, voice. In a few years Ray Crittenden became department chairman, teaching voice and chorus as well. Nelle Gothold Carlson, who was interviewed by Smith for this study, later taught voice; Homer Grunn, piano; Robert Pollak, violin; and Edith BokenKrager and then Dudley Warner Fitch, organ.

7. Juliette Laine, "Know the Truth: Mary Carr Moore, Noted American Composer, Discusses Truth," in *Progress* (Chicago), n.d., clipping in Scrapbook no. 11, 1933–36, Moore Archive, attributes convictions to Moore which are repudiated by Moore in a note in the scrapbook: "these ideas are Juliette's—with my name tacked on. It has caused me much embarrassment." Moore may also have referred in the datebook entry to pressures from her many associates who were Christian Scientists. Olga Steeb, Mrs. Frankel, the Sanger-Moore-House family (unrelated), and Fannie Dillon were among these.

8. Paul Delp, a professor, put the peak pre–World War II enrollment at just under two hundred; Etheleen Brown Fiske, a student, estimated it at just under three hundred.

9. James Deese, letters to Smith, December 6, 1979, and May 12, 1980.

10. Ray Linn, interview with Smith, June 4, 1980. Linn became an arranger, working in radio and films.

11. Dorothy Miller Dunlap, telephone interview with Smith, July 8, 1980.

Dunlap eventually served as president of the Manuscript Club. At twenty and married, she was considered an "older student." Moore arranged for her to study through Chapman College because it was cheaper than private composition lessons. (She did the same thing for Edward Earle when he came to her at the age of nine.)

12. Dorothy West White, interview with Smith, June 23, 1980.

13. James Sample, telephone interview with Smith, June 27, 1980.

14. George Reeves, president of Chapman from 1942, telephone conversation with Smith, June 27, 1980.

15. Moore datebook, March 10, 1933, microfilm, Moore Archive. A program in Scrapbook no. 8 lists the composition students whose works were performed that evening as William T. Wilkins, Mary Gertrude Halsey, Harold Lewis, Fern Puffer, Allen Hubbard, Sei-Hyung Kim, and William Phillips. Phillips became president of the Manuscript Club the following year, and Lewis often performed as a flutist on her programs.

16. Three-page typescript prepared by Moore, n.d., Moore Archive.

17. Schoenberg's salary increased to fifty-one hundred dollars in 1940–41, according to H. Stuckenschmidt, *Arnold Schoenberg*, trans. E. Roberts and H. Searle (New York: Grove Press, 1959). Schoenberg complained that his pay at UCLA was far too low. He compared his salary to that of fellow émigrés—who were receiving conducting fees for short engagements as high, sometimes, as his annual salary—rather than to other teachers. In addition, salaries in the film colony were far higher than in teaching. Musicians in the all-male Philharmonic were paid sixty dollars per week during the winter season and in the summer Hollywood Bowl season.

18. In a conversation with Smith on June 19, 1980, Paul Delp, who taught philosophy at Chapman, reported that his salary deviated from Moore's significantly only in the last two years reported by Moore, after she had turned sixty-five. Delp said he received about $1,650 in 1940–41 and about $2,150 in 1941–42. He was critical of administrators who paid themselves considerably more than the faculty received in those years (although even they received less than Schoenberg at UCLA). Nelle Gothold, who taught voice, simply commented that the college was "run very cheap" (interview with Smith, October 9, 1981).

19. Mary Carr Moore, letter to President George Reeves, July 10, 1942, President's office, Chapman College, Orange, Calif. Several years after Moore's retirement in 1946, Chapman moved to suburban Orange County, where it has enjoyed stable enrollments and steady financial support.

20. Moore's datebook entries of March 5 and July 10, 1934, list these names as participating in the planning sessions: "Ezri Bertrand, Charles Dufur, Mr. Spurlock, Mr. & Mrs. Charles Lamb, Jascha Gagna, Dr. Alexis Kall, N. Ochi-Albi, Alex. Schreiner, Miss Hall (scenario), Norman Sproul, Ed. Carman, self."

21. Jack Blake, telephone interview with Smith, May 22, 1981.

22. Constance Shirley, interview with Smith, October 31, 1979; Constance Shirley, letter to Jeannie Pool, February, 1982. Moore was evidently dismayed when Shirley chose to go to Schoenberg and was thoroughly surprised when

she picked up their friendship again later on. (Shirley played Moore's piano concerto on several occasions after her study with Schoenberg.)

23. Albert Harris, telephone interview with Smith, March, 1983. Harris went on to a career in radio and television, eventually earning a doctorate in composition at New York University. The inference that Zador helped Harris through his professional connections as well as through his well-known skill as an orchestrator is the authors'.

24. "She was forever promoting the music of students in her composition class, and she would drive us all over the place to get our works performed at lunch club meetings and the like" (James Deese, letter to Smith, December 6, 1979). Deese was a student around 1940.

25. In addition to Johnson the charter members were: Lois Cunningham, Francis Drake, Adelaide Jenkins, Virginia Kahler, Iris Kuhnle, Creighton Pasmore, Elsa Proehl, and Victor Trerice. Pasmore and Trerice concertized as a two-piano team on the West Coast before the Second World War; they became teachers at the Steeb School, as did Iris Kuhnle. Elsa Proehl (Blum) recalls the Manuscript Club in *They Pleased World Stars: A Memoir of My Parents* (New York: Vantage Press, 1960). Johnson became a priest (Father Austin Johnson) and continued to compose; about a decade later, he helped Moore with the use of the requiem chant in *Legende Provençale*.

26. Mary Green Pauloo, interview with Smith and Richardson, January 17, 1980.

27. Moore's idea for the Manuscript Club had several sources. Sarah had started two writers' clubs in Seattle, one for published authors and one for less experienced writers. Moore, too, had attempted a composers' club in Seattle. As early as 1889 there was a Manuscript Society in New York City, designed "to advance the interests of American Musical Composition." A similar society was established in Chicago soon after; it had a surprisingly large membership.

28. Composers' names in the 1942 "Catalogue of Published Numbers by Members of the Mary Carr Moore Manuscript Club" (Moore Archive) include Richard Bender, Morris Browda, Grace E. Bush, Blanche D. Byles, Arthur Carr, Hazel Valentine Caster, Don Chestnut, Hugo Davise, Ernest Douglas, Dorothy Miller Dunlap, Bessie Bartlett Frankel, Thordis Ottenson Gudmunds, Virginia Gurley, Mary Halsey, Augusta Hanson, Vernon Haskins, Graham Howard, Allen Hubbard, Martha Cooke Hulett, Ada V. Hull, Ruth Irving, Nora Jorgenson, Arthur Koopman, Iris Kuhnle, Eva Law, William Mathias, J. Chas. McNeil, Henry G. Millier, Lloyd Mills, Amy Moede, Laurel Nemeth (Saunders), Lora Perry (Chestnut), William Phillips, Adelaide Pouliot, Elsa Proehl, Vera Fern Puffer, Mary E. Rabe, Edwyl Redding, Barbara Reynolds, David Rike, Rita Robles, Elena Peabody Rouse, Richard Drake Saunders, Ella Serrurier, Helen Louise Shaffer, Lucile Simcox, Harold Porter Smythe, Elizabeth Sterling, Rena Stombs, Mary Sinclair Taylor, Wesley Webster, and Emele Wendel.

Names that had appeared in 1938, but not on the later list: Louis Danz, B. Lester Doty, Vernon Leftwich, Albert Denis Tessier, Elthea Turner, Alice Lee Wiley, and Mme. Claudia Wirsen.

29. One hundred ninety-three publications are listed in the 1942 "Cata-

logue," not including Moore's. All but fifty-four were published by Wesley Webster, who made a specialty of West Coast composers.

30. Mary Green Pauloo, interview with Smith and Richardson, January 17, 1980.

31. After Moore's death, the membership decided to continue with the club, but the emphasis gradually shifted from music to poetry, and the membership changed considerably. The club is now called "The Manuscript Club of Los Angeles, Mary Carr Moore, Founder."

32. Unidentified clipping, 1929, in Scrapbook no. 7, Moore Archive.

33. "Tenth Anniversary Year Book, 1938–39," Moore Archive.

Chapter 14

1. The presence of the movie industry in southern California was indicated in this *Year Book* (Los Angeles: Frank H. Colby, 1926) only by one small advertisement, from one F. Quentin Landwehr, who offered his services as a "Teacher of Motion Picture Playing."

2. Unidentified clipping, n.d., in Scrapbook no. 7, Moore Archive.

3. *Pacific Coast Musician*, June 25, 1927, 13. Moore made very few appearances as a singer after this.

4. Actually the second prize, the first having gone to Adolf Tandler for his one-act opera *Fluff*. Tandler's opera was not produced by the club. Moore's Quartet in G Minor won the third prize. Mildred Sanger, Laura Sweeney Moore, and Mildred Sanger House were a family group, unrelated to Moore, with connections to the Los Angeles Department of Playground and Recreation. They were involved in amateur dramatics and music and were at the center of a considerable circle of their own. They were strong supporters over the years of Moore and Moore's work, including her operas and the Manuscript Club.

5. Myra Nye, *Los Angeles Times*, November 26, 1927.

6. Helen Scott, review of the performance of May 18, 1928, *Music and Musicians*.

7. The women, in addition to Moore, were Carrie Jacobs Bond, Lucille Crews, Grace Adele Freebey, Kathleen Lockhart Manning, Frances Marion Ralston, Gertrude Ross, and Elinor Remick Warren. The men were Charles Wakefield Cadman, Herbert L. Clarke, Sol Cohen, Ernest Bloch, Arthur Blakeley, Wells Hively, Nino Marcelli, Charles E. Pemberton, Otto Rasbach, and H. J. Stewart.

8. This production never took place. Mrs. Lulu Sanford Tefft was a strong supporter of American opera and opera in English; she worked for performances of Moore's operas, especially *Narcissa*.

9. The fate of *David Rizzio* is discussed in chap. 15 below.

10. Patterson Greene, *Los Angeles Examiner*, April 14, 1930.

11. Scrapbook no. 8, Moore Archive, contains a typed list of them.

12. Emilie Hardy Peluso was later a member of the San Francisco Opera Company. She kindly gave an interview to Smith, November 2, 1979.

13. Moore datebook, March 21, 1931, microfilm, Moore Archive. Hereafter dates otherwise unattributed in the text indicate quotations from the datebooks.

14. Moore datebook, December 24, 25, and 27, 1928, microfilm, Moore Archive.

15. Moore was contemplating Eleanore Flaig's *Macabre* (see chap. 15) and Edna Buckbee's planned libretto on Lola Montez.

16. Elena Miramova (widow of Byron Carr Moore), interview with Smith and Richardson, January, 1980.

17. Eleanor Howett Zimmerman, telephone interview with Smith, July 20, 1985. Zimmerman had been a friend of Marian at Girls' High School in San Francisco.

18. Marian Moore Quinn, letter to Smith, December 8, 1980. Marian added, "I never heard that she only talked about her music. I doubt now that either of them would have wanted to go back together again because by that time, their lives were so different."

19. Moore datebook, June 25, 1931, microfilm, Moore Archive.

20. Etheleen Brown Fiske, interview with Smith, December 19, 1980.

21. Mary Carr Moore, letter to Margaret Ryan Sampson, n.d., courtesy of Margaret Ryan Sampson.

22. Lois Strahl Linn and Ray Linn, interview with Smith, June 4, 1980 (Lois speaking).

23. Moore sat on a panel judging applicants who wanted to perform on Federal Music Project concerts. Probably she had known Brahm Vandenberg earlier as a pianist in Los Angeles.

24. Moore worked on Dr. Lloyd Mills' concerto in 1932–33.

25. A bequest from the Pratts may have financed the San Francisco production of *Narcissa* in 1925.

26. The debts she specifically mentioned were associated with the 1932 production of *David Rizzio* and the cost of engraving the *Rizzio* piano-vocal score.

Chapter 15

1. This hope is expressed by Moore in a letter to Arthur Farwell, November 14, 1949, courtesy of Evelyn Davis Culbertson.

2. James Deese, letter to Smith, March 5, 1980.

3. Mary Carr Moore to Mr. and Mrs. Harry Noyes Pratt, undated letter ca. 1932, Special Collections, San Francisco Public Library.

4. Browne's mother, Celestina Boninsegna, sang roles in several Mascagni operas in Italian opera houses. She made her debut at the Met in 1906 opposite Caruso in *Aida*. Browne, whose name sometimes appears as Bruni, was supposed to be an illegitimate son of Col. Henry Mapleson, an English opera impresario who, among other things, took Adelina Patti as part of his company to San Francisco in the 1880s, when Moore was a young girl.

5. Even though Mary, Queen of Scots, was a popular heroine in nine-

teenth-century literature, there are surprisingly few operas that treat her actual reign. Donizetti's *Maria Stuarda* (1835) deals with the last days of Mary's captivity and her execution at the hands of her half-sister, Queen Elizabeth. Thea Musgrave's much more recent *Mary, Queen of Scots* (1977) deals with the same period in Mary's life that Moore and Browne treated, but with an entirely different focus and tone; it avoids the rumored Rizzio-Mary romance, which is historically inaccurate.

6. The opera's completion was announced in the *Los Angeles Examiner*, May 20, 1928, "Hall of Fame" column. Redfern Mason wrote of it in the *San Francisco Examiner*, December 30, 1928, noting the "suavity and passion" of the score.

7. Patterson Greene, *Los Angeles Examiner*, April 14, 1930.

8. March 27, 1931, on KHJ in Los Angeles.

9. Emanuel Browne avoided Moore for a time during this period. Later he admitted to her that he had lost all his money in the stock market and so couldn't afford to promote the project any further.

10. L. E. Behymer's papers at the Huntington Library are singularly uninformative about this production, so it is difficult to clarify his relation to it. The only comparable event he was connected with for which some of his papers survive is a Los Angeles production of Louis Gruenberg's new opera *The Emperor Jones*, which had already been produced in New York in 1933. Behymer's budget for that opera must have been ten times Moore's for *Rizzio*, to judge from available figures.

11. The 1932 prize was for "Four Love Songs," a cycle she had assembled for the competition. Moore left a spirited account of this trip, which involved quite complex rail and air connections. ("Suite in 8 Movements. An Episode in the Life of a Flighty Composer," n.d., Moore Archive.) The flights were planned at the suggestion of her older son Byron, a commercial pilot based in Detroit at the time.

12. Margaret Sampson told Smith in an interview on January 2, 1980, that Moore emerged from this session "with blazing eyes." Lindbergh was about Byron's age; Byron, also a pilot, had at least met him. At the time of the kidnapping, Charles A. Lindbergh was still a national hero for his solo flight across the Atlantic Ocean.

13. Carl Bronson, *Los Angeles Express*, n.d. (probably May 27, 1932), clipping in Scrapbook no. 19, Moore Archive.

14. *Musical West*, June, 1932.

15. Alfred Price Quinn, *B'nai B'rith Messenger*, June 3, 1932.

16. *Chicago Musical Leader*, July 20, 1933.

17. Morris Browda, *California Jewish Voice*, April 30, 1948.

18. April 2, 1982, at the University of Southern California, by the American Theatre of the Opera, for the Second International Congress on Women in Music.

19. James E. Seaver, letter to Jeannie G. Pool, February 8, 1982. Seaver, professor of history at the University of Kansas, has had a weekly one-hour radio program, "Opera Is My Hobby," on station KANU-FM since 1952.

20. James Deese, letter to Smith, May 3, 1982.

21. Sarah Pratt Carr had written a four-act play about Lola Montez in the 1880s, when Moore was a young girl in St. Helena. The library of the California Historical Society, San Francisco, has a thirty-five page typescript, "Lola Montez in El Dorado," in Box 2 of the Edna Bryan Buckbee Papers. The typescript, which is undated and missing a page or two at the end, is in narrative form. It includes plenty of material for an opera, but it is not a libretto. That Moore should have considered a treatment of Lola Montez at the same time Alban Berg was becoming interested in the similar if fictional character of Lulu is an interesting historical parallel.

22. Typescript, January 1, 1937, in B. O. Carr's scrapbook, microfilm, Moore Archive. Flaig was the daughter of Edmund H. Flaig, a Shakespearean actor. Eleanora Flaige is a common variant spelling of her name. The authors are indebted to Verna Arvey and Judith Anne Still for information about Flaig.

23. There is other evidence that suggests that she may have completed more than Act I not long after she started the opera. In a letter to Smith dated August 8, 1979, Herman Langinger tells of engraving Moore's opera *Love and the Sorcerer* when he worked as Wesley Webster's partner and engraver. In an interview with Smith a few months after the letter, he placed the date as around 1931. It is not clear whether Moore intended to have the first act engraved before the rest was done, or whether she intended what she had completed as part of a different, possibly shorter, work. There is no reference to this title in Moore's papers.

24. Lucy Sherman Robertson was a daughter of Aunt Harriet Pratt Clark (a much younger sister of Sarah) and Gen. Moses Hazeltine Sherman, who became wealthy as a developer of interurban rail lines in the Los Angeles area. Aunt Harriet had divorced General Sherman, who apparently had philandered, after Moore set the example by divorcing Claude. Sherman was so angry that he cut her out of his estate entirely, leaving it to his two daughters instead. Lucy's share was several million dollars.

25. Eugene Zador was born in Hungary and emigrated to Hollywood in 1938. His doctoral dissertation dealt with the use of the orchestra and form in symphonic poems from Liszt to Strauss. He had taught in Vienna before being exiled by Hitler's *Anschluss*.

26. Performed by the Federal Music Project orchestra in Los Angeles in April, 1941.

27. Rosing was a Russian-born tenor who directed the opera workshop at the Eastman School of Music in the early 1930s. After he went to Los Angeles, he started the American Opera Company along with Albert Coates. Apparently the only contemporary opera ever done by the company was Coates's *Gainsborough*.

28. Verna Arvey, "Eleanore Flaige, the Dancer Divine," *American Dancer*, April, 1930. Moore is quoted in this article, which discusses the language of *Legende*'s libretto.

29. Richard Drake Saunders, *Hollywood Citizen-News*, April 10, 1941.

"L'étoile du soir" is the only aria included in the collection of Moore songs published by Da Capo Press (1987), and on the recording of Moore songs issued by Cambria Records (1985).

30. Alfred Price Quinn, *B'nai B'rith Messenger*, April 18, 1941.

31. James Sample was a young conductor, fresh from several years' experience in France, when he went to southern California to work with the Federal Music Project in the late 1930s. After he became music director of the Southern California Symphony (the principal FMP orchestra in the Los Angeles area) in 1939, he worked frequently with Moore. In 1942, he began a stint of several years as an assistant to Wilfred Pelletier, a conductor who specialized in the French repertoire at the Met. He returned to Los Angeles as conductor of the KFI radio orchestra in 1945. There he also performed Moore's music on several occasions.

32. James Sample to Mary Carr Moore, May 25, 1943, as transcribed by Moore, Moore Archive. Sample confirmed the letter's contents in a letter to Smith dated October 19, 1983.

Chapter 16

1. Neeta Marquis taught English in a Los Angeles high school. Her papers are at the Huntington Library.

2. In "Waters of Eden," Moore's mother described the writing and producing of a pageant as an example of the creative potential to be found in a rural community. Pageants were so popular and widespread in the United States in the early years of the century that an American Pageant Association was formed in 1906. Arthur Farwell, outspoken champion of the American music movement and a friend of Moore, believed that the pageant was an important element in the growth of a characteristic American musical life. See Evelyn Johnson Davis, "The Significance of Arthur Farwell as an American Music Educator" (Ph.D. diss., University of Maryland, 1972). For more on SAAM, see chap. 19 below.

3. [Sarah Pratt Carr?], "Incidents in the Life of Mary Carr Moore," 1934, single typewritten sheet, Moore Archive.

4. Mary Carr Moore to Neeta Marquis, n.d., Neeta Marquis Collection, Huntington Library.

5. [S. P. Carr?], "Incidents."

6. Othemar Stevens to Mary Carr Moore, September 17, 1931, Moore Archive. Stevens wrote for the *Los Angeles Examiner*.

7. Bruno David Ussher, *Los Angeles Evening Express*, September 11, 1931.

8. Carl Bronson, *Los Angeles Herald*, September 11, 1931.

9. William Hamilton Cline, *Los Angeles Times*, June 21, 1931. There is no confirmation of this report of interest from the film colony, but Moore had previously made overtures in that direction. She had auditioned *The Flaming Arrow* at Universal City two years earlier without success. Earlier, Sarah Pratt Carr and a friend from the Southern Pacific Co. had corresponded about a possible film treatment of Sarah's novel, *The Iron Way*.

10. Katherine T. Von Blon, *Los Angeles Times,* March 5, 1934.

11. It is not known whether Laura Sweeney Moore offered a second libretto to Moore, although a copy of another libretto, *The Drums of Sacrifice,* 1935, is in the Library of Congress along with *Flutes of Jade Happiness.*

12. This forbidding image of the string quartet may have discouraged women from attempting them. Very few were written by American women before 1940. Ammer, *Unsung,* lists string quartets written by the following American women during Moore's working life: Amy Beach (ca. 1920), Helen Hood, Ethel Leginska (1921), Marion Bauer (1928), Ruth Crawford (1930), Radie Britain (1927, 1934, 1935), Louise Talma (1950s). Fannie Charles Dillon also wrote one in the early 1920s.

13. Phillip Kahgan, interview with Smith and Stephen Fry, October 27, 1983. Though Kahgan said that the performance had been a private one, not reviewed, it actually came at the end of a very long public concert, which was indeed reviewed. Moore herself called it "a perfect performance" in her catalog and reported "a great ovation" in her datebook. Moore's catalog states that Kahgan himself "requested" the string trio, but in 1983 Kahgan did not remember anything about the trio.

14. Pianist Emil Danenberg and conductor Modest Altschuler for one FMP performance; pianist Constance Shirley and conductor James Sample for the other. Constance Shirley, Ann Thompson McDowell, and Viana Bey all performed it either in the two-piano or the quintet version. One of these performances (Shirley, with Arthur Carr, second piano) was given at the World's Fair, on Treasure Island in San Francisco Bay, on August 23, 1939. The concerto was dedicated to Olga Steeb, who played it once in the two-piano version (with Creighton Pasmore, for an audience including conductor Pierre Monteux) and once in the quintet version.

15. Bruno David Ussher, *Los Angeles Daily News,* October 24, 1940. Dame Ethel Smyth (1859–1944) was a prominent English composer who wrote five operas, among other music. She published seven volumes of prose, including *Impressions That Remained* (New York: A. A. Knopf, 1946; New York: Da Capo Press, 1981).

16. Geoffrey Norris, "Rakhmaninov, Sergey," in *The New Grove,* vol. 15, p. 550.

Chapter 17

1. Information about the Federal Music Project is drawn from Cornelius B. Canon, "The Federal Music Project of the Works Progress Administration" (Ph.D. diss., University of Minnesota, 1963), and William F. McDonald, *Federal Relief Administration and the Arts* (Columbus: Ohio State University Press, 1969).

At its largest in 1938, the FMP employed about ten thousand persons nationwide. The Federal Theatre Project was drawn into disputes over the alleged Communist tilt of its New York City branch, resulting in the termination of the entire project in 1939. Mark Blitzstein's opera, *The Cradle Will*

Rock, which had a clear anticapitalist message, in particular created a scandal. For an account of this incident and a discussion of the Composers Forum Laboratory in New York City, see Barbara Zuck, *A History of Musical Americanism* (Ann Arbor: UMI Research Press, 1980). Zuck's account of the leftward leanings of musical Americanism in the 1930s contrasts sharply with Moore's experiences.

2. Pettis had introduced Moore's "Barcarolle" for piano and played it several times in his San Francisco area recitals around 1920.

3. The Composers Forum Laboratories are said, in Canon, "The Federal Music Project," to have been imitated in Boston, Philadelphia, Los Angeles, and Chicago. The laboratories were not held very frequently in Los Angeles, however. Moore mentioned them only once in her datebooks: "August 18, 1936. Took Ethel [Dofflemeyer] and Augusta [Hanson]—Composers forum, FMP."

4. *Pacific Coast Musician*, November 2, 1940.

5. Canon, "The Federal Music Project," pp. 175–76. Jazz was not recognized as legitimate concert music at that time, and therefore received very little support. If something like the FMP were undertaken in the 1980s, dance bands, opera, and ballet would all receive greater attention, mainly at the expense of concert bands. Audiences for FMP performances overlapped little with traditional symphony audiences; the low ticket prices brought out large numbers of new listeners.

6. *Pacific Coast Musician*, March 5, 1938, 7, reporting on a concert presented February 22. Other composers whose music was heard on that program were Frank Colby, Otto Mueller, Homer Grunn, Scott Bradley, and Elinor Remick Warren.

7. Ernst Bacon, former director of the San Francisco FMP, telephone interview with Smith, May 20, 1986.

8. Jacques Samoussoud and Modest Altschuler were FMP conductors, as was David Rubinoff. Moore's implied objection to Altschuler, a Russian who had organized the Russian Symphony in New York two decades earlier and introduced the music of several Russian composers in the United States, may have stemmed from his performance of her piano concerto three years before, or from her much earlier association with him at the Hollywood Conservatory. "Ditch Digger" refers to the unnamed FMP administrator who presided over this housecleaning—perhaps Jervis's successor.

9. *Pacific Coast Musician*, July 15, 1939, 4.

10. "Index of American composers," card file from Federal Music Project, Music Division, Library of Congress. The file lists most of the performances of Moore's works that are given here. Moore claimed to have conducted over sixty performances of her own works with orchestra over the years, including *Memories* (sixteen), *Narcissa* (sixteen), and *The Flaming Arrow* (eight).

11. Men such as her friend Henry Hadley, once conductor of the Seattle and San Francisco Symphonies, had many more performances of their music. According to Canon, "The Federal Music Project," Hadley's music was performed more than five hundred times by the FMP. Overall, the WPA had far less direct effect on women than on men. Early WPA reports indicated that

less than 5 percent of the workers employed overall were women. By early 1936, "projects were designed and placed in operation which would fit the abilities of this group of needy unemployed," raising the percentage of women to between 15 and 18 percent among those employed, according to *Report on Progress of the Works Program*, WPA, March, 1937, p. 37. Photos of the FMP Symphony in Los Angeles show that perhaps 15 percent of its membership was female, including its concert-mistress Eunice Wennermark. By contrast, the Los Angeles Philharmonic did not employ any women musicians in the 1930s.

12. In 1932, she had taken the scores of "Intermezzo," "Brahma," "My Dream," and *Saul* to Frederick Stock, who was conducting at the Hollywood Bowl that summer, and picked them up a week later. In 1934, she took the scores of the operas *Narcissa, Flutes of Jade Happiness,* and *Harmony* to Jan de Kolty, another conductor, again without success.

Chapter 18

1. See the publication note that accompanies "Immortal Birth" in *Music Lover's Magazine* (Portland, Ore.) 1, no. 2 (September, 1922).

2. Unidentified clipping in Scrapbook no. 8, Moore Archive, which contains items from 1930–33. The program on which the violin sonata appeared was sponsored by the Society for the Advancement of American Music (SAAM). Cowell's concerts are chronicled in Rita Mead, *Henry Cowell's New Music 1925–1936* (Ann Arbor: UMI Research Press, 1981).

3. Hugo Davise, interview with Smith, July 6, 1981. Davise (b. 1907), a member of the Society of Native American Composers, studied piano and composition and taught philosophy at Los Angeles City College following World War II. Davise and Moore worked together for American music amicably enough. They heartily disliked each other's music, even as they dutifully attended each other's performances.

4. Jerome Moross, "Hollywood Music without Movies," *Modern Music* 18 (May–June, 1941): 261. New York performances by the League and the ICG were reported on the West Coast by the *Pacific Coast Musical Review* in the late 1920s, but that San Francisco–based journal had suspended publication by 1932. The experiments of Americans such as Charles Ives and Henry Cowell, which were roughly parallel to those of the Europeans, were probably even less well known in the United States than were those of their continental colleagues.

5. Dorothy Miller Dunlap, telephone interview with Smith, July 8, 1980. Dunlap is a former Manuscript Club president who studied composition with Moore at the same time she studied piano with Davise. Their opposing aesthetic views gave Dunlap a very stimulating musical education, apparently.

6. Louis Gruenberg (1884–1964) settled in the Los Angeles area in 1936. His works often used jazz elements. His opera, *The Emperor Jones,* was given at the Met in 1933. Ernst Bloch (1880–1959) taught in the San Francisco Bay Area 1925–30 and 1940–52. Naturalized in 1924, he incorporated aspects of his Jewish cultural heritage into his music.

7. A California Society of Composers program. Stahl (b. 1896) was a member of CSC and later of SNAC. He was a violinist and conductor as well as a composer and painter. Florent Schmitt (1870–1958) was a French composer influenced by Debussy. Russian-born Alexander Borisoff (1902–?) was principal cellist in the Los Angeles Philharmonic; he also composed music for films.

8. *Hollywood Citizen-News, August 9, 1935.* This was not Moore's first meeting with Schoenberg. She had attended a luncheon in his honor at USC late in 1934, shortly after his arrival in Los Angeles. Achron, Cowell, and Still were probably the only persons listed who were new to her.

Verna Arvey wrote copiously about both music and dance. She also wrote several librettos for her composer husband, William Grant Still (1895–1978), whom she married in 1939. For a time she was a member of the Mary Carr Moore Manuscript Club.

9. Mary Carr Moore to Verna Arvey, August 7, 1935, Verna Arvey–William Grant Still Papers, private collection, Verna Arvey Still and Judith Anne Still. Probably Schoenberg's song cycle "The Book of the Hanging Gardens," is the work that was performed. Calista Rogers was the singer to whom she refers.

10. Arnold Schoenberg to Bessie Bartlett Frankel, November 26, 1935, *Letters,* ed. Erwin Stein (New York: St. Martin's Press, 1965), no. 168, written in English.

11. Schoenberg to Mrs. Elizabeth Sprague Coolidge, February 5, 1937, *Letters,* no. 174, written in English. Mrs. Coolidge had commissioned a quartet from Schoenberg and arranged for the Kolisch Quartet to play it at UCLA. The letter complained that UCLA skimped on his concert publicity "because the Budapest Quartet played the same evening in Mrs. Fraenkel's club and they and Mr. Behymer are afraid their box-office would suffer."

12. Mary Carr Moore, "Is American Citizenship a Handicap to a Composer?" *Musician* 40 (September, 1935): 5, 8 (an interview by Juliet Laine).

13. In B. D. Ussher, ed., *Who's Who in Music and Dance in Southern California* (Hollywood: Bureau of Musical Research, 1933), 45 percent of the names listed are women's. In J. Rodriguez, ed., *Music and Dance in California* (Hollywood: Bureau of Musical Research, 1940) only 30 percent of the names are women's. Moore's promising female composition students found other ways to support themselves.

14. Guy A. Fasoli, "An Occupational Study of the Vocations in Music in the Los Angeles Area," (Master's thesis, University of Southern California, 1942). Fasoli reports census figures that indicate that between 1910 and 1930 the number of women musicians in the United States remained relatively constant, while the number of men increased.

Chapter 19

1. *Wa-Wan Press Monthly* 6, no. 43 (March, 1907). Farwell later backed away from the views of his three Los Angeles followers, however. He did not

become a member of SNAC. A 1938 letter to John Tasker Howard at the Newark (New Jersey) Public Library contains the phrase "without being as aggressively nationalistic as in my younger days" as a preface to his statement about American music.

2. Born in Wisconsin in 1880, Homer Grunn studied in Chicago and Berlin before teaching stints in Chicago and Phoenix. He lived in Los Angeles from 1910, teaching and performing with the Brahms Quintet, the Zoellner Quartet, and the old Los Angeles Symphony. He composed five operettas, three ballets, and numerous songs, as well as piano pieces. He died in 1944. His music is still in the hands of his family. A song cycle, "From Desert and Pueblo," is his best-known work. His students included Ferde Grofé, Clarence Mader, and Harold Gleason.

3. The only extended account of Cadman's life is Harry D. Perison, "Charles Wakefield Cadman: His Life and Works" (Ph.D. diss., University of Rochester, 1978). Among other things, Cadman helped found the Hollywood Bowl. Perison (pp. 203–5) says that Cadman accompanied Moore's champion, Madame Anna Ruzena Sprotte, in what Perison calls "the first professional test of the acoustics of the Bowl" in 1919 or 1920.

4. *Los Angeles Express*, February 20, 1931.

5. *Los Angeles Examiner*, October 21, 1935.

6. Freer (1864–1942) was the only other American woman of Moore's generation to compose several operas. In addition to her own composition, she used her considerable wealth and prominent social position to champion American opera and opera sung in English. Freer founded the American Opera Society in Chicago in 1921. David Bispham was a famous American singer who had received part of his training at the hands of Freer's father and who had frequently sung in English; hence the use of his name for the medal. Between 1924 and 1930, thirty-three medals were awarded. The others awarded in 1930 went to Pietro Floridia, Karl Schmidt, and Charles Sanford Skilton. For information on Freer, see her own *Recollections and Reflections of an American Composer* (New York: Musical Advance Publishing Co., 1929); Agness Greene Foster, *Eleanor Everest Freer—Patriot—and Her Colleagues* (Chicago: Musical Art Publishing Co., 1927); and Sylvia Eversole, "The Music of Eleanor Everest Freer" (Paper presented to the Sonneck Society, Boulder, Colo., April, 1986).

7. The letter appeared on December 23, 1928. Her long letter drew a rather unsatisfactory reply from Otto Kahn, chairman of the Met's board, on December 30. According to Tefft's articles, she had studied voice, then taught at Cottey College in Missouri before going to Los Angeles. She was also the author of a short book on Cadman.

8. Lulu Sanford Tefft, "What's the Matter with English?" *Music World* (Los Angeles), November, 1930. *Narcissa* is on Tefft's approved list of American operas, along with Hanson's *Merry Mount*, Powell's *Evangeline*, Skilton's *Kalopin*, and Grossmith's *Uncle Tom's Cabin*.

9. Lulu Sanford Tefft, "American Music Values," *Music World*, August, 1931.

10. Lulu Sanford Tefft and Louis Woodson Curtis, "The Society for the Advancement of American Music," *Music World,* March, 1932.

11. "American Music Notes," printed brochure, in Box 4, Fannie Charles Dillon Papers, Music Library, University of California, Los Angeles.

12. The following have been identified: Amy Cheney Beach, S. Earle Blakeslee, Charles Wakefield Cadman, Frank Colby, Louis Woodson Curtis, Fannie Charles Dillon, Alexander Fadyed, Francis Hopkinson, Lou Alice Keller, Quinto Maganini, Kathleen Lockhart Manning, Mary Carr Moore, George Stewart McManus, Frances Marion Ralston, M. Hennion Robinson, William Grant Still, Harriet Ware, and Emele Wendel.

13. Ten names appear on a letterhead of SAAM dated 1931; five of them are women. Not all were composers.

14. Mary Carr Moore, "New Composers Group Formed," *Music and Musicians,* August, 1936.

15. Richard Drake Saunders, "California Composers Organize," *Educator,* 1936, 12. Grunn was announced as president and Charles E. Pemberton, chairman of the music school at USC, vice-president. Saunders was a critic for the *Hollywood Citizen-News* as well as a composer and teacher.

16. The list of composers includes Earnest Anderson, Zhar Bickford, S. Earle Blakeslee, Felix Borowski, Scott Bradley, Morris Browda, Charles W. Cadman, Arthur Carr, Frank Colby, Hugo Davise, Max Donner, Charles Ferry, Homer Grunn, Baruch Klein, Vernon Leftwich, George Liebling, Mary Carr Moore, James H. Morrison, Charles E. Pemberton, Frances Marion Ralston, Richard Drake Saunders, Willy Stahl, William Grant Still, Adolph Tandler, Elinor Remick Warren, Guy Bevier Williams, and Mabel Woodworth. The presence of only four women on the list indicates how few of them were able to offer orchestral music or instrumental chamber music, i.e., compositions in the "more serious forms," to use Moore's language.

17. Others included Arthur Leslie Jacobs's Festival of Modern Music; the New Music Forum; and the public readings of the American Society of Music Arrangers.

18. Liebling and Moore had taught together at the Hollywood Conservatory a decade earlier. Tandler had conducted the old Los Angeles Symphony and later the Tandler Little Symphony. Leftwich, a composer and arranger, was a member of Moore's manuscript club.

19. *Pacific Coast Musician,* January 7, 1939. The article is unsigned but may safely be attributed to Colby. The unfortunate Leftwich soon became secretary of the newly organized American Society of Music Arrangers. On a personal level, Leftwich and Moore managed to smooth things over; they frequently met on FMP committees, and Mr. and Mrs. Leftwich called on Moore at least once, in 1944. The Music Teachers Association honored both composers on a program in 1946.

20. Richard Drake Saunders, "New Group to Back Music of Americans," unidentified clipping (probably from the *Hollywood Citizen-News*), in Scrapbook no. 13, Moore Archive.

21. Bruno David Ussher, *Pasadena Star-News,* October 26, 1940, reviewing an FMP orchestra concert of October 23, 1940, the first in the season of

concerts sponsored by SNAC. Ussher's critical response to Moore's music cooled after the SNAC controversy erupted.

22. Mary Carr Moore, radio interview by Naomi Reynolds on station KMPC, January, 1944, transcript, Moore Archive.

23. Of the composers mentioned, Lionel Barrymore was famous as an actor; Barber was a younger American composer; Korngold and Zador were émigrés who were already active in the film colony.

24. Jerome Moross, "Hollywood Music without Movies," *Modern Music* 18 (May–June, 1941): 262.

25. *Co-Art Turntable* was published by Arthur Lange in support of his recording venture, starting in the fall of 1941. Ethel Dofflemyer became his editor. Under the pen name Henri Lloyd Clement, she contributed several articles, as did other members of the Society of Native American Composers, that advocate a position generally similar to Tefft's.

26. *Co-Art Turntable* 2, no. 9 (September, 1942).

27. For information on the iconoclastic Weiss, who had been a student of Schoenberg, see William B. George, "Adolph Weiss" (Ph.D. diss., University of Iowa, 1971).

28. The *Native American Composer* probably appeared only once, in August, 1942.

29. Charles Ives to Henri Lloyd Clement (Ethel Dofflemeyer), March, 1943, Charles Ives Collection, Music Library, Yale University. Weiss's reply, also in the Ives Collection, does contain extravagant language, aimed especially at the émigré composers. But Morris Browda, a Jew who had been active in both composers' societies, wrote a convincing article defending SNAC from the charge of anti-Semitism (*Co-Art Turntable* 3, no. 3 [March, 1943]).

30. Mary Carr Moore to Charles Ives, March 22, 1943, Ives Collection. Moore obviously believed that émigrés had prompted Ives's action.

31. The following performances have been identified:

May, 1937. Quartet in F Minor; Song, "Sunset"	January 19, 1941. Suite for String Orchestra
May, 1938. Quintet in F Minor	February 5, 1941. "Intermezzo" from *David Rizzio*
January 14, 1939. Three songs, three violin pieces	March, 1941. Song, "My Dream," with orchestra
February, 1939. Songs	April 6 and 9, 1941. "Aria of Rozanne," with orchestra
March 19, 1939. Excerpts from five operas	October 25, 1942. "Four Love Songs"
October 23, 1940. Piano concerto	January 9, 1944. "There is a Dream," organ and chorus
March 10, 1940. Song	
November 24, 1940. Songs	

32. Gerald Strang, telephone interview with Smith, July 7, 1981.

Chapter 20

1. Mary Carr Moore to Mr. and Mrs. Harry Noyes Pratt, two undated letters, ca. 1932, Special Collections, San Francisco Public Library.

2. Otto Hertzler, *Horse and Buggy Doctor* (New York: Harper and Bros., 1938). This country doctor's autobiography must have prompted some nostalgia for Lemoore days.

3. Moore datebook, December 1, 1940, microfilm, Moore Archive. Moore is referring to Lillian Quinn Stark, to whom *Saul* and "O Wondrous Soul" were dedicated

4. *American Opera and Its Composers* (Philadelphia: Theodore Presser, 1927). The second edition (1934) contains descriptions of *Narcissa, The Flaming Arrow,* and *David Rizzio.*

5. Mary Carr Moore to John Wesley Moore, January 8, 1944, carbon copy, Moore Archive.

6. Wesley's widow, also a pilot, was killed a month after Roosevelt's reelection in 1944, when a student pilot froze at the controls in flight and the plane crashed. Their son, then four, remained in Quincy, California, and was raised by his maternal grandparents. Moore visited him there on several later occasions. She had offered to raise him herself, presumably with help from Marian and Byron.

7. Sponsorship of a production of *Narcissa* was mentioned as an inducement when Moore began teaching at California Christian College in 1928. There was a formal agreement in December, 1929, that CCC would guarantee fifteen hundred dollars toward a production, and the Olga Steeb Piano School another thousand. She began rehearsals in January, 1930, but the production was shelved very soon, probably as a result of the gathering Depression. There were numerous club programs of extracts from the opera around that time. On April 15, 1936, her datebook reads "audition Narcissa WPA," but nothing came of this. The first act was performed under the direction of her Chapman colleague Ray Crittenden, at the Long Beach First Baptist Church on March 14, 1937, and was broadcast nine days later over radio stations KFWB and KFOX. There were two presentations, probably heavily cut, before opera reading clubs in 1940.

8. Louis Woodson Curtis was a member of the California Society of Composers and SNAC. He was director of music education in the Los Angeles Public Schools. Rev. Evans was president of the Hollywood Ministerial Association.

9. Witmark still had enough copies in stock to supply the San Francisco cast with scores in 1925, but he claimed at that time that the plates had been stolen. By 1929 Moore thought they had been shipped to Germany during World War I to be melted down for ammunition. Witmark reluctantly agreed to transfer the copyright back to Moore after the San Francisco production. Had the 1930 production come off, Moore wanted her friend Wesley Webster in San Francisco to print the new edition. Around 1936 Moore seems to have transferred the responsibility for *Narcissa*'s copyright to Webster, who inadvertently allowed the copyright to lapse in 1940.

10. Quoted in Ruth Dennen, "'Not Without Honor . . . ,'" *Pacific Coast Musician,* March 3, 1945.

11. Albert Harris, telephone interview with Smith, October 27, 1983. The

English-born Harris went to Los Angeles in 1941. He went to Moore for private lessons in harmony and counterpoint at the suggestion of USC's John Crown and formed a lasting friendship with her. Moore sent him on to Zador and eventually to a career in radio and TV music.

12. Richard Carr Moore, conversation with Smith, March, 1983. Richard was fourteen years old at the time of the production.

13. *Pacific Coast Musician*, April 21, 1945.

14. Isabel Morse Jones, *Los Angeles Times*, March 17, 1945.

15. Patterson Greene, *Los Angeles Examiner*, March 17, 1945.

16. Clarence Gustlin to Mary Carr Moore, March 22, 1945, Scrapbook no. 19, Moore Archive.

17. Awan formally canceled the indebtedness of the "*Narcissa* Committee" on June 1, 1945. His own bill had been five hundred dollars of the total.

18. Mary Carr Moore to Robert L. Sincock, June 28, 1947, Northwest and Whitman College Archives.

19. Moore to Sincock, October 6, 1947, Northwest and Whitman College Archives.

20. Moore to Sincock, November 3, 1947, Northwest and Whitman College Archives.

Chapter 21

1. A few months later, Viana Bey played the concerto a second time. This time, Leginska, who was Bey's teacher, phoned Moore and "called [her] down" for asking Bey to play without a fee, though Moore had presented her with some private composition lessons.

2. Later it was played by the New York Philharmonic under Constantin Bakaleinikoff. Earle credits Moore with helping him achieve these successes.

3. Cadman's biographer reports that Cadman struggled throughout his life with homosexual tendencies (Perison, "Charles Wakefield Cadman," pp. 395–407).

4. *Music and Dance in California and the West* (Hollywood: Bureau of Musical Research, 1948). Earlier volumes, under slightly different titles, appeared in 1933 and 1940.

5. The box of major scores donated at that time became the basis for the Moore Archive.

6. Pauline Alderman, interview with Smith, June 10, 1980. Alderman (1893–1984) was the first professor of musicology at USC.

7. Porter was interviewed by Smith on December 18, 1980.

8. The Dillon Papers at UCLA include correspondence with Percy Grainger, Josef Hoffman, and Marian MacDowell, among others. Of course, Dillon had studied abroad and in New York, as well as spending several summers at the MacDowell Colony in New Hampshire. Apart from the interest of these friends, however, her music was ignored at least as much as Moore's.

9. Schmidt, who was much older than Webster, had a profound effect on

American music around the turn of the century through his publishing activities. He published much of Amy Beach's music, for example. See Adrienne Fried Block, "Arthur P. Schmidt, Music Publisher and Champion of Women Composers," in *The Musical Woman: An International Perspective, 1984–1985*, ed. Judith Zaimont et al. (Westport, Conn.: Greenwood Press, 1987)

10. John T. Howard, *Our American Music: Three Hundred Years of It* (New York: Thomas Y. Crowell Co., 1931). Irene Millier, a member of the Mary Carr Moore Manuscript Club, wrote to John Tasker Howard, January 28, 1931, inviting him to write a biography of Moore similar to the one he had recently completed of Deems Taylor. Howard's reply of February 19 indicated his regret that he had "overlooked" Moore in *Our American Music*, which had just gone to press. (Letters in the Art and Music Division, Newark Public Library.) Howard corrected the omission in later editions of his book.

11. Mary Carr Moore to Mr. and Mrs. Harry Noyes Pratt, undated letter, ca. 1932, Special Collections, San Francisco Public Library.

12. See, for example, "The Privilege of Maternity," n.d., typescript, Moore Archive.

13. "A Grand Young Lady," *Pacific Coast Musician*, August 21, 1943, 4.

14. This tradition is very well described in Judith Tick, *American Women Composers Before 1870* (Ann Arbor: UMI Research Press, 1983).

15. Mary Carr Moore to Jessica Fredricks, undated letter (written in 1949), Art and Music Department, San Francisco Public Library.

16. Pauline Alderman, interview with Smith, June 10, 1980.

Bibliography

The following bibliography is not an exhaustive list of the numerous sources examined in the preparation of this book or cited in the notes. It does contain all of the titles known to include Moore, as well as those works on the history of American music, the musical culture of Los Angeles during Moore's years there, and the experience of women in music that proved most helpful. Of the many books outside the field of music consulted by the authors, only those that most significantly broadened our understanding of Moore's values and the circumstances which alternately nurtured and thwarted her ambitions as a composer have been included.

Primary Sources for Moore

All of Moore's music and most of her papers are in the Mary Carr Moore Archive, Music Library, University of California, Los Angeles. Items retained by Moore's descendants have been generously loaned to the authors and have been microfilmed for the archive. The nonmusic materials to which the authors have had access include:

"My Little Story." Typewritten autobiographical account of Moore's life through her midthirties. 98 pp.
"Out of the Far West." Typewritten notes by Sarah Pratt Carr concerning her daughter's early years. 15 pp.
Twenty-one scrapbooks assembled by Moore, covering her career between 1893 and 1950; and other family scrapbooks, including one containing information about the Carr relatives and one compiled by Moore's grandmother, Louisa Merrill Pratt.
Annual datebooks, 1928–52.
Moore's annotated, handwritten catalog of her compositions and various typed lists of her works.
Typed transcripts of radio interviews and typescripts of articles and talks.
Correspondence, primarily from publishers Wesley Webster and Witmark.
Various typewritten librettos.

Reference Works That Include Moore

Anderson, E. Ruth, comp. *Contemporary American Composers: A Biographical Dictionary*. Boston: G. K. Hall, 1982. Moore is also included in the 1976 edition.

Armstrong, Alice Catt, ed. *Who's Who in Los Angeles County, 1952–53: Two Thousand Illustrated Biographies of Leading Men and Women of Achievement in Los Angeles County.* 2d ed. Los Angeles: Alice Catt Armstrong, 1952. Moore is also included in the 1950 edition.

ASCAP Biographical Dictionary. 4th ed. New York: R. R. Bowker Co., 1980. Moore is also included in the 1948, 1952, and 1966 editions.

Baker's Biographical Dictionary of Musicians. 7th ed. New York: Schirmer Books, 1984. Moore is also included in the 1940, 1958, and 1978 editions.

Barnes, Edwin N. C. *American Women in Creative Music.* Washington, D.C.: Music Education Publications, 1936.

Bio-Bibliographical Index of Musicians in the United States of America from Colonial Times. Washington, D.C.: Music Division, Pan American Union, 1941. Reprint. New York: Da Capo Press, 1971.

Block, Adrienne Fried, and Carol Neuls-Bates, eds. and comps. *Women in American Music: A Bibliography of Music and Literature.* Westport, Conn.: Greenwood Press, 1979.

Bull, Storm. *Index to Biographies of Contemporary Composers.* New York: Scarecrow Press, 1964.

———. *Index to Biographies of Contemporary Composers.* Vol. 2. Metuchen, N.J.: Scarecrow Press, 1974.

Butterworth, Neil. *A Dictionary of American Composers.* New York: Garland Publishing, 1984.

Cohen, Aaron I. *International Encyclopedia of Women Composers.* New York: R. R. Bowker Co., 1981.

Craig, David Scheetz, ed. *Music and Musicians Puget Sound Yearbook: Including Seattle, Tacoma, Everett, Bellingham, Olympia, and Mount Vernon.* Seattle: David Scheetz Craig, 1914.

A Dictionary-Index of Musicians. Vol. 2, M–Z. Vol. 12 of *The Art of Music.* New York: National Society of Music, 1917.

Fletcher, Russell Holmes, ed. *Who's Who in California: A Biographical Reference Work of Notable Living Men and Women of California.* Vol. 1, 1942–43. Los Angeles: Who's Who Publications Co., 1941.

Fredricks, Jessica M., comp. *California Composers: Biographical Notes.* San Francisco: California Federation of Music Clubs, 1934.

Guide to Music and Dance in Southern and Central California. 1955–56 ed. Burbank, Calif.: Life with Music, 1955. Moore is also included in the 1951 edition.

Herman, Kali. *Women in Particular: An Index to American Women.* Phoenix: Oryx Press, 1984.

Hitchcock, H. Wiley, and Stanley Sadie, eds. *The New Grove Dictionary of American Music.* 4 vols. London: Macmillan; New York: Grove's Dictionaries of Music, 1986. Vol. 3, s.v. "Moore, Mary Carr," by Catherine P. Smith.

Hixon, Don L., and Don Hennessee. *Women in Music: A Bibliography.* Metuchen, N.J.: Scarecrow Press, 1975.

Howes, Durward, ed. *American Women: The Official Who's Who Among the*

Women of the Nation. 1935–36. Los Angeles: Richard Blank Publishing Co., 1935.

———. *American Women: The Official Who's Who Among the Women of the Nation.* Vol. 2, 1937–38. Los Angeles: American Publications, 1937.

———. *American Women: The Standard Biographical Dictionary of Notable Women.* Vol. 3, 1939–40. Los Angeles: American Publications, 1939. Reprint. Detroit: Gale Research Co., 1981.

The International Cyclopedia of Music and Musicians. 11th ed. New York: Dodd, Mead and Co., 1985. Moore is also included in the 1964 and 1975 editions.

The International Who Is Who in Music. 5th ed. Chicago: Who Is Who in Music, 1951.

Ireland, Norma Olin. *Index to Women of the World from Ancient to Modern Times: Biographies and Portraits.* Westwood, Mass.: F. W. Faxon Co., 1970.

Johnson, H. Earle. *Operas on American Subjects.* New York: Coleman-Ross Co., 1964.

Kurzgefasstes Tonkünstler-Lexikon. 15th ed. Pt. 2, vol. 2, L–Z. Wilhelmshaven: Heinrichshofen's Verlag, 1978.

Laurence, Anya. *Women of Notes: One Thousand Women Composers Born Before 1900.* New York: Richards Rosen Press, 1978.

List of American Orchestral Works Recommended by WPA Music Project Conductors. Washington, D.C.: Work Projects Administration, 1941.

Lyons, Louis S., ed. *Who's Who Among the Women of California: An Annual Devoted to the Representative Women of California, with an Authoritative Review of Their Activities in Civic, Social, Athletic, Philanthropic, Art and Music, Literary and Dramatic Circles.* San Francisco and Los Angeles: Security Publishing Co., 1922.

McCoy, Guy, ed. and comp. *Portraits of the World's Best-Known Musicians: An Alphabetical Collection of Notable Musical Personalities of the World Covering the Entire History of Music.* Philadelphia: Theodore Presser Co., 1946. Entry for Moore originally published in *Etude* 54 (May 1936): 328.

Mattfeld, Julius. *A Handbook of American Operatic Premieres.* Detroit: Information Services, 1963.

Metzger, Alfred, ed. *Musical Blue Book of California.* Season of 1924–25. San Francisco: Musical Review Co., 1924.

Northern California Musicians' Directory, Including Dramatic and Kindred Arts. Seasons 1916–1917. San Francisco: National Musicians Directory Co., 1916.

Northouse, Cameron. *Twentieth Century Opera in England and the United States.* Boston: G. K. Hall, 1976.

Pacific Coast Musician Year Book, 1926–27. Los Angeles: Frank H. Colby, 1926. Published as the October 9, 1926, issue of the *Pacific Coast Musician.*

Pierre Key's Musical Who's Who: A Biographical Survey of Contemporary Musicians. New York: Pierre Key, 1931.

Pierre Key's Music Year Book: The Standard Music Annual. 1938 ed. New York: Pierre Key Publishing Corp., 1938.

Pratt, Waldo Selden, ed. *Grove's Dictionary of Music and Musicians: American*

Supplement, Being the Sixth Volume of the Complete Work. New York: Macmillan Co., 1928. Moore is also included in the 1920 edition.

Reis, Claire, comp. *American Composers: A Record of Works Written Between 1912 and 1932.* 2d ed. New York: United States Section of the International Society for Contemporary Music, 1932.

Rodriguez, José, ed. *Music and Dance in California.* Hollywood, Calif.: Bureau of Musical Research, 1940.

Saerchinger, César, ed. *International Who's Who in Music and Musical Gazetteer: A Contemporary Biographical Dictionary and a Record of the World's Musical Activity.* New York: Current Literature Publishing Co., 1918.

Saunders, Richard Drake, ed. *Music and Dance in California and the West.* Hollywood, Calif.: Bureau of Musical Research, 1948.

Skowronski, JoAnn. *Women in American Music: A Bibliography.* Metuchen, N.J.: Scarecrow Press, 1978.

Slonimsky, Nicolas. *Music Since 1900.* 4th ed. New York: Charles Scribner's Sons, 1971.

————. *Supplement to Music Since 1900.* New York: Charles Scribner's Sons, 1986.

Smith, Julia, ed. and comp. *Directory of American Women Composers, with Selected Music for Senior and Junior Clubs.* Chicago: National Federation of Music Clubs, 1970.

Stern, Susan. *Women Composers: A Handbook.* Metuchen, N.J.: Scarecrow Press, 1978.

Stewart-Green, Miriam. *Women Composers: A Checklist of Works for the Solo Voice.* Boston: G. K. Hall, 1980.

Towers, John, comp. *Dictionary-Catalogue of Operas and Operettas Which Have Been Performed on the Public Stage.* Morgantown, W.Va.: Acme Publishing Co., 1910.

Trapper, Emma L., comp. *The Musical Blue Book of America, 1915–1916: Recording in Concise Form the Activities of Leading Musicians and Those Actively and Prominently Identified with Music in Its Various Departments.* New York: Musical Blue Book Corp., 1915.

Ussher, Bruno David, ed. *Who's Who in Music and Dance in Southern California.* Hollywood, Calif.: Bureau of Musical Research, 1933.

Who Is Who in Music. 1929 ed. Chicago: Who Is Who in Music, 1929.

Who Is Who in Music: A Complete Presentation of the Contemporary Musical Scene, with a Master Record Catalogue. 1941 ed. Chicago: Lee Stern Press, 1940.

Who's Who in the West: A Biographical Dictionary of Noteworthy Men and Women of the Pacific Coastal and Western States. Chicago: Marquis—Who's Who, 1954. Moore is also included in the 1949 and 1951 editions.

Who's Who on the Pacific Coast: A Biographical Dictionary of Noteworthy Men and Women of the Pacific Coastal and Western States. Chicago: A. N. Marquis Co., 1951. Moore is also included in the 1949 edition.

Who Was Who in America. Vol. 3, 1951–60. Chicago: Marquis—Who's Who, 1960.

Wier, Albert E., ed. and comp. *The Macmillan Encyclopedia of Music and Musicians*. New York: Macmillan Co., 1938.

Woman's Who's Who of America: A Biographical Dictionary of Contemporary Women of the United States and Canada, 1914–1915. New York: American Commonwealth Co., 1914.

Books, Articles, and Published Scores

Ammer, Christine. *Unsung: A History of Women in American Music*. Westport, Conn.: Greenwood Press, 1980.

Apel, Paul H. *Music of the Americas North and South*. New York: Vantage Press, 1958.

Biggs, Gloria. "Retirement Means More Music for Dr. Moore, Busy at 'Things She's Always Wanted to Do.'" *Christian Science Monitor*, October 6, 1949, 14.

Blair, Karen J. *The Clubwoman as Feminist: True Womanhood Redefined, 1868–1914*. New York: Holmes and Meier Publishers, 1980.

Blum, Elsa Proehl. *They Pleased World Stars: A Memoir of My Parents*. New York: Vantage Press, 1960.

Carr, Arthur A. *The Carr Book: Sketches of the Lives of Many of the Descendants of Robert and Caleb Carr, Whose Arrival on This Continent in 1635 Began the American Story of Our Family*. Ticonderoga, N.Y.: The Author, 1947.

Carr, Edson I. *The Carr Family Records: Embacing [sic] the Record of the First Families Who Settled in America and Their Descendants, with Many Branches Who Came to This Country at a Later Date*. Rockton, Ill.: Herald Printing House, 1894.

Carr, Sarah Pratt. *Billy To-Morrow*. Chicago: A. C. McClurg, 1909.

———. *Billy To-Morrow in Camp*. Chicago: A. C. McClurg, 1910.

———. *Billy To-Morrow Stands the Test*. Chicago: A. C. McClurg, 1911.

———. *Billy To-Morrow's Chums*. Chicago: A. C. McClurg, 1913.

———. *The Cost of Empire*. Libretto for the Opera *Narcissa* by Mary Carr Moore. Seattle: Stuff Printing Concern, 1912.

———. "A Gordian Knot." In Seattle Writers' Club, *Tillicum Tales*. Seattle: Lowman and Hanford, 1907.

———. *The Iron Way: A Tale of the Builders of the West*. Chicago: A. C. McClurg, 1907.

———. "Waters of Eden." Serialized in ten parts in *Alaska-Yukon Magazine* 8, no. 2–9, no. 5 (May, 1909–April, 1910).

Chase, Gilbert, ed. *The American Composer Speaks: A Historical Anthology 1770–1965*. Baton Rouge: Louisiana State University Press, 1966.

———. *America's Music, from the Pilgrims to the Present*. 2d ed. New York: McGraw-Hill, 1966.

Chmaj, Betty E. "Fry versus Dwight: American Music's Debate over Nationality." *American Music* 3, no. 1 (Spring, 1985): 63–84.

Couche, Margaret. "Mary Carr Moore: American Composer." *Music of the West Magazine* 9 (February, 1954): 13, 18–19.

Cowell, Henry, ed. *American Composers on American Music: A Symposium.* Stanford, Calif.: Stanford University Press, 1933. Reprint. New York: Frederick Ungar Publishing Co., 1962.

Curtis, Robert. "A Club Comes of Age" [Mary Carr Moore Manuscript Club]. *Life with Music* 2 (April, 1949): 28–29.

Drinnon, Richard. *Facing West: The Metaphysics of Indian-Hating and Empire-Building.* Minneapolis: University of Minnesota Press, 1980.

Eaton, Quaintance, ed. *Musical U.S.A.. How Music Developed in the Major American Cities.* New York: Allen, Towne and Heath, 1949.

Elson, Arthur. *A History of Opera, Giving an Account of the Rise and Progress of the Different Schools, with a Description of the Master Works in Each.* Rev. ed. Boston: L. C. Page and Co., 1926.

——. *Music Club Programs from All Nations.* Rev. ed. Boston: Oliver Ditson Co., 1928.

Elson, Arthur, and Everett E. Truette. *Woman's Work in Music: Being an Account of Her Influence on the Art, in Ancient as well as Modern Times, a Summary of Her Musical Compositions, in the Different Countries of the Civilized World, and an Estimate of Their Rank in Comparison with Those of Men.* Rev. ed. Boston: L. C. Page and Co., 1931. Reprint. Washington, D.C.: Zenger Publishing Co., 1975.

Elson, Louis C. *The History of American Music.* Rev. to 1925 by Arthur Elson. New York: Macmillan Co., 1925.

Estavan, Lawrence, ed. *The History of Opera in San Francisco.* Vols. 7–8 of *San Francisco Theatre Research.* San Francisco: Works Progress Administration, 1938.

Farwell, Arthur, and W. Dermot Darby, eds. *Music in America.* Vol. 4 of *The Art of Music.* New York: National Society of Music, 1915.

Flexner, Eleanor. *Century of Struggle: The Woman's Rights Movement in the United States.* Rev. ed. Cambridge, Mass.: Harvard University Press, Belknap Press, 1975.

Fredeman, William E. *Pre-Raphaelitism, a Bibliocritical Study.* Cambridge, Mass.: Harvard University Press, 1965.

Gagey, Edmond M. *The San Francisco Stage, a History: Based on Annals Compiled by the Research Department of the San Francisco Federal Theatre.* New York: Columbia University Press, 1950.

Hamm, Charles. *Music in the New World.* New York: W. W. Norton and Co., 1983.

Hipsher, Edward Ellsworth. *American Opera and Its Composers: A Complete History of Serious American Opera, with a Summary of the Lighter Forms Which Led Up to Its Birth.* Philadelphia: Theodore Presser Co., 1934. Reprint. New York: Da Capo Press, 1978. Moore is also included in the 1927 edition.

Hitchcock, H. Wiley. *Music in the United States: A Historical Introduction.* 2d ed. Englewood Cliffs, N.J.: Prentice-Hall, 1974.

Howard, John Tasker. *Our American Music: A Comprehensive History from 1620 to the Present.* 4th ed. New York: Thomas Y. Crowell Co., 1965. Moore is also included in the 1946 and 1954 editions.

————. *Our Contemporary Composers: American Music in the Twentieth Century.* New York: Thomas Y. Crowell Co., 1941.

Hughes, Rupert. *American Composers: A Study of the Music of This Country, and of Its Future, with Biographies of the Leading Composers of the Present Time.* Rev. ed. Boston: Page Co., 1914. Reprint. New York: AMS Press, 1973.

Katz, Esther, and Anita Rapone, eds. *Women's Experience in America: An Historical Anthology.* New Brunswick, N.J.: Transaction Books, 1980.

Kraditor, Aileen S. *The Ideas of the Woman Suffrage Movement, 1890–1920.* New York: Columbia University Press, 1965.

Lengyel, Cornel, ed. *Early Master Teachers.* Vol. 6 of *History of Music in San Francisco Series.* San Francisco: Work Projects Administration, Northern California, 1940.

Levy, Alan Howard. *Musical Nationalism: American Composers' Search for Identity.* Westport, Conn.: Greenwood Press, 1983.

McDonald, William F. *Federal Relief Administration and the Arts: The Origins and Administrative History of the Arts Projects of the Works Progress Administration.* Columbus: Ohio State University Press, 1969.

Martens, Frederick H. *A Thousand and One Nights of Opera.* New York: D. Appleton and Co., 1926.

"Mary Carr Moore—American Composer." *Christian Science Monitor,* April 16, 1929, 11.

Mason, Daniel Gregory. *Tune In, America: A Study of Our Coming Musical Independence.* New York: Alfred A. Knopf, 1931.

Moore, Mary Carr. *David Rizzio.* Vocal score. San Francisco: Wesley Webster, 1937. Reprint with new introduction by Catherine P. Smith. New York: Da Capo Press, 1981.

————. "Is American Citizenship a Handicap to a Composer?" *Musician* 40 (September, 1935): 5, 8. An interview with Juliette Laine.

————. "Keep Your Tools Sharp." In *Music and Dance in California and the West,* edited by Richard Drake Saunders. Hollywood, Calif.: Bureau of Musical Research, 1948.

————. *Narcissa.* Vocal score. New York: M. Witmark and Sons, 1912.

————. *Twenty-Eight Songs.* New York: Da Capo Press, 1987.

Neuls-Bates, Carol, ed. *Women in Music: An Anthology of Source Readings from the Middle Ages to the Present.* New York: Harper and Row, 1982.

Reis, Claire R. *Composers, Conductors, and Critics.* New York: Oxford University Press, 1955.

Richardson, Cynthia S. "Research in Primary Sources: The Pleasures and Pitfalls of Breaking New Ground." *Working Papers on Women in Music* 1 (June, 1985): 38–44.

Rosenfeld, Paul. *An Hour with American Music.* Philadelphia: J. B. Lippincott Co., 1929.

Salter, Sumner. "Early Encouragements to American Composers." *Musical Quarterly* 18 (January, 1932): 76–105.

Schoenberg, Arnold. *Letters.* Edited by Erwin Stein. Translated by Eithne Wilkins and Ernst Kaiser. New York: St. Martin's Press, 1965.

Smith, Catherine Parsons. Liner notes to *The Songs of Mary Carr Moore*. Cambria Records C-1022.

――――. "A Bicentennial Look at Women in American Music." *The Triangle of Mu Phi Epsilon* 69 (Summer, 1975): 2–6.

――――. "A Musical Apprenticeship in San Francisco." *Halcyon* 7 (1985): 41–58.

Southern California Writers' Project. *Los Angeles: A Guide to the City and Its Environs*. New York: Hastings House, 1941

Spacks, Patricia Meyer. *The Female Imagination*. New York: Alfred A. Knopf, 1975.

Stewart-Green, Miriam. "Women Composers' Songs: An International Selective List, 1098–1980." In *The Musical Woman: An International Perspective, 1983*, edited by Judith Lang Zaimont, Catherine Overhauser, and Jane Gottlieb. Westport, Conn.: Greenwood Press, 1984.

Swan, Howard. *Music in the Southwest, 1825–1950*. San Marino, Calif.: Huntington Library, 1952.

Tawa, Nicholas E. *Serenading the Reluctant Eagle: American Musical Life, 1925–1945*. New York: Schirmer Books, 1984.

Thomson, Virgil. *American Music Since 1910*. New York: Holt, Rinehart and Winston, 1971.

Tick, Judith. *American Women Composers Before 1870*. Ann Arbor: UMI Research Press, 1983.

Underhill, Lora Altine Woodbury. *Descendants of Edward Small of New England and the Allied Families with Tracings of English Ancestry*. Rev. ed. Vol. 2. Boston: Houghton Mifflin Co., 1934. The Pratt Family is discussed on pp. 893–1026.

Upton, William Treat. *Art-Song in America: A Study in the Development of American Music*. Boston: Oliver Ditson Co., 1930.

Weimann, Jeanne Madeline. *The Fair Women*. Chicago: Academy Chicago, 1981.

Zuck, Barbara A. *A History of Musical Americanism*. Ann Arbor: UMI Research Press, 1980.

West Coast Periodicals

Co-Art Turntable. Beverly Hills, Calif., 1941–43.

Impress. San Francisco, 1893–95.

Music and Musicians: Devoted Principally to the Interests of the Northwest. Seattle, 1915–37.

Music World: For the Makers and Lovers of Music. Los Angeles, 1930–32.

Pacific Coast Musical Review. San Francisco, 1901–33.

Pacific Coast Musician. Los Angeles, 1911–48.

Saturday Night. Los Angeles, 1920–39.

Things Worth Knowing in Music and Art. Los Angeles, 1925–29.

Unpublished Materials

Arvey, Verna (Mrs. William Grant Still), and William Grant Still. Papers. Private collection.

Behymer, Lynden Ellsworth. Papers. Huntington Library, San Marino, Calif.

Briggs, Harold E. "The North American Indian as Depicted in Musical Compositions, Culminating with American 'Indianist' Operas of the Early Twentieth Century, 1900–1930." Master's thesis, Indiana University, 1976.

Bush, Grace. Papers. George Arents Research Library, Syracuse University.

Canon, Cornelius Baird. "The Federal Music Project of the Works Progress Administration: Music in a Democracy." Ph.D. diss., University of Minnesota, 1963.

Carr, Byron Oscar. "Field and Staff Officers File: Union." National Archives and Records Service, Reference Services Branch, Washington, D.C.

Davis, Evelyn Johnson. "The Significance of Arthur Farwell as an American Music Educator." Ph.D. diss., University of Maryland, 1972.

Dillon, Fannie Charles. Papers. Department of Special Collections, Research Library, University of California, Los Angeles; Music Library, University of California, Los Angeles.

Fasoli, Guy A. "An Occupational Study of the Vocations in Music in the Los Angeles Area." Master's thesis, University of Southern California, 1942.

Ford, John Anson. Papers. Huntington Library, San Marino, Calif.

Frankel, Bessie Bartlett. Papers. Ella Strong Denison Library, Scripps College, Claremont, Calif.

Frankel, Bessie Bartlett. Papers. Department of Special Collections, Research Library, University of California, Los Angeles.

Hertz, Alfred. Papers. Art and Music Department, San Francisco Public Library.

Index of American composers. Card file from the Federal Music Project, Music Division, Library of Congress, Washington, D.C.

Ives, Charles. Society of Native American Composers File, Charles Ives Collection. Music Library, Yale University.

Jewell, E. Harvey. "Performance of Contemporary and American Music in Seattle, 1853–1912." Ph.D. diss., University of Washington, 1977.

Marquis, Neeta. Papers. Huntington Library, San Marino, Calif.

Music in Contemporary Life. Institute sponsored by the University of California, Los Angeles, Department of Music and the Musicians Congress, September 14–17, 1944. Collected papers. Music Library, University of California, Los Angeles.

Music Scrapbooks, 1926–40. Art and Music Department, Los Angeles Public Library.

Music Scrapbooks, 1890–1925. Art and Music Department, San Francisco Public Library.

Perison, Harry D. "Charles Wakefield Cadman: His Life and Works." Ph.D. diss., University of Rochester, 1978.

Preston, Jean. "Olga Steeb: A Biography." Senior paper, Music Resource Center, Department of Music, California State University, Long Beach, 1979.

Ruger, Morris. "Autobiography of Morris Hutchins Ruger." Typescript. Music Resource Center, Department of Music, California State University, Long Beach.

Schoenberg, Arnold. Correspondence, Arnold Schoenberg Institute, University of Southern California.

Sherman Collection. Society of California Pioneers Library, San Francisco.

Steeb, Olga. Scrapbook. Private collection.

Index